Marrying
Mongolia

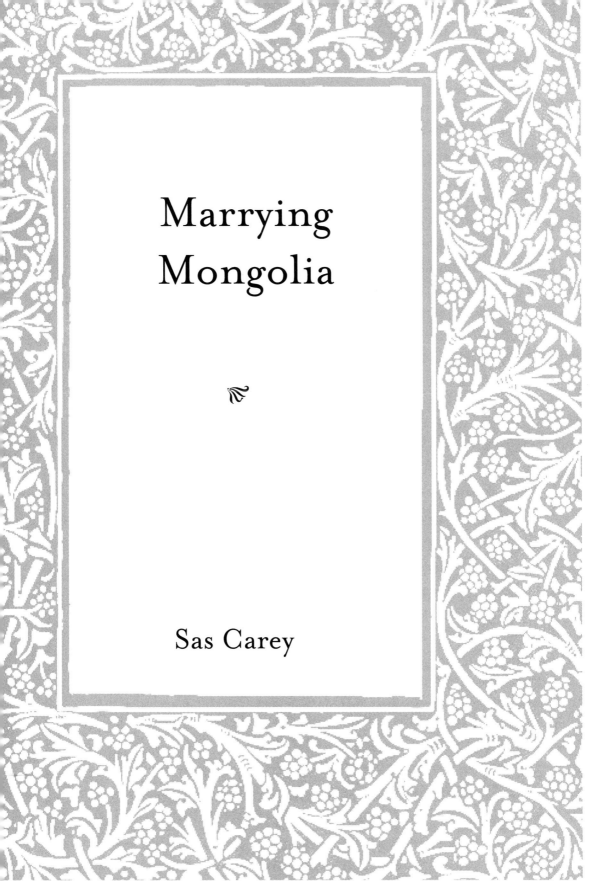

Sas Carey

Contents

(All photos by Sas Carey, unless noted)

ISBN 978-1-7366902-6-0
Distributed by Oxbow Books/Casemate

IPI Press
Post Office Box 212
Hanover, New Hampshire 03755

Dedication

Jean Arrowsmith who had the idea
Susie Cronin who helped in every way
Dr. B. Boldsaikhan who taught me

Note on Mongolian Words
All Mongolian words are listed in the Glossary.
The first time a Mongolian word is used, it is in italics.
Afterwards, for the smoothness of reading, it is in regular text.

Preface

I was born on the land of the Squaxin in Olympia, Washington. My early years were spent on the land of the Potatuck people, a subdivision of the Paugussett, in Newtown, Connecticut. Keene State College is on the land of the Sokoki or Ashuelot. The NorthEast Kingdom of Vermont is located on the native lands of the Nulhegan Band of Coosuk Abenaki. I appreciate that I have great privilege living on this earth, often at the expense of the original people.

This book was written on land which has served as a site of meeting and exchange among indigenous peoples since time immemorial. The Western Abenaki are the traditional caretakers of these Vermont lands and waters, which they call Ndakinna, or "homeland." I remember their connection to this region and the hardships they continue to endure. I give thanks for the opportunity to share in the bounty of this place and to protect its lands and waters.

As I work with indigenous people of Mongolia—Dukha, Darhad, Buryiat, and Khalkh—I am aware of the land struggles still going on—borders created between nations where families are separated and resources taken from the original people.

When the water is clear, the people will heal.
~Dadu, Mongolian Buryiat Shaman

Every February in the weatherized, sanitized, ease of my Middlebury life, as I look out the window at the swaying branches of the willow tree and ground covered in snow, I know it's time. I begin to dream of adventure, my body craves the challenge of living close to nature. Just like an animal with a yearly cycle who knows it is time for a change, I begin to look for a flight to Mongolia.

Газар, *gazar*, is the center of Mongolian life. In its cosmo-physical system you are part of the cosmos and physical world, not the center of it. It is where you are grounded. What your feet touch when you walk. Where you connect. Gazar is soil, dirt, ground, land, grass, country, earth, and world. Shamans say the spirits know you by your footprint on the gazar. When I first step on the Mongolian ground, an electric charge runs through me. We recognize each other.

In the хөдөө, *khuduu*, the countryside, we see a red lily at the side of the road.

Our traditional Mongolian medicine teacher Dr. Boldsaikhan, age forty-five, slams on the brakes of his Russian jeep, jumps out, digs up the lily plant, and says, "This is Tumsnii ulaan, a medicine plant for female disorders." At a nomad's gazar, the herder and my teacher choose a goat that he and his high school friends will barbecue without a pan or other implement. I couldn't be farther from Vermont. Past midnight beside a forest, we eat goat, sing, and drink vodka. The lily sits on the jeep dashboard.

We come to the тайга, *taiga*, the high altitude boggy forest, by horse. There are no roads, only trails. We ride horses over mountains and through mud and rivers to arrive at a settlement of *urts*, Siberian tipis, with reindeer close by. The dogs bark as we draw near to the home of the Dukha, Tuvan people, the smallest minority ethnic group in Mongolia.

My friend Batchuluun comes out of her white urts with her daughter Urna toddling behind her. "Welcome, Sas." Guide Battulga helps me get off the horse. I wobble a bit as my feet reach the uneven ground after riding so long. I arrive with a team of wranglers, a cameraperson, and a translator. It has taken us four hours by horseback to reach this spring-camp of the West Taiga reindeer herders. Since we are at 7000 feet in northern Mongolia just south of Siberia, I see snowcapped mountains as we follow Batchuluun into her family urts. She builds a fire to make reindeer milk tea. We sit on skins on the gazar.

I have been coming as a nurse-healer to this land of the taiga for almost two decades. I was fifty-eight when I first came to this part of Mongolia. Every time we arrive, I marvel that I am able to make it and I wonder if I am still up to the challenge of sleeping on the ground.

I remember why I am here. To come back to the gazar, earth, to feel a connection with land, and to experience life with those who live this way all year round. To offer myself as a nurse and a person who does energy healing. To document their true image and learn about shamans. I have craved this open sky, these nomadic people, the raw smells of leather, wood smoke, larch resin, and juniper incense, and the solid feeling of gazar under me.

At night I step out to see the stars. I glance at the sky to the North. The clouds pulsate with a certain quality of light. Three even rays radiate from a snowcapped mountain. The rays move, but not the way the trees or the clouds are moving. I have seen a green pulsating sky in Vermont and these shapes move the same way. Although they are not in color, I know that I am seeing the aurora borealis. I don't notice the cold. I can survive here.

Journeys have marked my life. Many are with men—first with my father—marked by his anger, then making peace. Calmness with my first husband in the Northeast Kingdom of Vermont and then other husbands, not so calm. There are journeys I make into myself and out—to become a healer, a teacher, a film maker. Mongolia is the first land journey I make on my own—discovering gazar in all its forms.

I have spent my whole life preparing for this.

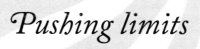

Pushing limits

Chapter One

⟶ *The Laundry Basket*

*A*ccording to a story Mom wrote a year later, in the fall of 1945 when I am four months old, I ride across the United States in a laundry basket. The laundry basket is in a 1928 Model A Ford.

My father Harry drives the car. He has nicknamed it "The Black Horse." My mother Ann sits beside him. Between them on the seat are my bottles with formula, extra diapers, and food. The laundry basket in which I lie is on the ledge behind the seat.

Harry is twenty-eight, trim with startling blue eyes. Many years earlier, a serious ear infection and subsequent surgery had made him deaf in his right ear. In the Army, he had been assigned to a unit of men with disabilities, which kept him from being sent to the front during the war. It kept him alive.

Ann is twenty-five years old with wavy dark hair and a quick smile. Since birth, she has been blind in her left brown eye. But she never misses anything with her right blue one.

As my father drives, she is on his deaf side and he is on her blind side. This way, they help each other.

The adventure starts on the porch overlooking Black Lake just south of Olympia, Washington—a few miles from the Pacific. It is October 1. World War II has ended, Dad is discharged from the Army, and my parents have decided to move back to Connecticut to share their first-born daughter Sally Ann with both sides of the family who live there.

Neither are sure the car will make it to the end of the 3600-mile journey.

🖎

My father had found the car a year before when visiting his sergeant's farm.

Chickens were nested in the seat and pecked at the flat tires. It had no horn, weak brakes, a broken lighting system, no windshield wipers, no heat, and no place to transport their possessions—or me, for that matter. And it wouldn't start. Still, Dad saw its potential and offered thirty-five dollars for it. The sergeant accepted.

Dad washed the chicken manure off and drove it home. Then he painted the body black and the motor gray, making it look like new. At the Army base, where he worked in the supply warehouse, he acquired a new battery and four new tires and inner tubes. He made the rumble seat into a storage area for our possessions and covered it with a black canvas Army tent. He hand-tightened the brakes. At least the emergency brake was strong, he assured himself. No windshield wipers were available. No horn.

Leaving in October and traveling the northern route required heat. Dad cut a three-inch hole in the passenger side floor for heat to come in from the engine and the exhaust pipe. Mom fit a Campbell soup can into the hole so she could heat baby bottles there.

Dad put two spare tires under the Model A's high hood and fit a laundry basket with me in it on a ledge behind their seat under the ceiling.

As they set out that day in October, Harry chuckles and says, "If the car burns up in Spokane, before we leave the state of Washington, we'll just take the train. I'm not going to worry about it. Let's have a good time. We'll go as far as we can."

This is the charm of my father. The adventurer. The Dad I want to be with. The Dad I want to be like.

But his fuse can explode at any moment, changing even the air. This is the Dad I come to know later. This is the quality that will explode through my life.

I don't know if on this trip the fuse exploded. My parents were both giddy when they started. They had recently lived through the Depression and the war and never imagined that they would drive across the country together in their own car.

According to Mom, I sleep well with the hum of the motor and their voices, with the scent of Dad's pipe tobacco blending with motor oil and canvas, and through the car's squeaks and clanks. I wake only for feeding.

❧

As it begins to get dark, my parents wonder where to stay for the night. In the mid-forties, there are no motels. They need to stop at a housekeeping cabin so they can wash diapers and make formula. When we follow a sign that says, Guest Cabins 5 Miles Ahead $2, we end up in a made-over chicken coop. Mom is relieved to find a clean room with a bed, a table, and electric hot plate inside. Dad is not so pleased to discover that the electricity is self-generated and weak. Water takes two hours to boil. With bottles to sterilize, formula to make, dinner to cook, and diapers to wash, Dad and Mom are exhausted when they climb into bed.

In the morning, I wake them up at six and they feed me. They drape the diapers over a pail to dry them from the hole in the car's floor and prepare for an early start.

❧

So where do we come from? It is likely that ancestors from both sides of my family came from Northern Europe and the British Isles to Massachusetts in the 1600s. My maternal grandmother Edith's family claims to have had an ancestor who came on the Mayflower. My DNA shows ancestors from Ireland, Scotland, Wales, England, and Northwestern Europe, with two percent from Eastern Europe and Russia.

My mother, Ann Titsworth, was born to Edith Dayton and Godfrey Van Duzer Titsworth. Edith's brother and future husband were roommates at Amherst College. I never met that grandfather, but think of him as fun and creative from the warm memories Mom had shared. Ann had four older brothers. One died of a motorcycle accident at the age of sixteen, when she was twelve. Edith's father was wealthy before the depression of 1929, if the number of useless stocks and bonds we later found were any indication.

My father, Harold Francis Carey (Harry), was born to Bridget Hughes whose parents immigrated from Ireland, and Wilbur Carey who came from a long British line. Wilbur, a heavy-set, stern man who was good at numbers yet illiterate, ran the Carey Trucking Company in Danbury, Connecticut. Dad was twelve when his mother Bridget died of lung cancer. His siblings were fourteen, nine, and six. One brother and one sister were obese like their father. The family barely had money for food or clothes and often got kicked out of apartments for lack of rent money. The state wanted to put the kids into foster homes, but Wilbur kept the family together. He lost his temper often, though. When Dad married Mom, he wanted the refined life she represented to create a peaceful harbor for our family. But, under stress, he would regress to the way he was treated by his father.

The adventuresome Dad always liked traveling. In 1938, when he was twenty, he went on a solo outing to Boston by bicycle. He rode from Danbury to Brooklyn, New York, boarded a ferry to Providence, Rhode Island and rode to Kendal Green Metro Stop, taking his bike on the train into Boston. He camped, cooked, and rode for six days and three hundred and twenty-five miles. When he returned, he began his first year at Danbury Teachers' College and was invited to share his experiences with other students. Mom was a freshman and attended that presentation.

Some years later, Mom tells me the story of that first sight: how when Dad stepped on stage to talk about his trip, the college audience laughed. He first thought his fly was down and walked off stage to check. Not his fly. His shirt was crooked, buttoned wrong. He fixed it and bravely went back on stage for his talk.

Mom says that she was impressed that Dad had accomplished his bicycle trip alone between high school and college. But he was not her type. He did not speak the cultured English she did. And she was aghast when someone mentioned him as a perfect boyfriend for her. She told her friend, "I wouldn't marry him if he were the last man on earth."

Mom reminds Dad of this on their trip, to which Dad laughs and replies, "Ha, ha, ha, handsome Harold, the housewife's friend, got you in the end."

≈

The roads are small and narrow and haven't been repaired since before the war. At the end of a 300-mile day, outside Missoula, Montana, they find a dirty log cabin, not chinked. Mom can see snow through the walls. She uses it to wash bottles while Dad heats water to wash clothes. Every once in a while, she opens the cabin door for ventilation because the old oil stove smokes and smells. So much to do with a baby! Still they smile as they eat canned spaghetti and make sandwiches for the next day. And Dad sings me to sleep.

> *Bell-bottom trousers Coat of navy blue*
> *I love my Sally Ann And she loves me, too*
>
> *Now we live in the country Out Olympia way*
> *And we are so happy And we are so gay*

The next day in Wyoming, Mom and Dad wonder whether to visit Yellowstone. A bad snowstorm is forecast. But since neither has been there before, Dad's "live it up" attitude wins. They stop. Not only do they find a high-class housekeeping cabin, with a bedroom, living room, and kitchen, but, best of all, the price includes a shared laundry room. My parents catch up on the diapers, prepare and eat more elaborate meals, sleep, and look at the buffalo, wolves, and geysers. It is a change of pace from traveling 250 to 300 miles a day at 35 to 40 miles per hour. The weather is fine, no snow or rain, with blue skies above Old Faithful.

Back on the road, while still in Wyoming, they see a sign, "Use second gear," at a steep, sharp mountain descent. The road is hairpin turns all the way down the mountain.

"That's for a normal car. What should we do?" Dad wonders about the weak foot brakes. He gently descends in second gear so he won't have to use the brakes, and near the bottom of the mountain, another sign says, "One way tunnel. Please use your horn."

"Oh, great," says Mom, "Now we're really in trouble."

"Don't worry. With the noise this car makes, we don't need a horn." Sure enough, at the end of the tunnel, there is a line of waiting cars.

There is plenty of time to tell stories, even if they have heard them already. Dad recounts missing school as a student. If he ripped his pants, he couldn't go to school. He had only one pair and had to stay home to sew them. When he outgrew his shoes, he had to miss school until he had saved money to buy another pair. He worked as a paperboy and at a felt hat factory to earn money, and shared it with his father.

The cornfields of the Midwest remind Dad of "the stubble of a bum's beard". They stay at more small, drafty cabins. After crossing the Mississippi River, Mom takes me out of the basket and holds me up facing the rising sun.

"Now we're in the East," she tells me.

As the car goes through the Wisconsin farmlands, my mother smiles down at me and softly explains that she was born here and, when she was seven, moved by train with her mother and brother to Connecticut. Dad nods appreciatively at the scenery and at her.

The day we approach Chicago is the only day they overrule my need to stop and have dinner at six. Dad decides that we will make better time if we go through the city streets at night, then we won't have to fight the traffic with commuters going to work in the morning. Dad says, "Since we're in Chicago, I know the 'Black Horse' will make it the rest of the way to Connecticut. We're nearly home now."

Ann and Harry continue to treat the old car like an elder who needs special care. Each time it stops for gas, the car needs oil, and they have to remove one of the spare tires from under the hood to add it. The tires need to be changed every couple of days because the car is out of alignment, but the Model A keeps moving forward.

In Pennsylvania, the trees are changing. After the lush green of

Washington, the stark Rocky Mountains, and midwest's ragged corn-fields, it looks like an artist has swirled colors on a pallet. Ann and Harry had forgotten the fall beauty of the East.

The weather holds out all the way to Connecticut, which is fortunate since they had never found any windshield wipers. "Carey luck, the luck of the Irish," Harry calls it.

Just over the Connecticut border, seeing a hitchhiker, Harry says, "You know, picking up a hitchhiker is dangerous. Of course, we don't have any space, anyway."

Ann remembers, "My father picked up a hitchhiker during the Depression once. After a while, he told the man, 'We are going to stop and eat a sandwich.'

When he gave half to the hitchhiker, the hitchhiker said, 'I was going to rob you, but not now since you have shared your food with me.'"

After twelve days, on October 12, the Model A turns off the road, crunches up a gravel driveway past a giant elm tree to a large two-story clapboard house. The front porch has rocking chairs and a white fence. We have arrived in Greenwich, Connecticut, close to the Atlantic Ocean, and we are now home. Ann's mother, Edith, whom I later call Gagie, and oldest brother Uncle Godfrey, (named for his father) come out to greet us. At first they can't see me hidden away in the laundry basket. In one movement, Mom ducks into the car and reaches me in my blue blanket with sleeves, hood, and all, out of the laundry basket. She hands me to her mother. A tiny, proper woman, my grandmother is too busy inspecting me and talking to me in her slightly British accent to take notice of the old car.

But Uncle Godfrey inspects it. As he walks around the Model A, glances down at the Washington 1945 license plate B–46271, the old tires, and the makeshift storage unit on the back, he shakes his head in disbelief. How could this contraption possibly have made it across the country? Harry answers the question on his face. "Not only did the 'Black Horse' make it across the country, the whole trip cost less than fifty dollars for gas and oil. Oh, and there was one repair bill for having the points adjusted that was fifty cents." Uncle Godfrey raises his eyebrows and his mustache turns up at the ends.

Chapter Two

*— All I want
is for him to
See me*

My father is two different people. A diamond in the rough. One is the diamond and the other one rough. One is fun and the other is painful to be around. No one in our family knows which one he will be from one moment to the next.

❦

One of my earliest memories is living in an apartment in Danbury, Connecticut. I am two and Mom is taking care of my new baby brother Harry in the living room. Dad is upstairs. I want to see him, but I am not allowed to go up the stairs. I call him, over and over. Finally, he stomps to the top of the stairs and yells at me, "Can't you just let me sleep? You woke me up."

Suddenly, my stomach hurts.

❦

I am two and a half when we move to Boggs Hill Road in Newtown, Connecticut. The GI bill helps us get a house on a dirt road with two bedrooms, a kitchen, and living room. The rooms are over a garage and an above-ground basement. The rural neighborhood has a house with a family of four on one side—so close we can see into their windows. On the other side our land borders the neighbor's pond and a large field with a barn in the center. New Yorkers own this property and seldom visit. Directly in front of our house and across the dirt road is an apple orchard with many kinds of apples, including golden delicious. Behind our house we have a garden, a small chicken coop, and small red barn. Past the barn are more apple trees and then undeveloped land with thick, prickly brush.

❧

At home with us, Mom is like one of us kids doing what we want. Before taking a train out West to start a family with Dad at Fort Lewis Army Base in Washington, she was a first and second grade teacher. I can see her in front of a class, loving and kind, giving her students creative educational activities even though the war was on. Humble and calm, and matter-of-fact about compulsory exercises, her classroom must have been a peaceful place.

Something Good

In the kitchen
When I am three
A large red Prince Albert tobacco tin
With a metal tab for opening the top
Holds crayon pieces
Saved by Mom the teacher

When she opens the tin
And I smell crayons
I know that something
Good is about to happen

She invites the older neighbor girls over for activities. They come up the outside staircase into the kitchen with its blue linoleum squares floor. Mom sits baby Harry, our neighbors, and me around the table and hands out white paper or a brown grocery bag for us to draw on. We need to fill the whole sheet and use the broken crayons and tape sparingly. If Gail and Marion can't come, I still have my invisible friends Sharjin and Ya-hoodi. They hide behind doors. I never know where they are but they are always around when Harry is busy. The record player plays thirties and forties songs like "Don't Fence Me In", and Mom sings "Shrimp boats are coming, there's dancing tonight . . ." Being home— just Harry and me plus my invisible friends before the younger kids, Julie, Joan, and Tom, are born—is like being in Mom's class. She has time to play, draw, and sing. Every letter she draws to teach us is beautiful—square and upright. It is almost like being in real school, like Gail and Marion are.

We hear Dad come up the outside staircase from work. As he steps inside the door, it feels as if he has a box of fire crackers in his pocket. I can never tell when one might be set off. The air of the house is immediately changed. If crayons are left on the table, I am afraid he will throw them away. Dad was in the Army and acts like an officer who might say, "Attention" at any moment. We need to be on high alert. Mom is rushing to set the table and get dinner ready. She swipes the crayons into the Prince Albert tin. He notices a red and yellow one in the corner and ends up yelling at me. I run into the other room. "Come back. You need to help your mother," he shouts as he sits at the table, waiting to be served.

☙

I hate the pigtails I have when I am in first grade. They always feel too tight. I hate having to rush for the school bus because Mom is braiding them at the last minute. But Dad likes my braids and he is the boss, Mom says.

Still, I keep asking Mom every day to have them cut off.

Finally, I wear her down. She agrees to take me to a beauty parlor in Danbury.

When we get there, the room smells of frizzy hair stuff, feels full with women talking. "Do you want to save the braids?" the lady asks, holding her scissors close to my hair. All sounds in the room stop. Everyone is watching as she snaps the sharp scissors. She holds the braids in her hand. "Do you want to save them?" She repeats.

"Yes!" I say. "I will give them to Dad so he won't be mad! The yellow-haired woman puts them into a brown paper bag and a new, free me stares back from the mirror.

We go through a hardware store where I run my fingers through nails in barrels and breathe in the smell of new lumber to climb the long stairs to Dad's Carey Insurance Company office. I carry the paper bag with my braids.

Dad is sitting behind his big desk. He looks at me, opens his mouth and shuts it again. His face is red. He gives Mom a sharp look. It is too quiet.

"Here, Dad," I say, "I saved the braids for you. You can keep them."

"NEVER!" he snaps. He stands up, grabs the bag and tosses it into his wastebasket. There is a sound of hammering in my ears.

Mom's face is white. She looks between Dad—sitting like a king behind his wooden desk, with his fingers back on his Olympus typewriter—and me standing beside her. I move toward the doorway, breathing the cigar-cigarette smell of the long wooden stairway.

Mom talks to him softly. His secretary Althea comes in, leans down, pats my head, and says, "Wow! Your hair looks nice! You look so grown-up."

I dry my cheeks and touch my hair. The ends are pokey bristles like my hairbrush. They are right next to my head.

"Who cares about Dad throwing them out?" I say bravely to Mom as she takes my hand to walk down the stairs. Mom looks straight ahead with her lips pressed tightly together.

But I don't believe my words. I can tell she doesn't either.

❦

In sixth grade, I am in love with Elvis Presley and keep track of the Top 50 hit songs in my diary. Every day I have to wait through forty-nine songs on the radio before I can hear #1 Love Me Tender by Elvis. So I decide to save my dime allowance each week to buy it.

When I have one dollar in dimes, I proudly walk to the record store, beside Cashman's Drug where all the teenagers hang out, and go in. The clerk hands me Elvis' forty-five single with a hole in the center and I close myself into the wooden booth to listen, as I have seen other kids do.

I walk out on the sidewalk and home holding the yellow record store paper bag with its black 78 logo on the outside. I've never bought a record before and strut along so everyone can see. Actually, I don't see anyone I know.

We have a square wooden record player-radio with a thin metal spindle. I put a plastic insert into the large hole of the 45. With the record settled on the turntable, I place the needle in the groove. The sound of that song sends shivers through my whole body. I play it again. I can't wait for Dad to come home. I am thinking about how he loves music and how he will be so happy for me. So far, we have jazz and Oklahoma! I know all the words to those songs.

When Dad gets home, he comes upstairs to Harry's and my bedroom where I have the record player all set up. His face is lifted with a smile.

"Let's hear!" he says.

I lower the arm into the groove and his smile drops as he hears, "Love me tender, love me true, all my dreams fulfilled . . ."

"You spent your money on this? I hate Elvis." He turns around and I can hear his steps pound down the stairs before half of the song is done.

❧

The first time we stay in a hotel is during a family trip to Niagara Falls when I am fifteen. All seven of us are one room. Dad goes out to do some errands and returns with food and presents—football pennants from colleges. When he lifts them out of a paper bag, I say, "Oh, I would like that Yale one." We go to the Yale-Brown football game every year and root for Yale.

Dad squints his left eye at me. His ruddy face becomes red like a balloon. All the air is suddenly sucked out of the room. The storm breaks with his loud voice. "Why does Sally Ann expect to get the first choice and best in everything?" I go sit in the closet.

Little things set him off because he is always sizzling underneath. It takes no time for him to shift. Maybe the deepest issue is feeling responsible for the death of his mother. "My mother really loved me," he told us once when we were older. "I was quarantined with scarlet fever, before antibiotics were discovered, and my mother stayed with me. Maybe I was too exhausting for her. At the end of the quarantine, she had lung cancer, went to a sanatorium, and died. I never got to say 'good-bye.'"

Still, we can't help loving him. Because he is also funny and affectionate. A polite and sincere businessman, well dressed, suave, smooth, and friendly. The man who kisses women "hello" on their cheeks after church and is the "most honest insurance man in Danbury, Connecticut." His charm makes his outbursts all the more confusing.

He's nearly always happy when hiking, fishing, dancing, skiing, sailing, camping and traveling. This is the Dad I want to be with. I always want him to look at me like he did in the picture with the laundry basket.

᭙

In my autograph book when I am twelve, Dad draws his sailboat called Carioga and writes: "Life is like sailing, sometimes calm, sometimes stormy, but most of the time fair winds blow. Keep the bow of your boat toward home. A peaceful harbor is there." I wish.

᭙

I don't know it then but my father's anger will ripple through my whole life. It will create a feeling of always being vigilant and waiting for the other shoe to drop. It will determine who I love and who I leave behind.

Chapter Three

— *Curious to Write*

$\mathcal{A}$t eleven, I am already curious, nosey, and interested in other people's lives. What gets me wanting to write is the desire to document what lies at the top of a scary staircase.

Staircases are my most recurrent dream. They don't have floors or sometimes even walls. I work my way up steps and steps and they end in nothing. Air. And no way down. Or maybe the next step is six feet above or below and I can't reach it.

Behind our house on Boggs Hill Road is our red barn. In the barn is a space left from where Dad had moved a steep staircase. The staircase goes to the barn loft. He never closed in the open square of floor at the top of the stairs. When I climb up the steep stairs there is a four-by-four feet hole. It is scary. I have to step diagonally from the top step to touch my foot on solid floor. We aren't allowed up there, of course, but I have to go.

The first summer day that I go, Mom is in the house with the three younger kids, Julie, Joan, and baby Tom.

When I climb up the ladder, I find dusty cardboard boxes full of newspaper-wrapped knick-knacks. I somehow know these used to belong to Mom before she was married and had five kids. There's a painted metal paperweight of Little Bo-Peep dressed in petticoats from the twenties. A black, carved, wooden Scottie dog. A fox hunt set with red clad metal jockey figures including dogs and horses. A plaster turtle faded to yellow.

With these treasures, I catch a glimpse of something sacred, mysterious. I find it hard to imagine Mom without us. Now all her time is focused on us. Yet one day, she had wrapped each tiny treasure in newspaper and packed it into this cardboard box. I wonder when. I watch Mom when I step into the house at dinnertime to see if I can figure it out.

My loft explorations seem historic, like mining. I want to keep track of my discoveries—when and what I find. When I get into the house that night, I feel like I have traveled far. I don't want to forget this important day, so I ask for a diary. I need to journal my explorations.

For Christmas, I get a daybook to write in. That first year when I am in sixth and seventh grade, I don't write every day. But from the next year until I am forty-two, I do. Then I write about dreams. Never mind that I don't know how to use fancy metaphors and adjectives. I am a plain writer. I just want to document things. It is what I do.

❧

At thirteen, I watch Mom closely, contemplating how she flows through life. Our time alone together usually comes after dinner when she washes the dishes and we kids take turns drying. Although I complain about the chore, I appreciate talking to her. If she tells me, "Don't talk to that boy." I tell her, "I like him. Of course, I'll talk to him." Later, I think, maybe she's right. I discuss it with a friend. I know Mom's right. And mostly I follow her advice. But I would never, ever, agree with her to her face. Still, I internalize her suggestions and each year, write my goals for the new year.

New Year's Resolutions at Thirteen

1. Be in bed and turn the light off by 11 PM.
2. Do exercises.
3. Get out of bed at 7:15 on school days.
4. Eat breakfast.
5. Stay on a high protein, low calorie diet.
6. Do homework fast and accurately. Stay on the subject.
7. Keep my room clean and neat.
8. Have a shower a day (every day).
9. Walk home from school for exercise.

10. Please, Sally Ann, for your friendship with your father,
    help your mother.
11. Never swear in front of boys. (No dirty jokes either.)
12. Wear deodorant and keep clean.
13. Have a good working attitude.
14. Be nice to Julie and Joan.
15. For heaven's sake, Sally Ann, when you belong to a club or
    activity you need to go. It is your duty to. (Youth group at
    church is the most frequently missed.)
16. Try to mind your father and mother about boys.
    (They are experts.)
17. DON'T CONFIDE IN EVERYONE and talk misleadingly
    about friends.
18. Don't pick pimples.
19. When you have a boyfriend, don't tell the whole world.
    (I mean a crush on a boy.)
20. When you know about an assignment, try to do it before it's due.
21. Try (very hard) to get at least 90s in ALGEBRA!!
    (You want to go to college, don't you?)
22. DON'T bite your nails.
23. Wash your face three times a day (and I mean wash).

Making resolutions and goals becomes a part of my life.

Once I'm a teenager, the goals begin to have an intensified focus on
hygiene and a lot of my inner conflicts are about food and exercise. The
food issues had been underlined two years before when I went for a physical check-up and the obese doctor's first words were "You need to go
on a diet. There is this new program called Metracal. You just drink this
during the day for one meal and you will lose weight. Eat fewer breads
and cookies and more meat." In our house, we all love sweets. All except
our thin mother.

Decades later, I am visiting my parents in a retirement community
when the topic of writing comes up.

"This is a good book I'm reading," says Dad. "No swear words. People
who use those words have a limited vocabulary and I have no need for
them in my life. I like a book where the author doesn't choose a com-
plicated word when a simple one will do. 'Write for people,' I say. Write
so everyone can understand you. *Angela's Ashes*, now that's a book I sent

to your brothers. Reminds me of my Irish ancestors. They lived like that before they came to this country."

"I thought the book was terrific," I say.

"You read it? Hrump. It's a man's book."

"I am writing about my childhood." I tell him. "You and Mom can't imagine the bad things I did."

"And we don't want to know, either." He dismisses me by raising his book between us. No matter. Mom has already told me that she wants to know everything I write.

Meanwhile, each of my words adds to the staircase. Now it spirals up into the sky. I step up.

Chapter Four

— *Water*

$\mathcal{M}$y mother looks between my toes to see if I have webbed feet like a duck. Because once I get into water, I don't want to get out.

I begin swimming lessons when I am six years old with Coach De-Groat. He sets up a swimming school for kids at Curtis Pond in Sandy Hook, a part of Newtown.

Every day, he drives around town in his Woody station wagon and picks us up. We sit on the floor in the back. When we get to the bump we call a "thank you, Mom," he steps on the gas and we all fly up into the air. If things get boring, he starts yodeling. And then teaches us to join by singing, "See the old lady, who? See the old lady, who?"

❧

I find a scene from those swimming classes on a website about high school teachers. The caption reads, "Honoring Coach DeGroat". In the black and white photo, twenty little heads, about half of them with bathing caps, stick out of the mud hole called Curtis Pond. Standing calf-deep at the edge, Coach de Groat is gently guiding a girl by touching her head. The other students are mainly watching him with their heads above water or socializing. As I look closer at the individual faces, I recognize four of my classmates. And then, I see myself. I am the one with dark pigtails, looking down at the water.

Maybe I am trying to persuade myself to stick my face in. Maybe I am pausing between breaths. For sure, I am not socializing. I am fully focused on the water. I look very diligent. Probably I am trying to avoid remembering that horrible, bubbly feeling of getting water in my nose and instead thinking about how more than anything I want to be in the deep side so I can climb the tree there, swing out on the rope, and jump into the middle where the big kids are.

Looking at the picture, I can see right away that our coach is teaching rhythmic breathing or at least blowing bubbles in the water as the precursor to exhaling under water.

I hear his voice, "One-two-three, one-two-three,"

I am six in the memory. I have an orange inner tube around my waist, turning my pigtailed head to one side and then the other, kicking my feet.

"One-two-three, one-two-three," Coach continues loudly.

I stop kicking and turn a minute to rest on the tube, just to admire. There is Johnny standing at the end of the wooden board, gripping his hands around the thick, knotted brown rope. He pauses and then he is flying into the water.

"Want to go over there?" Coach grins, noticing I am distracted. "Well, yes," I answer.

"Then you have to pay attention. When you pass Beginners, you can go over. Try breathing this time."

I try again, glancing at the rope swing to motivate myself.

"One-two-three." The litany of Coach de Groat continues. Right away I stick my head in the water, breathe in. My eyes sting. But I really want the reward of the deep water. When my head comes up, I'm sputtering, wiping my eyes.

Coach is smiling at me. "See? You can do it. Maybe next summer. People don't usually pass Beginners until they're eight. Maybe you can pass a year earlier."

I glance over to the swing. My neighbor Marion, who is three years older than I am, is climbing the steps on the side of the tree. A whole year. I don't know if I can wait that long.

❧

Our family is staying with some friends, the Eddys, at their summer cottage on a lake in Massachusetts.

I am ten. My brother Harry is eight. We row their boat out into the lake alone.

It's exhilarating. The farthest we have ever been. The most we've ever been trusted. I am so proud. I want to row. He wants to row. So we try sitting on the middle seat of the wooden rowboat and row in unison. That works for a while. A fish jumps and we are out of sync. I watch tiny minnows swim under the stern against the little wake our boat power is making. I dig those oars into the water, see how fast I can go.

We talk. We can say anything, softly. We know voices carry over water, so we talk in a whisper. Then we laugh loudly just from being so free.

We try whipping the boat around to face the opposite direction. We figure out how to move the oars, pushing one, pulling the other with the handles way up in the air. It works. Everything works out here in the water. We row like grown-ups. We explore the waves, the shapes on the different shores. We look over at the dock. It is amazing, but no one is standing there calling us back. It is the best place we have ever been. We still have time and check out everything—the other shore, the fish, and the deep water. We watch as we make ripples, smell fish. We study the reflections of the trees on the water. We talk about how much we love Mr. Eddy, even when later, he arrives to the end of the dock with his white nurse's pants on and waves us in.

Only someone who really understands kids would tie a long, long, long rope to a rowboat, so we could explore and also be safe.

❧

Living in Connecticut less than an hour from Long Island Sound, I am not a stranger to boats and water. As I get older, the boats are for boys in our family. We girls can ride in them, but only Dad and Harry sail the boats—they are seamen. They can raise the sails, lower the rudder, hold the tiller, and lift the centerboard on all four of our sailboats— sailfish, pram, twelve-footer, and eighteen-footer. Me? I am ballast. As the boom shifts from one side to the other, I duck my head and move to the high side. Dad has changed from the risk taker driving the Model A Ford in his younger years to being a cautious insurance man. He only sails when the weather is calm, which drives me crazy. I want wildness—to water ski or race in motorboats, not lie around waiting for a puff of breeze. On vacation, I love to stay with my cousins when we take Uncle Dean's thirty-eight foot motor boat out on Long Island Sound. We sleep at Montauk Point to the roll of waves and the taste of salt.

⁀

Coach DeGroat retired the year that I graduated from high school. When our class dedicated the yearbook to him, I interviewed him for an article. I asked Coach for some words of wisdom for the graduates and he replied, "If you want to be a part of the world, you need an education. If you want to enjoy life, you must look after your body, mind, and soul. These three are the basis for a well-rounded person and there must be a balance among the three."

I must have heard his advice on a deep level because it became an important principle in my life and work. I remember the photo of the girl with pigtails. Determined. Focused. She has brought me to where I am today. She swam on three continents. Across lakes, rivers, and ponds where she looked over to the deep water and jumped straight in.

Chapter Five

Pushing Limits

I love to take chances.

At three, I have my tonsils out and stay in a hospital. A doctor puts a screen over my face. He tells me to breathe in a bad smell. Then it is dark and I am throwing up in my bed. I keep moving away from the mess until I am crouched in a corner. The metal sides of the crib are high. I manage to climb over and walk toward a light—all the way down the hall. I see three nurses before they see me. They are in a corner with white hats, white aprons, white shoes, and white dresses. One nurse is knitting, one is writing, and the other one is talking. The one knitting sees me first, drops her needles and stands.

"What are you doing here? You are supposed to be in bed." Her voice is kind, but I'm scared.

My hospital crib can't hold me back, even though I know I am not supposed to get out.

❧

When I start school, my neighbor Karen Peck and her brothers become my models for pushing limits. We are in the same grade, although Karen is thinner and smaller than I am. She has blonde hair, brown eyes, and wears a crooked jacket. She already knows how to swagger up the bus aisle on our way to first grade. By the time she reaches my seat, I can't hold my giggles in. Her brothers, Artie and Jackie, sidle on to the back of the bus where they think they can get into trouble without the bus driver seeing. They begin to sing:

> *This old man*
> *He played one*
> *He played nick knack on my drum*
> *With a nick knack paddy whack*
> *Give the dog a bone*
> *This old man comes shitting home*

The bus driver calls them to sit up front.

After three weeks of bus rides to first grade, I tell my parents I've learned a new song.

"Let's hear it," they say, joining in when I start. As I come to the end, they look at each other.

Mom says, "Don't sing that."

Dad nods in agreement, "If you say that word again, your mother will wash your mouth out with soap."

I don't actually know what word he means. So I sing the song again.

There is silence. Then my mother stands and leads me into the bathroom. She closes the door, puts the seat down on the toilet and gets a new bar of Ivory Soap out from the high, secret cabinet. She sits me on the toilet seat cover, takes the white rectangular bar out of the white, blue, and red cover, and wets it.

My mother doesn't have a mean bone in her body. But she is consistent. I know this. When she and Dad promise to do something, they do it. I guess she and I are both a little scared now. She doesn't quite know what to do, me being the oldest kid. Maybe she wonders if I'll get sick or something. She clenches her lips together and narrows her eyes, then slides that new white Ivory bar between my lips, barely touching my tongue, barely leaving its slippery taste.

But, from that moment on, Ivory Soap represents something that I am not. It is too clean, smells too disgustingly proper, too sterile, and too pure for me.

Back on the bus, I join Karen and practice her brother Skippy's swaggering walk— the one he uses when he gets caught swearing and has to sit behind the driver. I cultivate that wicked look, that sneaky glance.

☙

I want what I want.

And when I don't get it, I'll walk three miles for it.

This happens when I am eight and want to go the Morgan's house to play with Judy and Diane and Chippy, my second grade crush. I want to wade in the brook beside the road, sit in their breakfast nook, and climb into the outdoor playhouse.

Mom is on the phone with Mrs. Morgan but keeps mouthing no every time I beg her to take us there.

I go outside and sit on the scratchy seat of the Buick in my shorts waiting for her to come drive us. But she doesn't come out. When I check again, she is still talking on the phone, shaking her head.

I decide I am going.

I motion to Harry, who is six, and Julie, three years old, as I walk out the door. They follow along, although they aren't usually as adventure-some and defiant as I am. We start up the hill. I turn around, expecting to see Mom in the driveway calling us back, but the driveway is empty.

It's a hot summer day. Julie, who has the lightest skin in the family, has cotton undies on and high white leather shoes. No shirt. We pass the neighbors' houses. No cars come. And when we reach Hattertown Road, we turn left and keep going. We have never walked this far. Still no cars.

After a while, I see a "No Trespassing" sign on the right side of the road hanging on a rope attached to two trees. I have heard the Pecks talk about a mica mine along here. It would be great to see it. We feel like explorers as we slip under the rope to follow a path through the woods. We crunch a few shiny chips as we walk. The dark wooded path opens. We are in a fairy tale. Bright sun reflects off a ring of cliff walls around us—walls of thick and thin sheets of glitter, some as long as my arms. I pick up a loose piece and peel away the layers. A transparent layer looks like something inside of our toaster. I choose a thick piece with many layers that fits into my pocket.

Later on, on another road, dogs suddenly barge out barking furiously. Julie and I are terrified. Harry picks up a stick. We keep walking even though my legs barely want to move, Julie has a rash from the sun, and Harry is defending us from more dogs.

We see the brook, the tree house, and then the Morgan's house.

Before we knock on the door, Mrs. Morgan flings it open and says, "Your mother has been here looking for you. I need to call her." I feel proud that we made it. I am bursting with the knowledge of the mica chip in my pocket.

When my mother arrives, I can see that she is sick with fear. Her big dark-framed glasses don't cover the tightness of her cheeks and mouth. Mom spanks me for the first and only time in my life.

Chippy sees it all.

❧

Harry and I sit in an apple tree near the barn at the back of our property. Just behind the tree, the land is full of brush, scrub trees, and rocks. The tree is far enough away from our house that no one can see or hear us, but close enough that we can hear Mom if she calls. His seat is in the small crook of a branch higher than mine. Mine is on a long, low, thick branch almost parallel to the ground—so solid that I can swing my legs when we are talking. Harry and I are planning where we could ride bikes if he had one. Riding is such freedom.

❧

The summer before my cousin Judy had taught me to ride her bike. Later our neighbor Gail let me demonstrate my new skill on her bike but it was too big for me and I crashed. After that, Dad decided to get me my own bike. He took me to a neighbor's where he'd found an old one with fat tires and foot brakes—one I could safely ride. All year I shared it with Harry and he methodically learned how to balance, steer, and apply the brakes, always in control.

He is not wild like I am, but he protects my wildness, so I love being with him.

On his eighth birthday, he gets a new, green, three-speed English bike with the latest thin tires. As soon as he figures out how to manage the different speeds and use the handbrakes, we're off exploring together.

One day I find Harry busy in the barn at his workbench opening paint to color spools from Mom's thread. He is making children's necklaces. I ask him if I can borrow his bike to go up to see Karen Peck. He starts to instruct me about the thin tires, the boys' high bar and the front and back hand brakes, but I'm in such a hurry, I barely hear him.

The hill up Mount Nebo Road is so steep I usually have to walk my bike up. Not this time. Today, I put the bike in first gear and keep climbing as little pebbles mixed with gravel skitter away from the thin tires.

After we play nine innings of softball with Karen's brothers, sister, and father, I have to go home. Karen grabs an old bike belonging to one of her brothers and says she will ride me down. At either house, we have to act a certain way, but the road is ours. I ride Harry's bike gently out the driveway, skidding on pebbles again.

At the mailbox, I turn the handlebars down the hill, press my foot on the pedal once and I am flying. Big stones, tiny stones jump from my wheels. I can feel my heart beating, my throat dry. The trees are blurry as I whizz past. The wind whistles in my ears. I have a metallic taste in my mouth. My knuckles are white on the handles. My foot is violently pushing back on the pedal to slow down, but nothing happens. Fear flies up from my belly through my chest, tightening my throat, hits my brain.

HANDBRAKES yells my brain, but only my right hand hears and smashes the metal to the rubber handle. My hands are vise grips holding on, the rest of me is loose, numb.

The front wheel digs into the dirt while the back wheel lifts off the ground, bringing the seat, pedals, and me with it, over the handle bars, and over the front wheel. I land with a thud on my chest with the bike on top of me, still grasping the handles. I can taste the grittiness of dirt but my lungs are empty. No sound comes from my lips. No movement of air in my body. I try to open my hands, lift my cheek off the dirt and pebbles. Nothing moves. I lie still.

Karen is hovering over me. "Breathe. Don't die, Sally Ann. Oh, my God, don't die. Breathe."

I hear her, but I can't breathe.

"Come on, come on! Breathe! Oh, please, please breathe."

A high-pitched pig squeal comes from my mouth. My chest expands, contracts, expands. I am breathing.

The sides of Karen's lips turn up, but her eyes are still dark with fear. I taste blood.

I lift onto my elbow and then my knees, still carefully holding Harry's precious bike. I take it home so gently, I am nearly carrying it, limping myself. Karen walks with me. I'm breathing. I act like I am fine, although from her face, I can see there is something wrong. Karen brushes a few tiny pebbles from my T-shirt and gets pale when she looks at my face. My fingers touch it and come back red.

When we get to my house, Karen describes what happened. Harry listens and watches me. He doesn't even look at his bike until he is sure that I am not hurt. When he goes outside to check his bike, he doesn't mention that some of the green paint is scraped off.

❦

Karen's mother Mrs. Peck invites me to dinner a few weeks later. Karen, her six brothers, one sister, and her father who drinks a lot will all be there. Their energy is very different from my family—thrilling somehow. For the visit, I feel it matters to transform my flat chest. In the top drawer of my mother's mahogany bureau is one lace bra. I borrow that and stuff it with nylon stockings.

Up at the Pecks, the father and boys are building a new house. I follow Karen up a ladder and walk gently on the new subfloor. The beams are up. It is airy and spacious with no roof or walls. I wonder if anyone will notice my new figure. Karen laughs, "Well, I see something grew overnight." I want her older brother Artie to notice. I don't want him to. I want Skippy to look at me in a new way. They are huddled together nailing two-by-fours.

When all eleven of us sit at the table, Skippy starts talking. "At school today Mary Jane tried to flush a baby down the toilet." I drop my fork on the plate. It clangs and splatters my mashed potatoes. What does this mean? Everyone looks at me. "Don't you know about this?"

I shake my head but can't talk. At home no one would ever talk about something violent or sexual or shocking like this. It takes effort to talk about the birds and bees. We are neighbors but live in different worlds.

Skip continues, "It turns out she lost the baby but it was early." "How far along was she?" asks Mrs. Peck.

"I heard maybe four months," says Artie. Skip nods.

I am having trouble swallowing my meat, trying to piece the story together. Does this mean she had sex? Does this mean she was pregnant? Does this mean she is a killer? Did the baby fit down the toilet? Who found her? What will happen to Mary Jane? How can I find out what this is about? Who would I talk to?

And somewhere in me, something opens. Something about differences. My family's way is not the only way. In my family, the stories and language are toned down to the youngest child and he isn't even one year old. There are other ways of being at a dinner table.

❦

We are ten when Artie teaches Karen and me how to smoke. I put the cigarette in my mouth. "Don't swallow it," he says pulling it out so it just touches my lips. He lights the match and holds it to the end. "Suck in," he says. I cough. Karen coughs. Even coughing, we are glamorous like the actors on our black and white television.

Cigarettes are twenty-five cents a pack. Usually Artie or Jackie gives me one. Sometimes we get some from our neighbors, the Barnes who live in New York City and leave their large renovated barn empty during the week. Karen and I just squeeze through the window to admire it. Cigarettes sit on the coffee table. They won't notice if we take three or four.

❦

One day after school, Karen and I are ready to smoke on our own. We walk into the Barnes' field where there is a haystack we can hide behind. I have brought a wax paper sleeve of Saltines to eat afterwards so we can cover up the tobacco smell. We smoke. Now what to do with the butt? I eat some Saltines and light the wax paper cover, putting the cigarettes on top so they will burn. The filters don't burn and I am nervous about leaving any evidence. I could put a little hay on top of the paper to make sure the cigarettes burn completely. And a little more hay. Flames move up the side of the haystack. My fear reflects in Karen's face. The pond where we skate is nearby but there is no bucket. I run home and tell Mom the haystack is on fire. She calls the fire department. With the sirens come about thirty neighbors who hear the sound.

"How did this start?" I hear mumbled around us. I don't say anything. I stand outside my house with the others and watch the flames reach the top of the haystack, as high as a house. Karen and I agree to never tell anyone we were smoking.

A couple of days later, a loud knock comes at our door. My brother Harry races up the stairs. "Don't go down," he whispers. "They are after you."

Mom comes upstairs, her face blanched and her jaw tight. "A policeman is here to question you."

The Newtown policeman Hiney Hanlon is standing in the hall. All I know about him is how he and Sneaky Pete stalk around the Edmond Town Theater and break kids apart who are making out at the movies. In person, he looks awkward, like Charlie Chaplin. I doubt that he visits ten-year-old criminals very often.

As I sidle toward him, I keep my back to the wall. I am defiant and humble at the same time. He introduces himself. My little sisters peer around the corner. My baby brother cries in his playpen. Harry is pacing. His face is red. He glances up at the policeman each time he walks past us. Before the officer says anything, my brother says, "She didn't do it. Don't take her to jail."

He ignores my brother. "Were you smoking?"

"She wasn't," says my brother, who always supports me. "No," I lie.

"Mrs. Carey," calls Hiney Hanlon, "Take your son upstairs. I need some answers from Sally Ann." Mom appears, her face drawn and pale, and does as she's told.

He asks if we started the fire. Why did we have matches? "Were there any boys with you?"

Boys? Now I am offended. Why? I want to ask. Can't two girls set a haystack on fire? I want to jeer at him.

"No." I answer firmly.

"Are you sure there were no boys?"

"Yes, absolutely sure."

"All right. Just be careful with matches in the future, okay?" He is probably laughing inside.

"Okay."

He turns to leave. As he opens the door, Harry is back. "You mean you're not taking her to jail?"

"No, I'm not taking her—not this time," he replies, pointing a finger at me.

No jail, but Karen is punished by her parents and, for a while, kept away from me, the bad influence. No one tells about the smoking. I can't figure out why he asked about boys. We can do anything boys can. Especially since I am eleven and old enough to have my own bra now.

☞

Our church youth group organizes a ski trip to Mount Snow in Vermont.

I am fifteen and it is not something I want to miss. Never mind that I don't ski. I hear there is also an outdoor swimming pool, which I can't imagine in winter but look forward to trying, and a skating rink. I can swim and skate.

We travel by bus. For the first two days, I alternate between the pool and the skating rink. But on the third and last day, I decide to try skiing. I am tired of being left out of all the ski stories. And it looks exciting. I rent skis and get a pass but don't have extra money for lessons. My friend Carolyn says she will teach me. She shows me how to snowplow and we go down the beginner slope twice before lunch. After lunch, she skis with my brother Harry, so I'm on my own.

I can't snowplow to a stop. But I like the feeling of skiing. I think I might as well see what it is like at the top of the mountain. If there is a beginner slope below, there must be a beginner slope above. Alone, I ride to the top on the chair lift. I haven't bothered to tell anyone, because, isn't this what you do here? Ski down the mountain?

From the hard, cold seat of the ski lift, the mountain looks beautiful, although I also notice bare rocks and dirt spots with no snow on the ground. We arrive at the top. I hardly have a chance to be scared, to wonder how to get onto the steep ramp, when I am lying down on it with the sound of large gears screeching to a halt above me. An attendant comes out of the booth and picks me up. Shaken, I go into the lodge to relax. I will have a cup of soup to warm up. That's what Dad would tell me to do. As I sip my soup and look around the lodge, the tables are empty except for one man. After eating and warming up, I am ready to go outside. I put my skis on and look for trail signs. I find a Beginner trail, but it is closed. Advanced Beginner: Closed. Intermediate: Closed. Only one trail is open— Black Diamond: Expert.

What choice do I have?

I have lost track of time and it is beginning to get dark. The bus will be leaving for Connecticut soon. I have to get down the mountain. The only way down is the Black Diamond Trail.

I walk step by step to the sign and look down the trail. It is a cliff of snow, going straight down. I breathe fear and feel nauseated. I shake. The mountain is empty, except for that one man who was in the lodge. When he sees my look of horror as I stare straight down, he yells, "Go across." I point my skis to the side. In a second, I am on the other side. I see a tree. There is no time for snowplow. I fall.

"Are you okay?" he asks as he glides close to me in complete control.

"Okay," I say, white with snow and fear. I fight to stand and as soon as my skis are on the snow they are zooming to the other side and my face is nearly touching a tree when I fall again.

"Okay?"

"Yes."

Again, I get up. But my skis are not pointed to the side. They are pointed down the hill for less than a second. Then I am speeding faster than an airplane. I can't see anything. My stomach is a huge knot. The soup is sloshing around. My throat is one big lump. I am speeding faster and faster. I crash. My skis are in the air. My leg twisted around.

"Okay?" says that angel man appearing from the white mist. "No, I'm not. I can't get up."

"Just stay here. I'll get the ski patrol."

I am cold and my ankle hurts. I lie in the snow. The toboggan comes. Two from the ski patrol lay me in the bottom and cover me. The sides are up to my nose. Cold seeps into my back. My ankle is searing pain. The treetops whiz past, but I smile to think I have my own ski story now. Suddenly, we stop. Medical people lift me and carry me into the Red Cross Clinic. Injured people in ski clothes crowd the room. A doctor assesses my ankle.

Torn ligament. I get crutches and am driven to the bus, which is waiting for me. I sit beside Carolyn, with my ski boot still on for immobilization.

"You went to the top of the mountain? Alone? On your first day of skiing? What are you, some kind of daredevil?"

Chapter Six

The Music of Feeling Close

When a guy throws pebbles that land near my blanket on the beach, I have to look around to see if he's throwing them at me. I have just finished fifth grade and will start sixth grade in the fall. I am eleven, but already I have breasts and my period. My family is camping at Black Rock State Park and the guy is a sixteen-year-old who invites me to take a hike with him up the mountain to the peak. Charlie is six-foot-three and two hundred pounds. He looks like a man, not a kid.

When Charlie asks me, my father isn't sure if it is okay for me to go, but I say he's just going to take me on a hike up the mountain to Black Rock. And Dad loves to hike. Maybe I think that's all there is to it, but maybe I think there could be more. I feel a thrill that Charlie would ask just me to do something and not ask my brother and sisters.

We climb. I am in front. He is behind me. He takes my hand and helps me over some rocks. When we get to the top, he lifts me and lies me down. He kisses me. He rolls onto me, completely dressed. It feels good. It feels like something that is maybe too good. He kisses me some more. He lies beside me. I have never been kissed. Something new awakens inside me. He stands up, takes my hand and pulls me up. We walk back down the mountain, stopping to kiss along the way.

Do Mom and Dad see my confusion? The startling realization that young as I am, I have been making out with a guy? That kissing is something powerful and new to me? That my whole body feels alive? In some ways, I wonder how they could miss it. In other ways, it is obvious why they would. Mom has a six month-old-baby and three other kids. They can't watch me all the time.

For the next two days, he takes me on other paths through woods. Other trails. Lies with me under pine trees on pine needles. Asks me if I know what petting is. No, I don't. He doesn't tell me but I get the idea, even though his hands don't wander over me. It is thrilling, this kissing and lying together. This new exclusivity, even for short hikes in the woods. Someone notices me. Relates to just me. So much attention. He doesn't hurt me. I feel the music of being close. The most exciting thing ever.

I write every action and every word of the conversation in my diary because it is so exciting. Also, because I don't know who to tell or what to say or if it is normal for my body to have these new feelings.

⁂

When Dad's sister Aunt Ruthie first saw me at five months old, she wrote this poem, which Mom saved and gave me:

> *I know a girl-my Sally Ann*
> *Little minx, a fairy hand*
> *Has made her eyes that blessed blue*
> *Has given her that smile.*
> *You'd look a million miles of sand swept land*
> *And find no match for Sally Ann*

My youngest aunt, she was always special to me. Aunt Ruthie has pierced ears, dark wavy hair, and a huge smile. Her skin is the color of the perfect suntan—the color I want to be—and she has bright light with a little mischief in her dark eyes.

She is married and has three little kids and is different from everyone else in my family. More open. The kind of person who would never wash with Ivory Soap.

Mom always says that since Aunt Ruthie has three daughters of her own now, she shouldn't give us big Christmas presents any more.

"Ruth, you don't have the money," Mom tells her each year as I open another perfect package—a Mickey Mouse watch, all the style, when I've never even had a watch before, or a frilly nightgown, which I love and something Mom would never get for me.

Aunt Ruthie just looks at my face and smiles.

❦

One winter Saturday when I am eleven and my sister Julie is six, we finish our violin lessons with Miss Russell, a stodgy, older woman. Miss Russell has moved from Newtown to Danbury, where Aunt Ruthie lives and Dad works. He has driven Julie and me to our lessons and we are walking to our aunt's where Dad will pick us up at noon.

On the way to Aunt Ruthie's, Julie and I walk by a junk store, one that's open to the sidewalk. I spy a springy thing with a wooden handle and a tag written in black letters 5¢. I have a nickel in my pocket, dig it out, and offer it to the man. We walk along carrying our violins in our left hands and I keep boing-ing the spring on my right leg as I walk. I don't know what it is, but Aunt Ruthie will. She loves "an-ti-kews," as she calls them. We ring the doorbell and climb the stairs to her apartment. The stairway smells of cigarette smoke. At the top is a baby gate. Aunt Ruthie's daughters are four, three, and two years old. I hear her shrieking at one. Mom says Aunt Ruthie is personality plus, but gets awfully angry at her kids. Maybe because she and Dad had the same model when they were growing up. She might yell at them, but she never yells at me.

We open the gate and climb another step. The apartment is dark with varnished wooden walls. The first thing I see is a painting of a man with a deeply lined face holding a rosary. I think he's Irish with bright eyes but mischievous underneath, like Aunt Ruthie and me. Whenever I'm here, he's watching. The Christmas tree is in the corner. My cousins, Linda, DeeDee, and Marcia are playing. Marcia is in the playpen, Linda is playing with her ball, and three-year-old DeeDee is following her mother around the kitchen.

"I thought I'd make you some butterscotch brownies," Aunt Ruthie says to us, licking her finger after the batter slides over it on the way to the baking dish. "In twenty minutes we can have a party."

"Party, party," mimics DeeDee.

"Do you want to lick the bowl?" Julie and I nod and she hands us a

scraper and a spoon. It is our favorite thing about baking. I hand her the
boing-ing thing.

"A whisk," she proclaims.

"What's that?"

"French people use them. They mix eggs and batter fast. This one is
unusual because of the flat bottom. Want to try it? Here's an egg."

"Okay, but first the batter," I say. When the last delicious spot has
disappeared from the batter bowl, I break an egg into a dish and whip it
with the whisk. Was that what she called it? Just a few strokes and the
white and yolk are mixed. "Works great," I tell her.

Aunt Ruthie opens the window and is pulling on a rope. The wheel
squeaks as her dry clothes come close enough to unpin, bring in, and fold.
It's a long clothesline, stretches way out the back to a tree.

"Party? Party?" asks DeeDee pulling on her mom's skirt.

"The brownies aren't finished yet, DeeDee."

"Party? Party?"

Six-year-old Julie takes DeeDee's hand, leads her into the living
room, picks up *Horton Hears a Who*! from the floor and starts pointing to
the pictures.

"So, Sally Ann, how's school going?" asks Aunt Ruthie when we are
alone.

"Mr. LoStocco became a teacher just out of the Army and makes us
shine our shoes every day. Checks us. Thinks we're all in the Army. It's
not too bad, though. The thing I hate is the boys. They are always saying
bad things to me."

"Like what?"

"Nothing."

She pulls her head inside the window, takes her hands off the line,
drops the clothespins into the bag, and leaves the diapers unfolded.

"What do they say?"

"They talk about my body."

"You mean that you are developed? That you are a young lady now?"
She sounds like Mom, I think.

"Something like that. Most of the girls are still flat. I wish I were,
too."

"You are beautiful. Look at you. Nice shape. Nice body."

"I'm fat."

"Fat?"

"The nurse weighed us in class. One kid after the other. Said the weights out loud to Mr. LoStocco who wrote them down. I was last. I nearly died. I weighed 139 pounds, the most of any girl and more than most of the boys. And I'm only eleven. Isn't that terrible? And to have everyone know. I wanted to die."

"Were the boys there?"

"Yup, they were putting on their black leather jackets to go out to recess. They are a bunch of hoods. I could hear them making comments. 'Did you hear that?' 'It's all on top!' 'I'd like to get my hands on her!' 'Quite a handful!'"

"Have you told your teacher?"

"He's a MAN! How could I?"

"What about the nurse?"

"I never see her."

"Sounds hard."

"It is."

Suddenly, Aunt Ruthie is off to pick up Marcia who's had enough of the playpen and needs her diaper changed. But I feel better having told someone who listened.

"Will you help me?" she asks.

"Sure." I hold the pins as she takes the diaper off. After depositing the wet one in the pail and washing her hands, she gives me a hug.

"Let's have that party now," she says, picking Marcia up and before she gets into the kitchen, everyone is sitting at the table, DeeDee on Julie's lap, and Linda in a chair. Aunt Ruthie deposits Marcia into the high chair and takes the brownies out of the oven with a potholder Mom made and we watch as they flatten.

"Nearly pure sugar and butter," Dad says about butterscotch brownies. "Can't beat that." Just as I am quoting Dad to Aunt Ruthie, I see his felt hat bobbing up the stairs to pick us up.

"Smells good," he says.

"Come join the party." She is pouring milk for everyone as the brownies cool. "How'd work go, Harold?" His family calls by his given name.

"Just fine," smiles Dad. "Wrote two new policies." But I know it's the brownies that make him smile, not the policies. A special joy of Dad's is sweet desserts. He's in a good mood all the way home. I look at the whisk in my hand and think how Aunt Ruthie whisked my problems away.

❦

When I am fourteen, Aunt Ruthie rescues me again. It is Thanksgiving and we are at her sister Aunt Mimi's and Uncle Marty's apartment. At about six feet tall and weighing about three hundred twenty pounds, Aunt Mimi tells jokes and laughs as she cooks the meal from turkey to dates filled with peanut butter and rolled in coconut for seventeen of us—and makes chicken cacciatore for Uncle Marty who likes Italian food. Meanwhile, Uncle Marty, a short, stocky man half her size, drinks beer. I try to avoid his roving eyes because I hate the way he looks at me. I don't trust him.

I decide to go outside and, on my way, stop at the bedroom to get my coat. He is right behind me. Blocking the doorway, staring at me. I don't want to walk by him. I never like to get that close. I'm not sure what to do. Maybe I'll just wait for him to leave. I hold my coat in front of me. Watching. Waiting. He is lurking, then comes closer. With his raspy voice and his alcoholic breath, he speaks into my ear, "Hey, Sally Ann, give me a kiss." I flinch.

Right then, Aunt Ruthie bounces into the room on the way to get something out of her coat pocket.

"Move it, Marty," she says shooing him off. "I need a diaper."

I breathe out sharply. I really love Aunt Ruthie.

"Are you okay?" she asks.

"I'm glad you came along," I say.

She gives me a big hug, grabs the diaper and says, "Come on, you can help me change Charlie." Charlie is my new baby cousin.

❦

My whole life, whenever I open the kitchen drawer to use that flat whisk, I feel Aunt Ruthie is still with me, whisking problems away, even though her life ended when she was fifty-five and I was thirty-three.

Chapter Seven

— *Somewhere Else*

I've always had a desire to leave, to explore somewhere else.

In 2000 I am talking with Marsha Wolffe on the phone about teas and herbs I might need for going to a high altitude place. My friend Mariah has suggested that I contact her since Marsha is at home in New York City. She spends most or her time as an assistant to the Dalai Lama's doctor in Dharamsala, India. After giving me a list of herbs, Marsha asks my birth date, and tells me, "You are a Taurus so you are content like Fernando the bull sitting in the field smelling flowers. But you are on the cusp of Gemini and you look at mountains and say, "I wonder, what's over there?" I get it. I feel she is looking straight into me, all the way into my childhood, to the wistful feeling of wanting to be somewhere else, visiting someone, learning about others' lives, somewhere without Dad around to tell me what to do.

❦

I am twelve when Mom tells me that I am not the kind of girl to wear make-up. That those girls will get into trouble. That they do things I shouldn't until after I get married. I'm still not exactly sure what she means. Not kiss a boy? Too late for that.

Newtown is changing. Due to space issues, the eighth grade, my year, is in the high school building. In the "basement" as we call the girl's room in the school, Zarin Patel, calmly leans over the sink with her face close to the mirror. She paints black eyeliner on. "Kajal," she says looking at me. Zarin is our school's first American Field Service (AFS) foreign exchange student. She's from Pakistan, a senior, and has been chosen to live in Newtown for a year. I can't take my eyes away from her doing this dangerous thing. I blink with confusion, yet feel entranced, unable to move as I watch her slowly trace those lines. I study her face in the mirror. What will become of her?

Or is it somehow right and good for this esteemed student because she is from Pakistan? Maybe these expectations don't extend to the whole world, just as all dinner table discussions are not the same.

I make up my mind to step out of my white middle class family's expectations to explore different cultures. I will find other ways. I will be an AFS student like Zarin so I can find out.

❦

At seventeen, I am sitting on the floor in the kitchen cleaning the oven when Mom hands me a large white envelope from AFS. I have been accepted to go to Denmark!

Where is Denmark? I get a map. It's strange when you hear a country name and know nothing about it but know that you are about to know a lot. The language. The food. The land. I will learn about the 482-foot hill that they call Himmelbjerget, Sky Mountain. The cold beaches. Bikes between cars on the roads. When I open that envelope, I move out of my home and classroom to Europe.

Living close to the ocean and being on boats my whole life has prepared me for traveling on the Seven Seas, the AFS cruise ship to Rotterdam. On this boat, five hundred American Field Service foreign exchange students from all over the country are on their way to Europe. Many, like my cabin mate Alice from Iowa, have never been on a boat before. Alice, along with Jane from Pennsylvania, Mary from New York and I share a small cabin in the bow with two sets of bunk beds. The bow rocks a lot, I notice, as I stuff my huge, heavy suitcase under a lower bunk.

❦

The crew is German—our enemies only seventeen years ago. When

55

we have a lifeboat drill, I notice that German or not, the guys give us seductive smiles as they hand us orange life vests. Rule number 1: No talking to the German crew. Okay, okay.

We dine in the hold, the tables set with crisp linen napkins folded in glasses. White tablecloths lie under numerous forks and spoons and plates. The meat tastes fresh. The steaks are juicy, thick. The potatoes are smooth on my tongue, tasting of fresh butter and milk. While we sit at the table, German men dressed in starched white uniforms wait on us. The vegetables crunch in my mouth and the raspberry sherbet reminds me of a hot summer day. I can even feel the skin pricks from the canes of the raspberries. We don't eat like this in my family. The little kids would mess up the table in a minute. I think back to dinner at home where we use melamine plastic dishes on a wooden table with an easy to clean Formica top. I sit up straighter.

Every day we study Denmark's language and culture. Dances, performances, and a masquerade party fill our nights. Other students going to Denmark dress as a pregnant couple with the words, "Free Love!" Funny and risqué, but still, I get a little bored around these "leader-type" kids— they are so perfect—and having to be on my best behavior. No swearing. No smoking. No relaxing. No being bad. I miss Karen and getting into trouble.

Halfway across the Atlantic, we hear about a hurricane coming. The air smells different. The next morning after breakfast, the boat swells reach eight on a scale of one to ten. I wonder if the water in the toilet will wash me—or if I will fall off—until I notice there are handles on the sides of the stalls. Eating the not-so-fresh soup at lunch is a game of chasing the liquid with my spoon from one side of the bowl to the other. Now I know why there are so many plates.

I walk on the deck. The air is still. No rain, just violent leaning and hundreds of teenagers with little bags in front of their mouths, looking white and greenish. I feel fine, so I fetch bags, hard candies, and blankets—my first nurse experience. I learn the truth about the cliché, being in the eye of the storm. When we are in the middle of it, the world is crystal clear, the ocean is shimmeringly smooth, and even the swimming pool on the top deck has no waves. But wait, I'm told. And later when we go through to the other side of the storm, there are number eight swells again. I like it.

After nine days at sea, when the butter is getting rancid, the lettuce is tasting a little wilted and the boat store is empty except for melted Babe Ruth bars, we see land—the White Cliffs of Dover, England. Suddenly, I am excited to see the Continent. Will it be very different?

We enter the Rotterdam harbor. My early experiences, even being ballast on a sailboat, made this journey easy. What I am not prepared for is my first view of the Netherlands—a giant Shell Oil tank.

☙

My eyes are full of stars as I get off the boat at Rotterdam and climb onto the train. I smile as I go to sleep thinking about the prestige in Newtown for being an AFS student-—writing letters to the Newtown Bee that will be read by the whole town, sitting on the back of a convertible in the Labor Day Parade, and giving talks to local clubs!

I wake up hearing Carin, our Danish chaperone saying that we are within twenty kilometers of the Iron Curtain—that close to our Cold War enemies. I try to see something but everything is black outside the windows. Some students get off at a German station, welcomed by balloons, signs, and crowds. At 5:30 AM, the train stops at Randers, Denmark and I get off at an empty outside stop and look around. No cars. I sit on a wooden bench. When I notice a kiosk, I walk over to find papers and candy and dig into my money pouch for Danish kronor. I buy a candy bar—Swiss Chocolate. Sitting back on the bench, I admit to myself that this is not the welcome I expected.

Slowly a white Volvo approaches. "This is Jette, your host sister," says Mr. Vagtholm as he steps from the car. His wife sits in the passenger seat and looks at her feet. I begin to speak and he says, enunciating in tones that sound like the Germans on the boat, "You will have to speak slowly, Sally Ann, so Jette can understand you." Jette is my age with blonde hair and enormous round glasses. I can't see her eyes. She keeps her head down, too, and doesn't look at me. Silence fills the car when I get in. I feel like some non-existent balloons are popping.

We drive along flat, green land with a few trees and some sort of building in every view, to Silkeborg and pull into the Vagtholms' driveway. The house is a half-timbered white stucco ranch with cross pieces of wood imbedded in the stucco and topped with a red-tiled roof. A big, shaggy dog greets us. I don't mention that I am afraid of dogs as we go in through the garage. Jette shows me to a room and explains where to put my things. The oak furniture includes drawers that pull out in the closet, a low wooden bed, and a matching desk—much cleaner lines than my fluffy bedroom at home. A *duna*, thick down comforter, covers the small bed and gives some softness. Before I even finish glancing around the room, Jette has disappeared without a word.

I stop at the tile-lined bathroom. It has an open shower, with a drain in the center of the floor, and a toilet tank that has a metal ball that you lift to flush. I wonder how you can take a shower without a curtain and stall or tub. Won't everything get wet? Later I learn there is running cold water and everything does get wet but it is okay.

In the dining room, there is an old-fashioned black square crank telephone, visible from the table. For breakfast they have Kellogg's Corn Flakes especially for me, along with Danish pastry and tea, their usual food. What we call Danish pastry, they call Wienerbrød, Vienna bread. The living-dining room has a grand piano and a television. The television stations are on from six to ten o'clock in the evening, not all day like at home. I am noticing small differences, but things don't seem very different, except the language. Then I begin to learn the way of life.

Every day Jette and I ride our bikes to various small stores to get the day's food. I can't believe the smell at the cheese store. I wonder how anyone could eat something that smells like that. Like others in the fifties and sixties, we eat Velveeta processed cheese at home with no smell. I soon learn to appreciate the taste and texture of real cheese. We go to the butcher, the grocer, and the baker. The food is wrapped in paper packages tied with string, which we place in the baskets of our bikes.

One day in the center of Silkeborg, as we wait at a stop light between two trucks, I see a Connecticut license plate on a car. Connecticut! I haven't spoken English with a native speaker for five weeks. Come on. I wave to Jette and we follow the car through a few side streets until it stops. A man and a woman get out. I can hardly keep from jumping up and down. "Hi!" I say in English, ecstatic when they answer me. "Where are you from?"

Jette motions we have to get going. Her mother needs the meat, cheese, and potatoes for dinner. Go ahead, I motion back. I'm not leaving here when I just found people from home.

Her eyes widen and she raises her eyebrows at my refusal. She gets a glassy look like when her parents argue, turns away from me and stomps down hard on her bike pedal. I am relieved to be left alone for the first time this summer and turn back to the couple from Connecticut. We could be baby birds chirping for food we talk so fast now. I feel my shoulders lower and my stomach unclench. And something more—I feel a swollen area around my eyes like something is ready to let loose.

"Come in, come in," says the woman as we walk into her house. "It's good to see an American. How long have you been here? How old are you? What are you doing here? Are you okay?"

"I'm seventeen. Well, I miss home."

"Do you want some soda?"

No tea? Soda! This is great. "Soda sounds wonderful," I say.

We visit and talk and talk and visit. I have been holding everything in the whole time I have been in Denmark. Almost like a clogged system with water pouring in for weeks and no way out. They aren't really from Connecticut like I am—they just have a summer house there. But now it doesn't matter. I am relaxed and happy. I am getting lighter by the minute.

Then I clench my teeth. I remember where I am. I know I need to get back to the Vagtholm's and I jump up. The couple gives me their phone number and tells me I am welcome to visit again.

When I get home, all hell breaks loose.

"Jette knows where I was," I say in my defense.

"Yes, but you have been gone an hour without permission. How did we know you weren't in some accident? How did we know if you could find your way back? Maybe you were lost. Don't you ever, ever leave Jette. Ever. Again." My Danish mother's round small face is red hot, her cheeks puffed out, like it will explode any minute. Her eyes are like darts and I'm the target. She yells in Danish. Every few minutes, Jette translates.

It's not just her English that's stilted. I can feel the weight come back—the heaviness of trying to act in a way that's not me. And I know that I don't want to live in an unhappy family where there is no joy. That night I write a letter to AFS.

"I realize that there are only two weeks left for my stay in Denmark," I write, "I just want you to know that I think this family and I are not a good match. I am used to five kids, lots of action, and lots of fun. This family is serious, unhappy, and the most they do is watch television from six to ten every evening. I'm not asking for anything. I just thought you should know that I think there's been a mistake."

The next day, Carin, our Danish advisor on the Seven Seas, calls. She says she's coming to get me tomorrow night. She will find another family, even though there are only two weeks left. Why be unhappy? AFS wants you to have a good experience. "Quietly pack your things and be ready to leave," she advises. "I will come tomorrow night."

I feel like a failure for not managing at the Vagtholms.

But I am delighted when I meet my new AFS sister Charlotte in Aarhus. We take a bus to their summer house. Her brothers are waiting at the bus stop. They lift my eighty- five pound suitcase and balance it on their bike. We walk for ten minutes up a little hill to a compact cottage. The ocean is in view and although the water is cold, everyone has a bath-robe to change into a bathing suit on the beach and take a quick dip. On the weekend, we all walk to a dance and don't stop dancing until it's time to walk back home at about one in the morning. My Danish mother is committed to teaching me how to make Rødgrød med Fløde, a strawber-ry pudding with a name that includes the most challenging words to say in Danish. From one day to the next, the Vang Jensens with their seven kids and their summer house are full of action, joy, and fun.

᠅

And back home in Newtown when I sit waving from the convertible during the Labor Day parade, I love the fame, but I am not sure I deserve it. I don't think I did a good job as an AFS ambassador, but Tad, our Jap-anese student, and I give talks and slide shows about Denmark and Japan nearly every week to Newtown's clubs and churches. It turns out I now know a lot about a country I knew nothing about a few months ago.

Everyone wants to hear about my trip. In the short time before my senior year of high school starts, I get asked out to a block dance, a play, and the movies. For a week or two, I feel popular and active. I take a walk around our back yard where the fish in the tiny pond are still swimming, the pears are getting ripe, and the Carey kids are shooting the basketball into the hoops on the larch trees. Karen and I talk. Dad takes us camping for a weekend. I'm home.

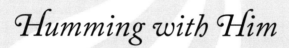

Humming with Him

Chapter Eight

 *Green Chevy*

The Newtown Bee

Harold Careys Are California Bo

i a maximum of ambition and a minimum of belongings, the Harold F. Carey family of 31
Thursday for a 10,000 mile, six-week trip to California and scenic points along the way. Th
find arrival in Los Angeles, a possible side trip to Canada, and a return to Newtown on /
'amily include, from left, Harry Jr, Julie, Sally Ann, Joan, Ann, Thomas and Harold. T
many friends, wishes the Careys a safe and pleasant trip.—Bee Staff photo

*I*n the summer of 1963, after my eighteenth birthday, I travel with
my family from Connecticut to the Southwest, up the West coast, and
head east in a 1962 green Chevrolet station wagon with a travel trailer.

Riding along, we entertain ourselves with reading, writing, and knitting. We have been traveling for a month and lately, it's been one dusty,
bumpy road after another. Plus no escape from Dad and his moods.

❧

My father is driving, Tom, seven, is on the front bench seat between
Dad and Mom. The rest of us sit and lie in the back. Harry, sixteen, is
behind Dad and I am behind Mom. We have the elite window seats. Julie, twelve, is between Harry and me. Joan, eleven, is in the revolving area
where we have a foam mattress behind the back seat for lying down and
relaxing. There are no seatbelts to hold us in place. We all take turns in
the way back, as we call it, but Harry and I always get our window seats if
we are sitting.

Harry's side has a disadvantage. Dad smokes a pipe. When he taps
his pipe's burned tobacco into the ashtray, Harry moves his hand to the
window handle. He listens for Dad's throat clearing—to be prepared in
case he spits out the window. Harry learns to roll the window up fast to
avoid a wet breeze on his face. When he avoids it, we giggle softly, but

when he isn't fast enough, we groan and he has to get a cloth handkerchief out of his pocket.

I've just graduated from high school and feel claustrophobic being in the car for so long, without my friends and with no way to be in touch except to wait and wait for letters. Maybe I get mail once a week—if I'm lucky. We've crossed into South Dakota and the last time was in southern California. I want some excitement, that is, flirting, romance, dancing, dating. And not just from the book *Hawaii* that I am reading. I long to meet someone.

We are headed to McLaughlin, South Dakota to visit Reverend Philip Frazier, a Dakota (Sioux) preacher on the Standing Rock Reservation. I look forward to it as I remember him as a gentle soul. He had visited our church in Newtown the previous spring and told us about the open land and the lack of resources, especially for teenagers. I loved a story he told about flowers being of all colors and how they look beautiful together in a garden—how people of different colors make a beautiful world.

Out the window, dust blows over flat land. We go up a little rise every once in a while. Every way I turn my head the vast, prairie brownness stretches forever.

When we arrive at the Fraziers' house after six long hours of riding, they are not there. Instead, Dad finds an envelope taped to the door with our mail and a map. With the map comes an invitation to a Mission Revival Meeting—an annual event that has been held every year for one hundred years. We will drive one-hundred-forty miles to Red Scaffold. At least I have a precious new letter from Karen and a postcard from my grandmother to read.

As we turn around and retrace our steps for seventy miles, Dad taps his pipe on the ashtray and clears his throat to start talking. "Dr. Frazier went to Mount Herman School and graduated from Dartmouth in 1925. His church is called Little Eagle Presbyterian Church..."

I hadn't thought about it at the time, but as I write this, I wonder how a man who refers to himself as "a full-blooded Sioux Indian" becomes a minister.

I find out that his grandfather Artemas Ehnamani was converted to Christianity by missionaries while in prison after the Dakota War of 1862. Although the details are unique, the unfair story about our white settler ancestors' treatment of indigenous people is familiar. The Dakota

War started because US government Indian agents refused to pay the Dakota their stipends or distribute their food. The children went hungry. The reason they had no food was because the government had moved them to uninhabitable land where the Dakota were unable to farm or hunt. When a Dakota stole some eggs and killed five white men, a Da kota war council was held and they decided to try to drive out the whites. More people on both sides were killed and President Lincoln eventually approved the execution of thirty-eight Dakota, the largest number of people ever executed in one day by the United States government. Just for being Dakota, people like Ehnamani, who had no part in the fighting, were put in prison on Santee Reservation, Nebraska.

Christianity must have resonated with Dr. Frazier's grandfather. Or maybe he felt some safety in it, because he converted. After his release he became pastor of the largest Dakota church, Pilgrim Presbyterian. Dr. Frazier, his grandson, was born in a teepee on the Santee Reservation in Nebraska in 1892.

Dad shifts into low gear. "Along with being a minister, Dr. Frazier is the supervisor of the Sioux Indian Mission of Standing Rock Reservation. With the help of other New England Congregational Churches, our church sent a sound movie projector to Little Eagle Church. It made a big hit with the kids and adults."

❧

I look out the window on the word "kids". Maybe I will meet some young people. I understand that it is a privilege and opportunity to see the country. But Dad is getting tired of driving and grumpy. I have a lump in my throat, invisible protections up, an irritated digestive sys-tem—not knowing when Dad might explode. He usually does when he gets stressed. I try to keep quiet because at any moment the energy of the car could change. Maybe a mission meeting where there are lots of people will give me an opportunity to be away from our family togetherness.

Four hours after leaving Reverend Frazier's house, I look up from reading when I hear a sound and see a flock of turkeys cross the road. They glide away from a small arrow and sign that says Mission Meeting. A small white church appears on a hill and we look below us to see little white dots. Acres of them. Maybe miles of dots with one solid sheet of brown beside them.

"The mission tent," says Dad pointing to the brown. "We had tents like that in the Army."

"It's bigger than a circus tent! Looks like a big encampment," says Mom.

Two lean men whom I assume to be Lakota Sioux, wearing cowboy hats, dusty clothes, and boots greet us. They are about my age. The tall one with shoulder-length black hair welcomes us and the shorter one wearing a black hat bends down to Dad's window. He says that we can camp in the second row as he nods in that direction.

"Thank you," says Dad. He moves his elbow from the window, prepares to drive on, puts his foot on the brake and pauses. "By the way, where did they get the name Red Scaffold?"

The two men exchange a look. One indicates a direction with his chin. The other one answers. "Over there, white men hung our people."

"Oh, I'm sorry." Dad's face is tight.

We are all silent as Dad presses the gas pedal and the car lurches forward.

Chapter Nine

Meeting in South Dakota

*B*rown kids with black hair in a circle on the powdery dirt ground calmly play marbles until our car gets close. Then they sweep them up, opening a path between the trailers and tents for us. After some tension in the car, Dad is in a good mood. He seems to be in his element—having an adventure. The mission meeting will start at seven. We don't have much time so we set up camp at top speed using our vast experience. We've already set up in a campground in Illinois near where Lincoln lived, at the Grand Canyon, Yosemite, Crater Lake, Glacier National Park, Los Angeles, and Olympia, Washington. Harry and Tom put their tent up in record time while we three girls help Mom and Dad make our beds in the trailer. With its gas stove, refrigerator, and gaslights, it feels like a mansion here. And by six-thirty we have eaten and are walking along a path with sparse green vegetation into the mission tent.

The Fraziers are already up front. Dr. Frazier smiles and says, "Hi Harry," to Dad. "Glad you made it! So nice to see you!" I remember his broad shoulders, warm eyes, and a welcoming grin as he shakes our hands. Mrs. Frazier, a heavyset woman with grey curly hair and glasses, sweeps the platform with a hymnal. "Come sit with us. Join the choir." Immediately, I am glad we are here.

Why not? Mom and I sit in the front row on a bench, Julie and Joan behind us. We are facing an audience of thousands of indigenous people. As I glance around, I notice that all the women are wearing long skirts.

My sisters and I are the only ones in the whole tent with Bermuda shorts on. It's embarrassing and probably disrespectful. We will wear skirts tomorrow. The songs are in English and Dakota. I try to follow the Dakota words from the hymnal. Mini wakoni wa hey ukan. Ota, ota, ota. "Beside the still waters," the Dakota woman next to me whispers. "Reverend Frazier translated the words into Dakota." She points to his name on the hymnal.

The theme of Reverend Frazier's sermon is acting in a Christian way. Being kind to all people. Praying. And giving up habits that get in the way of kindness. Just hearing his voice I feel my shoulders relax.

A middle-aged man wearing jeans and boots with his baseball cap in his hands saunters up the aisle. Looks up at the preacher and speaks loudly, "I used to be a bum on the street. I told the Lord if he gave me a pickup, I'd stop drinking and get a job. He did and now I have a job as a diesel mechanic. I am here to praise the Lord!"

"Amen!" fills the tent.

One by one, members of the audience come forward to speak. The stories they tell are about adultery, drinking, salvation. This service is nothing like one in our sedate Congregational Church.

Reverend Frazier touches one man on the head and he faints backward on the floor. I twist my neck to watch. My mouth hangs open. The woman beside me whispers, "He was touched by the spirit." People are gathering around him, holding him. After a few minutes, when we are singing the next hymn, I see him get up, shake his head, wipe his face with his handkerchief, and hobble back up the aisle. What kind of spirit can do that?

❦

Eventually, Reverend Frazier gives announcements. "These are the Careys from our sister church in Connecticut. Parents and five children. Already in the choir," he grins. "Stand up, so we can see you. You've come so far. Welcome! And our other guests—some of you know them—four college boys from New Hampshire—Ken, Larry, Pete, and Ronnie. They have been here all week building a youth center. They raised their own money and gave up their summer jobs to come help us. Stand up, boys. We appreciate your help."

Boys! I crane my neck at movement half-way back in the audience. I can see the silhouettes of four guys, maybe with beards and sideburns—like Maynard G. Krebs on television. One has both sideburns and a beard. Finally I am out of that car! When the service is over, I weave my way through the crowd to the boys.

I stop in front of the one with sideburns and an Elvis haircut and introduce myself. After a minute of talking, he turns to the leader.

"This girl is from Connecticut," he says.

I introduce myself as Sas, a nickname Dad always calls me when he is in a good mood.

And with a Boston accent, the slim leader with the dark hair, beard, and sideburns, says, "You're from New England? Gee, can I touch you?" He pokes my arm with his index finger and guffaws so loudly, the Lakota and Dakota filing out of the tent glance back. Seeing them look at him, he laughs again, and puts the back of his hand over his mouth to hide his chuckles.

What a relief to talk with this person, Ken, who looks about my age. I laugh and feel easy, finally free from my family. "You're building a youth center? How do you happen to be out here?" Our church sends tooth-brushes and he builds a whole youth center.

As a pacifist, he wants to serve others instead of fighting in the Vietnam war. He started his alternative service at an Amazon jungle hospital in Peru, then decided to do something in his own country.

He brushes his hand through his hair. "I was picking cotton in South Carolina, and now we're building a center for teenagers here. You can learn a lot about other people by working and living with them. Pretty impossible to have stereotypes when you know them."

I have a feeling about his actions being nonconformist, but different from Karen and me being rebellious. More thought out. Service. Kind of gritty, like my mouth in this windy, dry place. Maybe you have to be gritty to do service.

"What did you do in Peru?" I ask. He pauses as we both notice the mission tent getting empty and turn to walk out.

For eight months he did whatever they needed—from feeding chickens to visiting patients in a thatch-roofed hut with the doctor. Before he went, he raised money for medical supplies, a Land Rover, and for passage through the Panama Canal. The hospital in Pucallpa, Peru modeled itself after the work of Albert Schweitzer's in Africa, he explains.

I take a breath. Albert Schweitzer? The quintessential service giver, who said, "The purpose of human life is to serve, and to show compassion and the will to help others."

"What are *you* doing so far from home?" he asks me.

Back and forth, we share our travels—Denmark, Peru, my family visiting friends and camping at state parks around the country. His experience picking cotton with Blacks.

Service. Dad, on the World Service Committee of our church, was just talking about it. What exactly does it entail?

"Are you religious?" I ask.

"I think of myself as a Quaker."

Hmmm. We had an austere German neighbor who tutored me in Latin—the only Quaker I ever met. I don't know much about their beliefs, although Mom went to his memorial service and told me that it was silent with people telling stories about his life. She found it very moving.

Ken explains that he is drawn to the Quakers because they are against war, like he is. "What I don't understand" he says poking a rock with a stick, "is if the Bible says that Jesus's most important teaching is 'Do unto others as you would have them do unto you,' how can Christians go to war? One man on my draft board attends my Congregational Church. That seems wrong."

I've never thought of it that way. What other obvious connections have I not made? We soon arrive at the trailer and I drag myself inside to go to bed. Dad's snoring serenades me.

As soon as it's light in the morning, I peek out the curtain on the trailer window wondering if the day before had really happened. Ken is standing just outside. I glance at the clock—seven-thirty—check my hair in the mirror, and step out the door.

"Let's go rock hunting," says Ken, before I have even eaten breakfast. Rock hunting? I like the idea of walking around the prairie, the two of us, alone.

We walk until we come to a rise that looks like the bank of a dried river.

"Look at this one," he says leaning over. "I like the red in it." We bend over the rock, brush against one another.

"How old are you?" I ask.

"Twenty-one. You?"

"Eighteen."

"Just out of high school, huh? New to the world? Innocent?"

Normally, I would be pissed off and self-righteous—I have been to Europe already and across the US. But then, I think of the people and places he has seen and experienced—the Amazon Basin, cotton fields, and now plains. I just sigh and watch him put the back of his hand over his lips, questioning with his eyes. Maybe he caught me giving out some of my automatic negative response.

Ken is standing over me with a rock in the shape of a branch in his hand. "Look at this!"

"Looks like petrified wood. We saw some in the Southwest," I mention.

"Did you see a lot of Indians there? Navajos? Hopis? Zunis?"

I describe the Navajo women dressed in long skirts and velvet tops with silver and turquoise jewelry, the Hopi craft center with beautiful woven rugs and the sand painting that took all day and then was destroyed at sunset.

In Peru, the women all weave and dye their own cloth for their clothes, he tells me. He finds weaving fascinating and is disappointed, here at Standing Rock Reservation, that only a few very old men and women know how it's done. In fact, only two older women still weave cloth. White people are responsible for their cultural genocide, he says. In the mid-1800s we started boarding schools to teach indigenous children the colonialist ways. The students were forced to cut their hair and punished if they spoke their own language. Not weaving is a part of the bigger picture of what has happened to the indigenous culture.

I wonder. I want to learn the old ways. When people learn new ways, is it necessary to throw out the old ones? Is there a way of respecting both? The US government has made the Dakotas move again and again. I feel sad energy from them and from the land under my feet.

The bell rings and we walk back for lunch. Way before we get there, I smell frying. At the mess hall, we sit on a bench with the Indians. The tables form a long line with chicken and fried dough in the middle. I can't eat. My belly is too jumpy being with Ken. He doesn't notice, though, as he concentrates on cleaning his chicken bones.

In the afternoon, Ken has set up a meeting with teenagers. We sit on a little prominence waiting for them to arrive. Usually, I hate waiting, but I could sit here with Ken all day. When the young people gather, he asks them what they need. They say movies and games would help. I notice some teenagers about my age nudging each other when a girl says how tempting it is to drink because there is not much to do. Sounds like teenagers in Newtown or maybe anywhere. They need activities.

When Ken walks me to the trailer, Dad says, "Hey, we have some great steaks that need to be cooked. Why don't you invite your friends over for dinner tonight?"

Ken says he could cook. My eyes widen in surprise. Who does this? Who is he? How does he know how to cook, too? Then he asks, why don't we cook together? Really? I have had dates, but nothing like real life, doing something together. We comfortably dance around each other in the small space of the trailer. When the steaks are ready, we serve my family and the three other New Hampshire guys outside.

As soon as everyone is seated, Dad wants to know everything. "What do you do? How did you get here? What kind of help are you giving? Who is sponsoring you?"

"No one," says Larry choosing the last question. "It was Ken's idea. He raised the money. Pete's parents gave us an old car. We figured, why not? We have time—no school, Pete's job hasn't started. I don't have to go to the Peace Corps training for a few weeks. And school for Ronnie and Ken doesn't start until next month."

"That's very ambitious of you to do this at your young ages," says Dad—so impressed that he forgets to make them sing a song—his usual practice when I bring a boy to dinner.

❦

Ken and I do the dishes. When he washes a plate and hands it to me, his soapy hand grazes mine. My hand feels zapped. Then his shoulder brushes against my arm. Suddenly my arm is a spotlight of energy. By mistake, my breasts graze his back as I reach to put the glasses away. My face flushes. I can feel the blood coursing through my body. More than anything, I want to be alone with him.

We go to the mission tent instead. Dr. Frazier says, "A good Christian smiles, has fun."

As the "I led a terrible life..." part begins an hour and a half into the service, the four boys, Corney, a Dakota, and I sneak out to follow his advice and have some fun. Who wants salvation—when there is fun to be had?

Once outside Ken reaches for my hand. We walk away from the others—up the hill toward the church. When we get there, he touches my face lightly with his fingertips, looks into my eyes, reaches his arms around me, and leans over to touch his lips to mine. His beard is prickly as it grazes my cheek. Lightening streaks around the horizon as our bodies feel electricity. We barely take a breath. What seems like less than five minutes later, he warns that a storm is about to break, so we'd better get under cover. And a movie is starting—shown on the gift projector. All through the movie, Ken holds my hand. When the movie ends, we walk back to their car and climb in. In spite of the cool night, the air gets steamy.

"Do you play chess?" he asks.

"No," I say. He laughs and then I get it. "Oh, you mean, the stalemate? You mean every time you make a move, I stalemate you?"

"Yes, and you've been winning all night."

"I like kissing." Nothing more, either, I add to myself.

"In Dakota they would call you, Wawona wasete. It means, 'good girl'." He squeezes my hand. "Wawona wasete," he says, again, kissing me as he opens the car door. "It's late. Go now, before we fall asleep. I'll probably regret it later. I feel like a starving man turning away a full course dinner. Good night."

I gently open the metal door of the trailer. "Do you know what time it is?" Mom whispers. "It is two o'clock! Where have you been?"

"I've been right outside," I whisper back, climbing quietly into my sleeping bag, and lie still. My mind is flying.

I don't sleep too long, though, because Ken is in the car—about fifteen feet away. I look out at four in the morning to make sure he is still there. At six I wake up, write in my diary, and step outside.

Ken isn't up yet, so I talk to Ronnie. "What have you done to him? When we went through towns, we stopped and whistled at the girls, but

Ken never even looked at them. Casanova Ken, as we now call him, will probably organize a work camp to Connecticut next year.

"I hope so," I smile.

After breakfast, the boys are ready to leave. Ken sticks his head out the car window. "Good luck with that tournament!" he says, grinning at me, as he tucks my address into his Bible.

The dust settles from their car, and my heart sings as I remember something he told me: "Your life speaks so loudly, I can't hear what you are saying." That's Ken. I fold his address and slip it into my bra, next to my heart. I hope he writes me. Such an amazing guy—he knows how to farm, lead discussions, drive across the country, organize work camps, build a youth center. He acts on his beliefs. He has faith and can even cook. I've never met anyone like him.

"Did you have fun with those boys?" Dad asks, not glancing up from a book he's reading in the shade of the trailer.

I reach down to pick up a rock so he can't see my red face, just thinking about how much fun.

Chapter Ten

— *Ken's First visit to Newtown*

"Girls NEVER write first," Mom tells me me when I show her the ten-page letter I've written to Ken after meeting him. "You need to wait until you get a letter from him" she says. I keep writing even when I begin my freshman year of college. My heart aches for the excitement that I found with Ken in those few days, but it's been three months and there's no word from him.

At Danbury State College I start dating a junior named Bob. I'm not going to sit home at this prime age and wait for a letter that might never come. In October, Bob takes me to a formal ball, buys me my first orchid corsage and promises to build us a house with a white picket fence next door to his parents in Connecticut. We could teach school. I find this b-o-r-i-n-g when compared to imagining a future with a person like Ken. I cringe when I hear his Danbury accent. He's not the one.

❦

Finally, during the second week of November, I get a letter. Ken says he'd lost my address in his Bible. Aha, maybe he doesn't read it as much as I thought; I'd had him pegged as a Bible reader. In any case, he says he is planning go by bus to visit his friend Larry in Washington DC. Larry had been in the Virgin Islands training for the Peace Corps when his heart enlarged three times. He nearly died. The Peace Corps has flown him to a hospital in Washington DC where he is recovering. Ken will stop in Newtown on his way back to New Hampshire. I feel like jumping up and down.

And then he's here, right in my living room, talking to Mom! A long way from the reservation. It's so powerful having him here; I have to keep busy, coming in and out of the room. Dad is at work and Ken is sitting on a footstool facing the sun porch. I am watching silently. What will he do next? He has tied some red yarn together—is trying to figure out how the Shipibo-Conibo people in Peru weave with back strap looms. Mom is knitting mittens for the church gift tree.

"How does it work? How do you get those strings lined up? What will hold it together?" asks Mom, watching Ken over her knitting. I don't remember Mom hanging out with any other love interest of mine.

Ken says, "This looked so easy in Peru. The women just leaned back against the yarn like this." He leans back, the strings twist, and the stick separating the warp strings falls out. "Ahem!" He laughs. "Well, anyway, they lean back and pop the shuttle back and forth." He can't demonstrate now because there is no separation between the threads. "This is what's wrong with modern society. We are losing the important things—like how to make material for clothing. I wish you could have seen those women. They could set up on any tree or pole. Then knot the string, smooth out the warp, I guess it is called, and move their hands so fast, it was a blur. It was magic. Or so I thought. I can see it wasn't magic. It was work. To those women, weaving was living. A life skill."

Ken is the god in my life, even though I now know that he's not reading his Bible that much. I am watching the interaction, laughing at the way he switches "r" and "a", like "park the car" being "paaak the caa" or "Allah" being "Aller". Of course, he has a Boston accent—he was born in Massachusetts and his mother and father were, too.

I had waited all the day before for him to call so that we could pick him up at the bus station. Did he call? No. In the evening, there was a knock at the door. Ken stood with his bulging tweed wool overcoat, a stocking knit hat, and a few days growth of beard.

When he brought his hand out from underneath his coat, it held a metal coffee can. Julie, Joan, Harry, Tom, Mom, and I stared at the can. Dad in his armchair kept his eyes on the newspaper. Inside the metal can something moved. "White mice!" breathed Joan. I'm not big on animals, but my family is. In that one moment, he won over Mom and my younger brothers and sisters.

We kids knew that Mom had had a white mouse as a child. She reached into the desk in the living room and flipped through a pile of papers to find a story that she had written about it. She read it to Ken and to all of us.

Pete, the White Rat
by Ann Titsworth

My brother has "Pete," a white rat that is very tame, in a cage in his room. He lets the rat out when he is in his room. There is a little ledge behind the mirror on his bureau where Pete likes to walk. If you get at one end and whistle, Pete turns around as quickly as he can and comes walking along to see you.

One afternoon my brother came downstairs and said, "Mother, may I get a new toothbrush? Pete took mine." Pete also took six marbles and a necktie into his cage. He wove the necktie around his nest.

It is very cute the way he takes things. Every night my brother takes a jar of milk upstairs for Pete, and if he doesn't give it to Pete right away, Pete gets some himself by climbing on the edge of the jar, putting his head way down in, and drinking.

He also thinks he has to store for the winter. So whenever there is some food that my brother is going to feed him, he takes it in his cage to store it.

Pete once got up on the edge of the goldfish bowl and put his paw in to get a drink of water.

One night my brother was awakened at twelve o'clock. Pete tickled him on the cheek with his whiskers. He must have pushed up the top of his cage to get out.

My brother says, "He's a good little pal."

❧

Mom says Ken's white mice look like good little pals. I'm not so sure, but already Mom and Ken are bonded.

Chapter Eleven

 *Beginning November*

*I*t is November 22, 1963 and I am going to Boston to meet Ken without my family for the first time. I still have to get through gym class and then I'll be done for the weekend. To go away for a weekend unsupervised to meet a guy is completely new to me. My heart pounds when I think of it. But for now, I have to sit with all the other girls against the wall in the corridor at Danbury State College waiting for the teacher to lead us outside. Like everyone else, I wear a regulation pale yellow gym suit with snap fronts and pantaloons rolled up to the top of my legs. Someone whispers that she heard President Kennedy was shot. I don't believe it. As far as I know, the last president who was assassinated was Lincoln and that was a hundred years ago. (Later I remembered two others, Garfield in 1881 and McKinley in 1901.) In modern times, presidents wear bulletproof vests and have security. We're nearly twenty years past World War II. People don't get killed randomly these days.

And yet, our always-frowning gym teacher comes out of her office and announces that President Kennedy has been shot at a parade in Texas and taken to a hospital. Now our class will go outside to practice field hockey. "Line up," she orders when we get outside. One-by-one we dribble the field hockey ball part way up the field and pass it to someone. That person stops the ball with her stick and tries to shoot it into the goal. Nothing is different about the class except that each time I catch someone's eye, I see tears. The President. What has happened? Will he live? Everyone's face is sullen and white. I pray that he doesn't die as I swing the field hockey stick. I imagine the other girls are praying, too.

After class, we all go to the locker room wondering if President Kennedy is alive. Our teacher checks the radio and reports without any emotion that the president has died. And in that moment, life in the United States changes. With my head down and eyes wet, I dress, and prepare for the weekend.

The purpose of the train trip is to attend an American Friends Service Committee (AFSC) work camp in Roxbury, a Black community of Boston. I will meet my love Ken there. Yet, with the day's events, I wonder: do trains keep their schedule when a US president is killed? I have no idea exactly what will happen. In my mind are thoughts of freedom, romance, service, and tragedy.

Even before the tragedy, I'd wondered if I could I manage this weekend. I love the idea of service but the reality is new to me. Am I strong enough to work in impoverished areas? What will the families be like? What will the apartments be like? Will it be hard work? It feels like a test to see who I am as a young adult and if I am worthy of being with a humanitarian like Ken. Even while he is in college, he spends weekends at work camps in the "projects" of Boston.

An hour later, as the train gathers speed, I glance across the aisle where someone has left the morning New York Times with news that is already old. On the back page is a small photo of Vice President Lyndon Johnson. The headline says, "JFK considers a New Running Mate." I wonder if Lyndon Johnson has already been inducted as the new president.

❦

When I arrive in Boston, Ken meets me with a big hug and kiss and takes me by MTA to Dudley Station in Roxbury. We walk to a settlement house where we will stay. On the way, his eyes are soft as he explains that the house is a place for middle class students to lodge while they support and organize with the Black community for justice, equality, and power. Again, I have a wave of self-questioning. But Ken has been here before. My feelings are complex, his energy draws me so strongly I have to focus on the sidewalk so that I can hear his words.

Inside the settlement house Bob and Mary, workshop directors for the American Friends Service Committee (AFSC) program, sit at a long table with twenty young people. We join them for a dinner of chili con carne. So far, so good. After dinner the directors explain that the purpose of the weekend is to improve housing. Tomorrow at breakfast, we will get assignments to visit Black families and support them in some practical way. My home town in Connecticut is nearly all white. One Brown girl, Johnette, graduated with me but I didn't know her well. I don't know what it will be like to be with the Black families in their apartments. I have never been in any apartment building in any city. Even so, I am eager to meet the community and experience the work challenge. AFSC works with the organizations Congress on Racial Equality (CORE) and the Student Nonviolent Coordinating Committee (SNCC). They both are in the news as they work for racial equality.

℞

For perspective of the times, Martin Luther King Jr. had given his speech "I have a dream" three months before on August 28, 1963 to 200,000 people who marched on Washington. President Kennedy introduced the Civil Rights Act on June 12, 1963. It hadn't passed yet, and wouldn't until on June 10, 1964. The Civil Rights Act of 1964 would outlaw discrimination "on the basis of race, color, religion, national origin and sex in public accommodations, employment, and federal funded programs."[1]

℞

I will stay in a girl's dorm later. But after dinner Mary and Bob ask if Ken and I will babysit their two sleeping children. We discover that this means spending time in their bedroom with the kids asleep in the next room.

The situation is a dream. There's only a double bed. No chairs. No way to be apart. We laugh. I guess Ken is surprised, too. But it's great. We have escaped from the world.

Our first time alone with soft touching, clothes pressing, lips search-

[1] www.civilrights.org

ing, and, so conveniently, on a bed. Delicious. When Mary and Bob come back and we separate to go to our dorm rooms to sleep, my whole body is alive and humming.

In the morning Ken's and my assignment from CORE is to check the apartment of a family where a rat had bitten a baby in her crib. We are to patch holes in the plaster and paint the walls. Mrs. Hunter meets us at the door and then is busy feeding her children and watching television with them. I paint a dining room wall while Ken patches the bedroom wall. I keep looking over at him, so competent and sure of himself. Every time I look I feel a zap in my body remembering our hugging last night. At noon, Mrs. Hunter hands us soda in a sticky glass. I feel good here, doing something. I drink the soda, ignoring the film. She apologizes for the glasses and tells us that her kitchen water faucet is broken so she can't wash the dishes. I look at the pile of dirty dishes and wonder how she can manage.

I never knew helping could feel this right.

When we leave the Hunters there is a positive change in the apartment and in the attitude of the family. The kids hang on to us. They don't want us to go, but we are finished and eager to share more experiences.

❧

Ken wants me to meet another family he enjoyed knowing during past work camps. The Roberts live in "the projects." While there, I take it to mean that projects are apartment buildings with outside concrete stairways for poor people. I later learn that projects are government-subsidized housing. The goal in the beginning was for people with lower incomes to live in more convenient locations rather than moving away from the city for affordable housing. Later, the projects were blamed for concentrating poverty in certain communities.

The apartment is a third floor walk-up. When Mrs. Roberts opens the door, we see a mother with eight kids. She says, "Hi Kinny," greeting him as an old friend. One look and she says, "Oh, you brought someone. Are you two going to tie the knot?" This is all new to me, asking such a blunt question before I even know her. She sees our closeness.

On her black and white television she points to Day Two of the three-day funeral proceedings of President Kennedy. It is the first news we have seen. Tears in her eyes reflect the light of the picture. The little kids wander in and out. The older two don't leave their places on the floor in front of the TV. Tears stream down their faces. "We won't turn it off," Mrs. Roberts says. "He was always good to us folks. Supported integration."

Two sisters, seven and eight years old, ask if they can touch and comb my long, straight brown hair. They sit me in a chair in front of the television. As they comb, a horse- drawn casket with President Kennedy drives from the Rotunda. Just behind the caisson, Jackie Kennedy, with a black veil over her face, walks with Robert Kennedy and her two little ones, Caroline and John. Behind them are President Lyndon Johnson and First Lady, Lady Bird.

I don't know how to talk about our President being killed. Or what this all means. I am not used to representing myself in this way. I still live with my parents. Maybe I disappear into Ken. Seeing things through his eyes. Accepting him as the authority. He wants me to speak my mind. I have no words yet.

I am surprised at the non-stop sobs of the young teenagers watching the news and at Mrs. Roberts who chokes back a sob every time she glances at it. President Kennedy represents hope to her. The two-year old boy playing on the floor toddles over to give his sad mother a hug. And his three-year old sister glances up at her mother with big eyes and walks to her. With tears dripping, their mother gives each one attention and pats the baby asleep on her lap. There is action all around me. Love. Attention. I can feel the energy of the family.

I don't know what I feel about the President being killed. It is wrong. I am shocked and sad. But more doesn't reach me. My heart is fully engaged with this new experience and being with Ken. I am present in this apartment full of kids with the girls gently combing my hair, saying how easy it is to comb. Everything mixes together.

℘

I was confused about Kennedy becoming President. My parents are Republicans. I can not vote for three more years. In the 1960 election, I handed out Republican pamphlets for Nixon. My father was against Kennedy because he was Catholic. Like my father, many Protestants believed that, as president, he would answer to the pope who could then actually rule the United States. After President Kennedy won, I didn't hear any mention of his religion or the pope. Ken says that Republicans take care of businessmen and Democrats take care of all citizens. My father is a businessman.

Already I am in a sensitive emotional state from the new feelings about Ken. I cry along with Mrs. Roberts. Ken does, too. For humans committing violence to others. For the little Kennedy kids, like these kids, who have no father now. For Jackie who—like Mrs. Roberts—is without a husband. And I cry just because when I see someone else cry, I cry, too.

But with the Roberts family, we sense something more. Real grief and despair. The Roberts lost a President from their state who cared about race relations. Someone who cared about them. Mrs. Roberts tells us that when he was a senator, John Kennedy contacted Georgia's officials to help get Martin Luther King out of jail. In June, she saw President Kennedy talking about giving the right to vote to everyone with a grade school education.

"That would mean that we could vote, go into any business, and sit anywhere we want. President Kennedy was our President." Her kids know this. Her friends know this. Ken knows this. I am learning.

The funeral procession ends at Saint Matthews Cathedral and the world is silent for five minutes as Cardinal Cushing begins the mass. Ken, the Roberts family, and I sit still in the apartment. The kids soften their sobs. The shared moment of silence draws us together. Ken's and my eyes meet.

When we leave, I realize that seeing the news makes the President's death real. To hear what the President has done to help Black people makes me want to do something. I find it beautiful that Ken and Mrs. Roberts are friends and glance sideways, wondering how I got so lucky.

Climbing down the concrete stairs, Ken says, "My dream is to adopt Black kids."

Coming from the crowded warmth of the Roberts' apartment, having my hair softly combed by the two girls, sharing grief, I feel a yearning in my heart, too.

Chapter Twelve

~ *Art and Life*

You have your antenna out. You're just walking through the world and you're picking up these signals of emotions and spirit and history and events, today's events and past remembrances. People who are very attuned to that atmosphere usually end up being artists of some sort. Because they're so attuned to it, they have a desire to record it. If that desire to record it is strong enough, you learn a language to do so. Whether it's paintings, films, songs, poetry . . .
~Bruce Springsteen

*W*hen summer comes, I need to leave. Harry had left in December to be an AFS student in New Zealand for a year. Up until he left, Harry had softened Dad in his usual peaceful way. I am outspoken, like my father is, and it sets him off. I can't believe I have had to live with my family during my whole freshman year of college. Without Harry to buffer Dad's anger, my life has been unbearable.

Mom and Dad agree to let me spend the summer in Keene, New Hampshire where Ken is. My goal is to spend time with my love. I will take a summer class at Keene State College and get a job, while I board out of town with Mrs. Ruse, an older woman. This is the plan and they approve. Yet, Mom cries when I leave and whispers that she doesn't think I will come back.

A lot of things happen at once—sculpture, apartment, factory work, love.

Ken and I have spent our school vacations together since November.

Now I yearn to be with him completely—spiritually, emotionally, and sexually. He picks me up at the bus station in the dark. We can't go out to the woman's house at this late hour and none of his roommates are in his apartment. That leaves us one option—to sleep together all night for the first time in his twin bed. We are each other's first lovers at nineteen and twenty-two. A night of softness, touching, smoothness happens. All lovely.

The next morning we take a ride out to Mrs. Ruse's house. When I step into the dark, dreary space that smells of dust, I don't want Ken to leave me there, but he does.

At Keene State College, I choose a sculpture class so that I can be near Ken in the art building. He is an art major, building a loom in the next room. Smells of wet plaster from our eighteen-inch blocks and cut wood from next door permeate the room. The class is horrifying and magnificent. I stand all day with my hunk of plaster on a stand and peacefully chip away at it, letting something emerge. As I chisel and en-vision and get encouragement from the professor and Ken, I feel focused. No hurry. Thoughts fly away. I lose track of time. No one pulls on me to help with dishes or to take care of a brother or sister. Dad is not here to interrupt my train of thought to get me to do something for Mom or him.

❧

The horrifying part—of taking the class—is I believe I have no artis-tic ability. In first grade I scribbled over a black dog on a mimeographed worksheet and ended up with a big fat D on the paper and time out in the hall where everyone saw me and asked me what I had done.

And further, as part of Swimming School after first grade, I took a craft class to make a candleholder. First, we rolled out clay like a piecrust. Then traced a three-inch circle and three smaller petal shapes from the clay slab. After attaching the petals to the circle, we formed a coil to hold the candle and placed it in the center. Mine was stiff and ugly. A Black girl named Jane across the table from me attached her petals and pressed them with her thumb, making flowing and gentle curves. When they were glazed and fired, I found my name on hers. I told the teacher that this one wasn't mine. The teacher insisted that my name was on it. Maybe the teacher wrote it herself. I saw this decades later as possibly overt racism. I couldn't do anything. And Jane accepted the one the teacher handed her. She took my ugly candlestick holder home. I watched her lift it up. Her face did not show any expression.

My parents complimented me on the one I took home and burned a candle in it, but I felt sick every time I looked at it. I wondered if her parents knew that the one she had was not hers. If they knew of her grace and sensitivity, her artistic touch. If they knew she was cheated. I was confused about what happened and found no way to change it. All I did know was that I was no artist.

❦

Boarding with Mrs. Ruse isn't working for me. My first Saturday there, after telling me which room I can go into and which ones I can't, she tells me I will clean her root cellar. I pull up a metal ring on the kitchen floor to open a trap door. She points as I walk down the four wooden steps and bend over in the darkness to find shelves of liquid vegetables and tiny animal carcasses. I gag at the smell of rot and mold and try to hold my breath for as long as I can. I put the decayed food into bags and carry them, soft, leaking, and slippery, up to the garbage can.

The only good thing about having this boarding situation is that without it I wouldn't have gotten permission to come.

❦

Ken and I work for a company run by two Greek men that silk-screens cards and bumper stickers for places like Fort Devens and Ballantine beer. The business is factory work in a hot room with toxic paint smells and bad lighting. A production line keeps the product moving. Someone runs a squeegee over a screen fixed with a pattern, transferring it onto paper. After a sheet is printed, someone has to cut it with a powerful paper cutter— and quickly—to keep the assembly line moving. The next step is to punch out parts of the print with our hands. Cutting the paper is Ken's job—until he nearly cuts his thumb off and ends up in the hospital.

In the sculpture studio, I happily carve at the intersection of mother and child. With one extra nick from the chisel, the child part doesn't work anymore. I chip it off and my mother and child sculpture turns into the bust of a woman. Like me. I like it and the teacher likes it. Maybe I am becoming an artist—doing well in the sculpture class and also creating something with Ken.

☙

After Ken comes out of the emergency room of the hospital with stitches and a bandaged hand, his accident becomes the perfect excuse to move in together, because he needs help—with only one hand functioning. We sit on a curb on Main Street holding the Keene Sentinel newspaper open to rent ads. Right away we find an available place in a building behind the church at the end of Main Street. If we look up, we can practically see it from where we are sitting.

When we rent the fifty-dollar-a-month, second-story apartment, we have each other and nothing else. After opening the door with our key, we stand in the large empty living room, looking through a doorway to an empty bedroom, to the bathroom with a claw-foot tub, and turn to check out the galley kitchen with a small gas stove, a refrigerator, cabinets, and a sink. This is enough. We don't have a pan, so we eat SpaghettiO's from a can with two forks we have bought from Woolworth's store on the way home. It's really fun. Who wouldn't want to be with someone who knows how to manage on nothing, weave, build, and softly make love? We sleep on the hard wood floor and wake up smiling.

The next stop is a second-hand furniture store. My list includes a bed, a table, chairs, a pan, a teakettle, two plates, silverware, two glasses, two cups, and two bowls. We fairly dance around the store, looking at everything, imagining where to put it in our apartment and discussing the pluses and minuses of each item. In the end, we buy a table made from a door, chairs, and a bed frame with a bookcase, headboard, and drawers under the bed. When we add some kitchen utensils, we have everything we need for under $38.

Once Ken and I have spent a week together, I know what heaven is—having our own life and making decisions together without anyone yelling at me. When I compare it to being home where my father is in charge, I see Dad's anger directed at me. Here I dare to say no and I have a will. I can't imagine another half a year at home without Harry. Now that I have escaped for a summer to be with Ken, I know can't go back.

We are happy just staying here until a friend tells us this could lead us to jail. What? Ken thinks we can live together for seven years and have a common law marriage, but she tells us that cohabitation is illegal in New Hampshire in 1964.

We decide to get married. Ken is the perfect person to marry—harmonious, communicative, creative, and opens my heart in new ways. Ken is my whole world. I call my parents from a pay phone and tell them we want to get married right away. I can transfer to Keene State College. At first, my mother listens quietly. Mom's life has been to love her children and give all of herself to us. As the quintessential mother born on the second Mother's Day, all she wants is for us to be happy.

As a girl, I dreamed of the perfect wedding on June 27, the wedding day of my parents and mother's parents. But after telling her we want to get married right away, Mom cries all night. She can't bear rushing though the wedding preparations. A couple of weeks won't do. Meanwhile, Ken is not happy thinking of all the trappings of a wedding—rings, gown, presents, cake, guests. He wants simplicity and would rather move together into a tarpaper shack in the woods. Maybe we should wait a little. We schedule the wedding for two months later on August 8 in Newtown.

❦

When Ken becomes part of my life, I am Sas. I like the name Sally Ann, especially having my mother's name as part of mine. But, everyone shortens it to Sally and I hate the shortened name. Since first grade my parents complained every time someone missed the Ann part. They saw it as one name, in spite of having a space and capital A for the second part. Very few people used my whole name. Tired of correcting people, I pre-empt the problem by using Sas.

Who I am becoming is not what was expected of a Connecticut high school National Honor Society member, American Field Service president, and foreign exchange student. I assumed I would go to four years of college, meet a man, marry him after graduation, and live in a white house with green shutters and a wide green yard. I would go to the Congregational Church, vote Republican, and be active in the community like my parents.

All that changes with Ken. I doubt if I could find anyone anywhere more attractive and experienced in the kind of life I want to live. I want a worldly life with lots of experiences. Already I can see that every moment with him will be new and exciting.

☙

A week after postponing our wedding until August, Mom and Dad say we are invited to see the Dakota Reverend Philip Frazier receive an honorary doctorate of divinity degree at Dartmouth College, two hours north of us in New Hampshire. They pick us up in Keene and we arrange to meet them on the street. We are nervous that they will discover that we are living together. But they don't. We ride to Hanover and find a place to park among the tens of thousands attending the graduation on the village green. We sit in the back. From here the graduates are tiny dolls. After the ceremony, we fight the flow of the crowd to find Dr. Frazier and congratulate him. When he sees us, he says, "Oh, there you are! Where were you? I had seats in front for you. You are my guests and I hope you can join me for the luncheon with the other honorary degree recipients and their guests at the Hanover Inn." On the way to our table, we notice that one of the honorary degree recipients is the famous Secretary of State Dean Rusk, proponent of the Vietnam War. We don't say anything at this fancy event.

Back in Keene, our classes finish. I complete a plaster fish sculpture in addition to the woman. It is more abstract and more like a sculpture than my "two dimensional" woman, as Ken calls it as he dries the dishes I have just washed.

With the summer course done, we focus on our next step—the wedding.

Chapter Thirteen

⁓ *Wedding*

*O*ur two families meet for the first time at Ken's parent's house in Manchester, New Hampshire. Conveniently, my family stops on the way from a Prince Edward Island vacation. Manchester is not far out of the way. The parents get along fine, although his father is the soft one like my mother and his mother can be loud and critical like my father. All goes well at their house and I join my family the rest of the way home to Connecticut to prepare for our wedding. Ken goes back to Keene to work.

In our green 1962 Chevy station wagon, with the trailer in back, we have the same general seating arrangement as we did on our trip out West the previous year. Julie, thirteen, Joan, twelve, and I sit in the back seat with me behind Mom who is in the passenger seat. Tom, eight, lies in the way back with his shoes off and a blanket over him figuring out averages from his baseball cards. Julie knits a sweater and Joan works on a wedding present for Ken and me. It is a green afghan, already three feet long. I address wedding invitations. We miss Harry who is still in New Zealand.

As we cross the line between Massachusetts and Connecticut, we distinctly hear s-s-s-s, a hissing sound, as if air is escaping from a punctured tire. My sisters and I assume this stretch of the highway is making the sound. Then Dad feels it and gently pumps the brakes. When they don't work, he carefully maneuvers the car to the side of the road. I open my door, ready to get out.

And gasp. Flames from the back tire almost lick my face. I blurt out, "Fire!" Slam the door shut, put the wedding invitations behind my seat so that I can get out fast, slide to the road side and climb out. Everyone rushes out the highway side to get away from the fire.

When Tom and Joan bolt out of the door, they turn toward the rear of the car where the trailer is, while the rest of us turn toward the front. They don't realize that there will be no way to rejoin us without passing close to the burning car.

Dad yells to Tom and Joan, "Keep going. Get away from the car. The gas tank might explode." He signals to them. The four of us climb a fence, run through a field, and beyond to a house. Trees line the road beside the trailer so Joan and Tom keep going along the highway, farther and farther.

Dad knocks and asks the woman at the door to call the fire department. Tom and Joan keep running farther from the car and us. After the woman calls, she gives us lemonade. We four stand silently drinking it as we watch flames engulf our car, our clothes, bedding, tent, cots, and art supplies. There is nothing we can do. Time ticks along.

Still no fire engine comes. The car windows crackle and melt, folding over. My diary and the wedding invitations burn. Tom's baseball cards that he has earned by sweeping the floor at the campground in Prince Edward Island burn. Julie's almost-finished knit sweater and the Joan's knit afghan burn. Mom's and Dad's wallets. The car and everything in it are blackened and still the fire roars. Where is the fire department?

Just as we watch the flames lick the front of the trailer and hear its windows begin to crackle, the fire department arrives with two police cars. They stop traffic and stand back. Right then, the gas tank explodes, the blue, orange, and yellow flames burst twenty feet into the air.

When the explosion dies down, the fire department gets it under control and saves the trailer. Tom and Joan join us. Tom's eyes are wide, his socks caked with dirt, since in the hurry he had to leave his shoes in the car. We praise them for being so brave as we all wait and watch for a tow truck to take our car and trailer to a garage. We follow in a police car. The police tells us that the delay was caused by the fire department getting an incorrect address.

No one was hurt, not even the firemen when the gas tank exploded.

Insurance agent Dad will write up the claims, but you can't replace knitting. It takes time to re-order wedding invitations. And Dad tries to tell Tom that the cards aren't worth much, but Tom knows even then that they are.

Standing at the garage peering into the wet blackened Chevy, we wait after Dad calls his secretary. Her family is borrowing our second car while our family is on vacation. Billy Benedict, her son, arrives in the old Ford two hours later to take us home. The Ford just happens to have a trailer hitch, so Dad attaches the trailer with its crinkled glass and sooty front and we all pile into the car to ride home in the dark.

Dad and I return to that burned car the next day and search through the soggy, sooty rubble, making a list of destroyed items on a brown paper bag. I find my wallet with singed high school pictures and coins in the space where I sat. Behind the seat, one char-edged wedding invitation, but Tom's shoes and baseball cards and the rest of the invitations are gone. I wonder what kind of omen it is for my wedding.

☙

Contrary to what Ken would like, we aren't moving into a tar paper shack. I guess he wants to spend his life with me even when we plan "all the trappings." A fifties girl's whole life is lived for her wedding. The culture has us dressing up from when we are little. We act out make-believe weddings. What are proms and formal dances but preludes to a wedding day? No way will I avoid having a real wedding.

Mom and her mother Gagie make my gown, as the newspaper announcement says, with "a fitted lace bodice of French illusion lace … the floor length satin skirt was laid in full, soft pleats." Mom and Gagie also make pastel bridesmaids' dresses for Julie, Joan, and Ken's sister Carolyn—organza in yellow, lavender, and green taffeta. A jeweler takes a diamond from a locket I inherited from my great aunt to create an engagement ring, so I can match Mom with her engagement and wedding rings.

A week before our wedding, I am back in Keene when I get a letter from Dad:

> *I think you were always working for your own identity in our*
> *large family and this individualism of yours was bound to con-*

flict with my ideas of our family group. Parents are supposed to
make individuals out of their children, and it is this business of
wanting you to ourselves and our desire for you to stand on your
own feet that caused some of the troubles.

I'm not sure I registered the truth of his words then. But later I realize that his anger erupted when I wanted to "stand on my own feet" and make my own decisions, like when I got my pigtails cut, bought the music I liked, or sat in the living room, not helping Mom. That was exactly our conflict.

And then the day comes. We have joined the Quakers, but they don't have a building of their own. We arrive at the Newtown Congregational Church in a Black Thunderbird. Dad walks me down the aisle. Organ music plays. Then the wedding is in silent Quaker form. Friends read Kahil Gibran's poems from the silence. A college friend Ida, perhaps the first Black person ever in the church building, reads "On Love". Ken and I say our vows to each other and exchange gold bands. Mr. Singer, the minister, pronounces us man and wife, even though we've asked him not to.

And so, on August 8, 1964, Ken and I are married.

Chapter Fourteen

➤ *Haystack Mountain School*

*I*n spite of burned wedding invitations and Ken not being super enthusiastic about the wedding process, our first year of marriage is full of lovely freedom. The two of us are in charge, planning, learning together as I start my sophomore and Ken his junior year at Keene State College. Our life is peaceful in the apartment with our simple lifestyle. We have added a tank with Beta fish, guppies, and angel fish and watch them instead of television. Piles of boxes of still-packed fancy silver and china dishes from our wedding sit in the corner of the living room. We are in love. That's what's important.

Thank goodness Ken knows how to manage—cooking, working, and going to school—because I am on my own for the first time. I know how to cook a few basic dishes and mainly sweets, like cakes, cookies, and brownies, food to get into Dad's good graces. When Ken invites a couple to dinner, I have to call Mom from a phone booth in the corner drug store to ask her how to make a pot roast. I cry from missing her. Yet, from the first night at the apartment when we slept in sleeping bags in an empty room, life has been easy between us—with one exception. Ken has a habit of not tightening the tops of containers and I have a habit of lifting containers by their tops. One day I lift the top of a bottle of grape juice and our refrigerator turns purple—every shelf—and down to the floor. I gasp and then laugh as Ken gets the sponge and I grab the dishcloth.

Ken's friend Ben Taylor, a sturdy broad-shouldered person with thick glasses, is the only other upper class art major at Keene State College. His projects and Ken's art work are flexible and individualized. My studies are in education, not so flexible. As a nineteen-year old, I have trouble answering to the name Mrs. Mayberger in English class, but the teacher has just read *How to Win Friends and Influence People* by Dale Carnegie and calls everyone Miss and Mr. I am the only Mrs. I don't feel like a regular student. At this conservative school, Ken, one other student, and I are the only ones opposed to the Vietnam War. It gives me a strange feeling.

The summer before, Ben had attended Haystack Mountain School of Crafts in Maine, one of the most prestigious craft summer schools in the country. As the year progresses, he thinks it would be a good place for us. He helps us apply for work scholarships. We need a break from living in the center of Keene and want to be around artist types who understand our views against the war. One winter day, Ken and I drive to Maine to check it out. Haystack's Quaker director Fran Merritt and his wife invite us to stay at their home. I am charmed with the wood cook stove, antiques, and the couple. With Fran we ride to Haystack at the end of the road on Little Deer Isle—a site enveloped by evergreen trees with ocean below us. We walk on the boardwalks, our eyes feasting on the modern shed-style, shingled buildings. Below us, on this blustery day, we watch and listen as huge waves with chunks of ice smash against the cliffs. Raw power. We are sold. I have reservations about my ability to create art for six weeks, but the site could not be better.

As summer draws near, Ken dismantles his six-foot Jacquard loom and re-erects it in the weaving studio at Haystack. I study at that studio for our first three-week session with Mary Walker Philips, a famous knitter. Drawn to texture and color, I sit in the sun with the ocean view, creating objects with strings. I weave on a loom and knit on wooden needles I make from dowels with Susan Erb. She is just my age and is (shockingly) planning to travel alone with her boyfriend to Mexico. A single woman traveling alone with a boyfriend has the same stigma as co-habitation. She tells me her parents are artists and they are fine with it. The students and teachers at Haystack are individuals, artists, bohemians—and war resisters. What a relief to be among them! Susan and I find our days full of brilliant purple, turquoise, and green yarns. We feel the rhythm of loom beaters and breathe the ocean scents as we sit on a deck in the sun and share stories.

Yet the clay studio pulls me. I wander over to watch the students throw pots on the wheel. Over and over and over until they get one right. A thousand pots you need to throw before you get a perfect one, they tell me. This is a revelation. I thought talent made an artist. Maybe I can learn. For Ken's and my second three-week residence, I take pottery.

Even though I failed with the candlestick as a seven-year old, I love the feeling of wet clay in my hands and the magic of using a wheel to throw a pot. To glaze and fire that bowl so that it comes out of the kiln with a creamy white speckled finish— that is magic. At the end of those three weeks, I want to become a potter.

❧

I am also drawn to the artists' way of light hearted-ness and risqué behavior, like a famous potter and writer sitting casually topless on the deck. That is, they relax when they are not at work making a thousand pots. These seasoned artists have a carefree and free-flowing way of creating beauty once they have mastered their craft.

❧

Every day, the ocean is inviting me to swim. Looking, watching star-fish at the ocean's edge. The seeing, hearing, smelling, touching, visceral-ness of it all, like taking a walk in the woods, slowly, with the shadows sideways on rare orchids. All a part of the creative process. I don't have words but feel at home.

As we drive off Deer Isle and see autumn colors, I feel a shiver for the coming winter with its blandness of city life for my junior year of school.

Chapter Fifteen

— *Where is here?*

"*W*e're here."

Ken pulls the car off a narrow, snowy road into more snow. It is 1965 during the spring vacation of my junior year at Keene State College. I am twenty years old and Ken is showing me some land where he wants to live. Our friends, Dee and Jay, whom we met through Quakers, have bought forty acres and, as is common in the sixties, have invited us to live on it with them. We have visited Dee and Jay in a log cabin where they now live in southern Vermont. This spring semester Ken and Jay have been builting a log cabin on this land in the north. We will have a place to stay if and when we move here at the end of the semester.

I am wondering where "here" is. All I know is that we left Keene four hours before and are now somewhere in Vermont, near the Canadian border. The snow banks are as high as the car. The road, the trees, everything is white. Ken matter-of-factly unloads snowshoes for me—the wooden rawhide kind, wide and heavy—and he puts his skis on. We climb over the snowbank.

The only sound is the wet crunch of snow compacting under our steps. I stumble between evergreen trees. The balsam smell matches a pillow in my father's drawer. We come upon a frozen brook with water gurgling under the ice, and walk up a grade to a field rimmed by more evergreen trees. The sun is moving higher in the sky, and the snow is softening. Ken has a spring in his step like a jackrabbit. I lag behind, trying to keep up. With wide snowshoes, I have to hold my legs far apart. They ache from lifting to walk. I slip through the thigh-high snow every few steps and have to climb back up. Sometimes Ken whips over to give me a hand.

Here is another test to see if I can keep up with the challenges and adventures he has in mind. Starting in my childhood, I've always needed to touch the ground, the water, the trees, to breathe the rain and snow. Experiencing nature gives me a feeling of realness. Yet, I wonder if I will survive if we decide to come back and settle on this land.

❧

When my last exam is over in May, we move out of the apartment and pack our goods into a green Volkswagen bus. We take a tent, bedding, pans, plates, and our cat Phobia in the car as we drive up to the land.

Ken knows how to build, but we have no money. At first we choose a site with an already-built cellar hole. Jay and Dee decide to give us land if we move to the other side of the brook onto an eight acre plot. They buy a warehouse in Island Pond for its lumber. Ken's contribution is the labor—taking the building down to use the wood for both houses. He knows how to do this because of the farm work he did after high school. When he left the farm, he got some goats and chickens of his own, and built a shed for them in his parents' back yard.

I learn that this old lumber is especially high quality—its boards are un-planed and full width. Dad gives us some storm windows, which we plan to use for the house.

❧

We have plans galore, but move into a tent.

The next day, I put on my LL Bean hiking boots and my denim overalls, and drive with Ken to the warehouse in Island Pond. He has taken down the walls during spring visits and now his goal is to take the boards apart and stack them. With two sawhorses, he sets up a workstation for me. My job is to remove and straighten the nails for our house. For weeks, I stand in what I think of as my combat boots in the sun or with the mist coming off the pond, holding a claw-foot nail puller and hammer. As I work, I think about how this is not what normal girls do in 1966.

Women are not taught to be tough. Women do not wear high boots. Women do not stand outside all day to prepare nails. Women stay in the house to knit, sew, and cook.

How does it happen that I am standing here pulling and straightening nails? Everything with Ken is an adventure. I feel happy that I am helping build our house. And that it will be surrounded by nature.

❦

80-year-old neighbor Fred Tangway stops to see how I am doing. After checking for a couple of weeks, he says, "I never married, but, Mister Man, if I had met a woman like you—could pull nails and straighten 'em up—I would've." He shakes his head all the way back to his lake-side house. Work ethic is important among rural Vermonters.

❦

To live in a rural town with a population of 287, we have people to meet and things to learn. Newark town road commissioner Alfred Cole, a middle-aged man, makes a road to our property. The road has not been "throwed up". This means ours is still a town road and if someone lives on it, the road commissioner has to make it passable. He cuts evergreen trees down and uses his red grader to widen the road, making drainage ditches on the sides. We are the first young people to move into the town of Newark since a mass exodus in the nineteen thirties. Sometimes while talking to us, he turns away to hide his glee. Even beatniks, like us, are welcome here.

While Al upgrades the road to our property, he checks on us. With his baseball cap pulled down over his eyes, he asks how we plan get the lumber from Island Pond. We say we don't know and he offers to let us use the town dump truck—on one condition. The law says, he tells us, that you need a Vermont license to drive it. I am the one with a Vermont driver's license since I just had my birthday in May.

Me? Drive a dump truck?

The next morning I am in the truck driver's seat headed toward Island Pond. Beside me, Ken shifts the gears. The vibration and noise of the truck cover up the butterflies in my stomach.

That night back in the tent on the land, after transporting the wood and piling it on the ground nearby, we awaken to a screaming sound. It pierces the silence. It is too close, just outside our tent. I don't dare move. I lie rigid like one of those pieces of wood, not breathing. I am sure that this is some strange animal from the edge of the earth. I've never heard such an ear-splitting sound. I open my eyes and in the moonlight steal a glance at Ken, and he at me, at the same moment. I am not imagining it. We move closer and closer, waiting for the sound to die down.

It isn't until morning that we realize the sound had been our cat Phobia in heat. We had no idea that she was old enough—or that there were other cats here at the end of the world.

This is my most terrifying night.

❧

We meet the townspeople. Senior citizen Merton Cross complains about Newark, the people, and the weather although his asthma and wheezing take some of the force out of his protests. And one day when we have no car and need to get to Connecticut, he kindly drives us.

Dick Chapman, with his muddy grey clothes, lives in an A-frame on the way to Island Pond and speaks of his "chimbley" and invites us over for "pannycakes".

Our distinguished mailman Ray Walters, in his sixties, tells us he used to travel the mail route on a horse, with a barn at the half-way point so he could switch horses. Now he drives a Buick. He tells me, "I want to be the best mailman I can be. I don't care what someone does as long as they do the best that they can. If a person is a garbage collector, he should be the best damn garbage collector he can be." He is definitely "the best damn mailman!" Meeting him every morning at the end of our road is usually the highlight of the day. We don't want to miss his eleven o'clock sharp delivery, since he offers the neighborhood news along with the mail. When he retires, I write a letter to the Postmaster General of the US about Ray and he gets a citation.

The old timers tell us the warehouse in Island Pond that Ken is demolishing used to hide liquor boxes smuggled from Canada during Prohibition. Every day Ken takes the boards apart, one by one, and I continue to straighten the nails. Fred Tangway shares more stories. He comes from a family with eleven kids who immigrated from Canada. "The old man was a rooster," he says. And with a nod to the warehouse, tells us, "I built this christly building."

Some old friends come to visit us and stop at the summer camp of a young couple on the main dirt road. They tell our friends, "Oh, them two? They're world famous in these here parts." Maybe because Ken does weaving or because we live in our house year-round? Or because no one has moved into this town for thirty years.

When we need food and Ken kills a deer out of season, blacksmith Jim McPherson comes over to teach him how to butcher it. Jim cuts his finger on the sharp blade. I notice his blood dripping onto the deer meat. Soon after this I become a vegetarian.

And from the closest year-round family, the teenage son cleaning a gun accidentally shoots and tragically kills his father.

These are our back-to-the-land neighbors. The rawness of rural Vermont life in the sixties.

❦

One day as we walk up the new, old dirt road to our house, Alfred Cole turns off his red grader and looks down at my bare arms and legs.

"Ain't heard of black flies, have ya?"

"You mean little gnats?"

"Well, something like that, but more. Ever wonder why we have so much land up here?" He answers his own question with a guffaw. "It's because of them black flies."

"That bad?" wonders Ken aloud.

"That bad and worse. You'll see. Better put on some long pants, long shirts. You have a net for your head? You ain't seen the welts yet."

Swarms of tiny black bugs vigorously attack us, the first human flesh they have come across in thirty years. In the morning and around dusk, Ken wears his bee bonnet. But I don't. Ken shakes his head in disbelief at the clouds of black flies. I hate wearing extra clothing, so living in the tent, carrying beams, hammering nails, tarring roofing paper, or planting the garden, I don't cover myself. I get welts. Sure, I have lumps all over. Sure, they itch. They also go away.

At the end of the summer Al, finished for the day, climbs down from the grader. "Ain't seen nothing like you," he says, pointing to my bare legs. "Guess you're made to live here. If you can take them black flies, the winter in these here parts won't be nothing." I'm still not sure, but Ken nods in agreement.

༄

I never question how Ken feels about me. We are busy living our life. He treats me kindly with love and respect. I assume he loves me unconditionally like my mother does. He doesn't blow up at me like Dad does, so I accept him as I would my brother Harry or my mother. As a couple we are kind, passionate, and affectionate.

༄

The frame of our house is twenty feet by thirty feet. I have a magical feeling every time I look at it—a piece of land and then a home. I see it filled with our things. I feel how it will be walking inside. It will smell like the earth and wood smoke, I know. But, before the house dream comes true, we plan, measure, cut, carry wood, and nail. Ken is the mastermind, although he incorporates my requests—that the kitchen look off into the woods, that there is a pantry, a small, cozy bedroom, and a bathroom. Ken makes it happen—we work together with peaceful nature around us. We have no electricity so we use a buck saw. Even sawing the lumber is muted and something we do together.

During the month of June, we get the frame up, the siding boards nailed on the studs and just before my parents come to visit on the Fourth of July, we tar and nail the roofing paper. Ken tars and I nail. At the end of the day, I ache, but the roof is on. When my parents arrive, we are excited to show them what we have accomplished—the roof on already! Dad nods and wonders when we will have windows and doors. Having no door on the bathroom with its chemical toilet annoys my father but, Boy Scout that he is, he has brought a little collapsible shovel and makes his way out into the woods. Then he nails boards for us. They have brought food. Mom and I cook it over a Coleman camp stove.

❧

Before we get the windows in, but after we begin to put our food in the pantry, a raccoon comes in at night and, with a crash, breaks a glass bottle of catsup all over the shelves and floor. Slowly then, the windows are in, the trim around them. The tar paper is attached to the outside boarding and the outside doors of weathered barn boards are hung.

By contrast, Dee and Jay are living in the little cabin Jay and Ken built. They don't seem so intent on having another place to live. We are putting all our energy into preparing for the winter by making our house as warm as possible.

Eventually, our house is like this: walk up the steps to the small porch, open the door, and in front is the living room. On the right wall is the kitchen sink. Through a doorway beside the sink is the pantry. Then the gas stove and a table with chairs. The table we made from an old-fashioned wagon wheel from a local barn. We plan to put plexiglass on top of it, but right now without money, we are managing with chicken wire. If you spill, you get it on you! In the living room will be Ken's Jacquard loom, the one he built in college. Later beside it is a forty-eight inch Macomber loom purchased with all my savings from babysitting and working during high school. Our Volkswagen bus seat serves as a couch in front of the Ashley wood stove. The bathroom has a claw-foot tub, a basin and a chemical toilet. Ken carries all of our water from the brook. Two small rooms are beyond the wood stove—a library and our bedroom. The outside walls shine with foil over pink fiberglass.

We have a red plastic radio attached to a car battery where we get CBC, Canadian Broadcasting Corporation. The sad news of Martin Luther King's and Robert Kennedy's deaths reach us over that radio. We can't understand why violence is happening out beyond our walls. Ken and I often go for weeks without seeing anyone else in our peaceful and loving home.

Chapter Sixteen

— *Locals and Visitors*

*A*nd then, it's winter and I'm pregnant.

"There!" Ken says, sloshing most of the water from the two pails into the five gallon brown crock. Some of it spills on the pine wood floor and Phobia's kittens run to get a drink. The snow on Ken's boots is melting, but not too fast, while the cat's water is still frozen from last night. He takes off his wool-lined leather mittens, hangs his quilted jacket on a hook beside the door, and pours the rest of the water into the canning kettle so it can heat on the stove. Water comes from the brook. There is still no electricity and no telephone.

Now I can get to that pile of dishes, I think, looking up from my treadle Singer sewing machine. While the water heats, I reinforce the material Ken has woven before I cut it. Thank goodness for our main-stays, three-by-one-and-a-half-inch woven "smell cushions". They are stuffed with balsam from the trees felled while making the road. They retail for three dollars. We get a dollar-fifty, but if a store orders a dozen, we have food money for two weeks. It is nearly the end of the year and income from the tiny cushions has netted us $273, which is what we have had to live on.

The wind streams in around the double storm windows left over from a cabin Dad renovated in northern Connecticut. We put them in side-ways, like picture windows— along the front of the house. I can smell the burlap of the curtains as I push them aside to look out. I think of the pile of grain bags it took to make them. The curtains are double and we can usually close them again against the wind. But not today. The snow blows in when the gusts come, otherwise, it's falling silently. There is no line between the lawn and the driveway. And beyond, the evergreen boughs are heavy with piles of snow. All I can see is the windshield of our disabled Volkswagen bus. It looks like green goggles staring out at the house. The bus worked to move our full-sized gas refrigerator all the way up from Connecticut. Then died. Here we are eight miles on a dirt road, thirteen miles from the nearest town, with no transportation. I really don't mind.

I smell lanolin and feel the thud of Ken's weaving—the beater against the thick wool. He leans one way and the other in a mesmerizing rhythm as he shoots the shuttle across. Metal harnesses clang and heddles tinkle as he presses on foot pedals.

I am sitting right in front of the Ashley wood stove and my back is a lot colder than my front. Balsam needles to stuff into tiny woven smell cushions dry behind the stove adding their scent. Wood smoke mixes with balsam as steam rises up from the water heating. The rhythm and fragrances are soothing. The whiteness outside is serene. I focus on my sewing again. My right toe presses the treadle forward. My left heel pulls it back, while my upper body moves side to side, too. When this sewing machine belonged to my aunt, it was electric. Before we moved here, we went to an antique store to change it over. The owner, looking at us like we were crazy, took the motor off and fit the head into a treadle cabinet. Everyone besides us wants to be modern.

Suddenly, we look up. "Do you hear something?" I ask. Ken nods. First, we feel a vibration. We hear a hum. It gets louder by the second.

Now the whole house is vibrating with the rumble. Newark's huge red grader is barreling up our driveway spewing snow up higher than the top of our house. When the source of the vibration feels like it is an inch from the wall, the snow suddenly stops flying. The silence is deafening. Alfred Cole climbs down from his high seat with a metal pail dangling from his hand. He laughs as we open the door and he hands us a container of fresh milk from his cows. Then he notices our blanched faces and wild eyes.

"Oh, just thought I'd bank your house with snow to make it warmer. Ain't a big deal. It's what we do up here." He lifts his cap and runs his fingers through his hair. His eyes study the floor but I can tell they are laughing.

"Great present!" I stare at the milk. We can't run to the store to get any, even though I'm pregnant and could use it—I glance toward the buried VW bus. The only milk I get is Carnation powdered milk, which tastes terrible. I manage to add some to tomato soup (one of our staples), mashed potatoes, or eggs from our chickens.

"Better go. Got eighteen inches of snow in the Hollow. Drifted to three-foot overnight. Well, I hope the snow bankin' keeps ya warm."

From then on, Al visits whenever he's plowing the roads. One day, he jumps from the grader with a half-gallon of ice cream! It's been months since we had ice cream. We gather bowls and spoons.

"You ain't got a freezer," he reminds us, as we sit around the wagon wheel table. "You cain't save any of it, so eat it all." Even with the cold outside, we have learned that it isn't consistently cold enough to keep something like ice cream frozen.

Ice cream was rationed when I was a kid. I never just ate ice cream. I have stolen ice cream out of the freezer when I wanted more. I have shared it with my brothers and sisters. As a teenager, I worked as a waitress in an ice cream parlor. But I have never been handed a half-gallon of ice cream and been told to eat it all!

The three of us dig into the box of striped Neapolitan. It's like heaven. Al keeps removing his hat to hold it in front of his face for a minute. We can still see his smiling eyes as he watches us with delight as we eat. We are laughing at the incongruity of the day. How it can change so fast, one minute our normal rhythm and then a whole half-gallon of ice cream to eat. How can it taste so good? I know I am in our house, but each taste transports me. One minute I am picking tiny wild strawberries. The next Mom has made rich chocolate frosting for my birthday cake. Then I am drinking a thick vanilla milkshake at the ice cream parlor. I guess there is such a thing as enough ice cream, though, because eventually I can't eat any more.

Al climbs back into the grader, starts up that big engine, backs out of our driveway onto the road and toots as he goes on his way to plow Newark Hollow.

❧

Our house is cold. The cat's water on the floor of the kitchen is frozen again. It seems like it is every morning. The roof of the house has a very low angle but hot air rises and it is warmer over the ceiling under the roof. We move our bedding out to be closer to the wood stove and higher up, putting our mattress and our sleeping-bag comforter there. We climb a ladder and squeeze into the three-foot high space and fall asleep. In the night we are awakened by one startling scream. It's not the cat this time. Ken climbs down and discovers that our bred rabbit outside in her hutch beside the chicken coop has given birth to one large stillborn baby. He doesn't want to tell me because I am pregnant, but he does. To put the fear memory out of my head, we move back to our bedroom where it is colder, but farther from the rabbit.

❧

Ken's and my isolation continues until a few weeks later when Al stops and says, "I'm comin' back tonight to take y'out to dinner." Is there a restaurant up here in the boonies? We haven't explored the region too much since our VW died at the end of the summer and we ran out of money. Ken gasps. My eyes widen. Al sneaks glances at us under his hat's brim.

In a few hours, he comes to pick us up, but he looks different. We can't quite figure out what it is. "Is he drunk or something?" we whisper when we go back to our room for some money. Then we get it—he is wearing false teeth and that changes his whole face. Well, this is a big occasion!

❧

The restaurant is cozy with pine-paneled walls and a few customers sitting at tables smoking cigarettes. The menu lists meatloaf, macaroni and cheese, pot roast, mashed potatoes. Al tells us to order anything we want. At home our diet is rice, soybeans, kidney beans—foods that are dried or canned—and those we make, like bread. This is like eating at our parents' when we were younger. We feel like a king and queen eating them now.

Sitting in the red vinyl booth, I see our life—our cocoon, the house we built ourselves and which we haven't left for many weeks. Our craft-work. Feel the drafts from the windows onto our hard VW bus "couch". Here country music is playing. The whole place is a breath of stale human air after all that fresh air of our country lives and it feels invigorating.

❦

Then it is the spring of 1967 and I am almost seven months preg-nant. The snow melts and it's mud season. The main dirt road is closed. For a couple of weeks, we need to walk an extra mile to meet Ray for the mail. With mud season, there is no need for Al and the snow plow and our friends probably don't know if the road is open yet, so no visitors come.

Part of the reason that we live in remote Newark fifteen miles from the Canadian border is so that we can escape, if we need to. With the Vietnam War being fought, Ken often talks about how the government rounded up the Japanese in World War II and how today they could round up pacifists in the same way. I understand the idea is very scary and real to him, but I wonder if he isn't a little paranoid.

Normally, when a car does turn onto our road a mile away, we first feel a faint vibration, then a hum, and soon a friend's car appears. One day, we look out the window, after hearing a soft drone, and a shiny black Dodge is already parking at the end our driveway. Our friends know how deep the ruts are in mud season and they drive noisier Volkswagens and trucks. This is someone new.

We look at each other out the corner of our eyes as a tall strong-look-ing man in a black trench coat and fifties felt hat gets out of the car. Our first thought is "the establishment". We know right away that he is from the very life we moved here to avoid. Just one look and we remember why we are living up here at the end of eight miles of dirt road. We smirk a bit watching his shiny black shoes sink down into mud with each step as he walks up our driveway.

I watch Ken's questioning face as he opens the door. The man removes a card from his suit jacket and says, "I'm from the FBI. I am here to investigate…"

My knees shake and my ears hear a roaring. I can't hear his words. Until that moment, I thought Ken was exaggerating what could happen. Is he here to arrest us? To round us up? Are we doing something wrong? I don't think so. I want to hear what he is saying, but my brain can't discern the words. I know that the FBI has files on everyone, but I thought we were out of sight. I am shocked and horrified that they can find us all the way out here. Will we end up in jail? Just exactly what have we done? The roaring in my ears is loud. I still can't hear any words. The government believes that if you are against the war, you are un-American. We are supposed to be patriotic, fight for our country. Maybe that's it.

☙

The FBI agent sits on our Volkswagen bus seat couch, earnestly explaining something, but I only hear a buzz. I watch Ken's mouth move, so I guess he is answering. Out of the sound, I hear the name of a friend, Ron B. Is he in jail? The whirring in my ears is blocking sound. The whirring gets softer, but I still can't stop my knees from knocking together.

"Do you think he is really a pacifist?" I hear in a stern voice.

Ken answers, "Yes, he is. I met him at Quaker Meeting." After a few more questions, the FBI agent stands. We stand. He begins to walk out the door onto the porch.

Ken calls, "How often do you investigate conscience objectors?"

"Just when we don't believe them."

"What percentage would you say that is?"

"About 95%," he answers. Then turns to walk down the porch steps back through the mud to his car.

"Nice that our government trusts us," Ken says sarcastically as he leans against the closed door. We collapse on the couch, but don't relax until the faintest thrum from his big fancy car disappears.

Chapter Seventeen

⟶ *Birth*

I am eight months pregnant when another visitor comes in the late spring of 1967. Peter Wendland, Director of the Vermont Arts and Crafts Council, would like Ken to demonstrate Jacquard weaving for Lady Bird Johnson, who is coming to Vermont. The plan is to take the six-foot wide and eight-foot high Jacquard loom that Ken made and set it up at the Stowe base lodge. But the loom is so big Ken has built our house around it.

Ken's goal is to continue the weaving tradition that he discovered in Peru, that was lost at Standing Rock Reservation, and is disappearing from New England. In college when he visited factories during his senior project to learn weaving techniques and to buy supplies, he discovered that woven cloth labels can be made with intricate designs because they use Jacquard looms. He wondered if it would be possible to use the same process for weaving larger designs for wall hangings. That's why he built the loom.

The way the Jacquard loom produces complexity is by using a punch card system for weaving, later known as the dot matrix system. This was invented by Joseph Marie Jacquard in Lyon, France in 1801—and became the same dot matrix system used by early computers and printers. Today's mobile phones, televisions, and printers still use this technology.

In other looms, wooden frames hold metal heddles (long needles) with a hole for a warp string to go through. Two, four, or eight frames determine the number of repeating options for patterns. With a Jacquard loom, there are unlimited options. Each heddle is individual with a weight on the bottom. Ken punches holes in cards to create patterns. One hole lifts one heddle with one string. One card represents one row of the pattern where the shuttle goes under the warp yarn that is lifted. The punch cards laced together and a different row of strings is lifted by each card. It is quite complex.

No one else in Vermont does hand weaving on a self-built Jacquard loom. In fact, maybe no one else in the US does. So when Vermont hosts an event for the first lady, Lady Bird Johnson, Ken is invited to demonstrate his weaving along with fourteen other crafts people from the three northern New England states. We have no way to transport this large loom, so Peter Wendland drives his truck from the state capital to pick it up. Ken and I have no idea what he has in mind. One look and Peter sees what Ken and I know. The loom won't fit through the door. The choice is to take it apart or remove the doorframe. The loom being more intricate, Ken decides to take the doorframe down with Peter's help.

It isn't every day we get invited to demonstrate for the first lady of the United States and get exposure for our work. In fact, we hardly get invited anywhere, so we three make jokes about taking the house apart to see her. Since it is June, a little extra air in the house for a few days is no problem.

At the Stowe lodge, we wait eagerly for the contingent of governors, including Vermont's Phil Hoff, their wives, and Lady Bird to return from a gondola ride to the top of the mountain. Then the politicians, security, and press go from one display to another, like a spotlight moving over the room. As Lady Bird nears our display, we get into our positions—me with my pregnant belly squeezed behind the table of woven goods and Ken sitting tall on his weaving bench. He steps on a lever to change the punch cards, which makes the fancy heddles go up and down. She watches Ken create material. He is doing what he does every day, so is in the calm rhythm of shooting the shuttle across the warp. When she turns to our display, she picks up one of our balsam smell cushions, holds it to her nose, sniffs, and says in her Southern accent, "These would be great for a guest room." With her Southern accent, the words "gr-eat" and "gu-est" have extra syllables.

For dinner, we know we are out of our element when we are led to long tables laden with food. The three governors, their wives, Lady Bird, and other politicians sit at their own table. The fifteen craftspeople and one hundred media members sit together at other tables. What is shocking to us coming from our small house in the woods is the amount of food. Like the loom, this dinner has no limitations. Here is more food on one table than we ate all winter—maybe all year. Roast beef. Grilled salmon. Baked potatoes. Green beans. Tossed salad. And then layer cake with ice cream for dessert.

We think that the conversation will be stilted, but it isn't. A reporter about our age sits across from us. He describes taking the gondola to the top of Stowe Mountain. The photographers line up and move like a ballet with Lady Bird. For him the gondola ride is a waste. His job is to take a photo only when Lady Bird steps onto a lawn, as he works for a gardening magazine. Since there is no lawn on the mountain, he can't take any photos. But to be part of the press group, he pretends. He points and clicks along with everyone else. His is a film camera, but there is no film in it.

When Ken and I stand up from the table, we feel full and heavy. Glancing down, we are both horrified at the amount of food left on the plates to be thrown away.

❧

In the summer of 1967 Ken and I are in love with the land, the cedar trees, and the beech tree behind our house that takes three people with outstretched arms to reach around. We love the sound of the brook where we get our water, the smells of balsam and pine needles that crunch as we walk, and the maple trees we tap in the spring. We are mostly in love with each other.

In July, when I am in labor, we walk around in the garden and check on the potato plants, tomatoes, and lacy carrot tops. With each powerful contraction that grips my body, I stand still and hold onto Ken. Then walk again when it lets up. We have read *Husband Coached Childbirth* together. We also have *A Midwife's Textbook* on hand. Ken has delivered goats and sheep, so he knows all about birth. I have 100% confidence in him and in our decision to have a home birth.

Everything is ready—the oxygen, the plastic sheet on the bed, the suction bulb for the baby. Even though I have read the books, I know nothing about how long it will take or what labor will be like or who will come. I am not scared, though. I am sure my body knows what to do.

We even have a car that works—a white 1961 Saab whose doors open from the front. I read a nine-page letter from Susan Erb Farrow, my friend from Haystack Mountain School of Crafts, about her home birth nine months ago. The plastic under the sheet crinkles as I roll over to put the letter back on the bookshelf.

When Ken's mother found out that we were planning a home birth, she took me aside and asked if he was making me do it. No, I said, this is our decision. She said that if it's because of the money, she would pay for the hospital. I said no.

We've decided against a hospital birth because there was no guarantee that Ken could be present. In St. Johnsbury there is only one delivery room and if anyone else is using it, he would need to wait outside. We try to ask our doctor for Pitocin, which helps to contract the uterus after birth, but he doesn't take us seriously when we tell him that we're having a home birth. There are no midwives nearby and we don't have a phone anyway. Ken and I are doing this alone together.

Night falls and we settle on the plastic covered bed. We doze off and on. The kerosene lamp burns. Ken has been feeling my contractions and holding my belly. At nine o'clock, as I am stretched out on the bed, amniotic fluid gushes out. I figure it will be over soon. He is lying beside me putting pressure on my back when my legs fly up and I look at the silver insulation on the wall for something to push against. The transition period has started. I think the birth should be soon. Ken moves to sit at my feet so I can use him as a footboard. I think now certainly the baby will come, but no, it takes six more hours—24 in all.

Finally, at 3:18 in the morning on that July day in the house that we built on our land—with the door open to the balsam trees and the sound of the brook, our son comes not with a cry but a "Whoosh!" and is born into this place. There is a rawness to birth—the metallic smell of blood mixed with sweet, mysterious fluids. Born into the light of a kerosene Aladdin lamp, and then cleaned up with water from the brook. Soon the birds sing and it starts to become light. I have our baby on my belly. Out the open door the balsam trees are swaying in the breeze, more fragrant than ever before. The birds are singing louder than I've ever heard them. My son is beginning to latch on to my breast with a force that I didn't know skin could survive. When the sun comes all the way up, it is a different kind of light, brighter than any light I've ever seen.

Our son has long dark hair, five fingers and toes on each side, is perfect, and is the most beautiful being I've ever seen. The smell of wood smoke from last winter lingers on the wall's gray barn boards at the foot of the bed. The plastic over the insulation rustles in the early morning breeze. The outside door swings, bringing in the early morning fragrance of evergreen trees. I glance at the two-by-eight studs from the warehouse in Island Pond that frame our house. Our creation is welcoming a new life. It is miraculous.

The placenta does not come and we wonder how hard to press. Ken gets the midwife book out. Although there doesn't seem to be any problem, we diaper Kai and dress him in undershirt, hat and gown, and wrap him in a blanket. I dress with the cord still connected to the placenta and put my trench coat over my clothes. I am smaller—the coat closes in front! We drive to the doctor at 5:30 AM. Ken is so stressed that he loses a dime in the payphone at the Lynburke Hotel as he tries to call. Deer play in the fields. The sun is rising. The world is new. We call him Kai after my favorite Danish uncle. It is hard to find a short name to go with Mayberger.

At the doctor's, after a shot of Pitocin and strong pressure from his hands, out plops the placenta. As the doctor checks Kai, he says, "With these home births, the babies are usually fine. It is the drugs that slow them down."

We stop at our friends Claire and Mike's to call our parents, and write a note for our mailman to take on his route. Then we settle in at home to a quiet, harmonious time—the three of us in our peaceful home. Well, at least until the neighbors start coming with pies, casseroles, and Jell-O salads.

The bill we later receive from the doctor says, "Delivery of Placenta $15."

Chapter Eighteen

⏤ *Starting Over*

*All we have to decide is what to do
with the time that is given to us.
~JRR Tolkien*

*I*n the winter of 1968, the wind swipes across the field, over the brook, up our driveway, and finds its way in through the spaces around the picture windows again. We both shudder at the same time while the snow continues to swirl outside. Kai is six months old and sleeping in his crib when Ken picks up *The Hobbit* from our bookshelf. I have read it but he hasn't. We sit in front of the Ashley wood stove as he reads the first paragraph aloud.

> *"In a hole in the ground there lived a hobbit. Not a nasty, dirty, wet hole, filled with the ends of worms and an oozy smell, nor yet a dry, bare, sandy hole with nothing in it to sit down on or to eat: it was a hobbit-hole, and that means comfort."*

The words irresistibly draw me in. The wind disappears. I feel only warmth, abundance, comfort, and—as he reads—magic. We lose track of time. Kai cries. I nurse him. Then it's dark and we notice the growl of our stomachs. Ken sits at the table, still reading, and holding Kai as I boil water for spaghetti and open a can of sauce. Ken puts the book down to eat, but we don't interrupt the flow with talk. He puts some wood into the stove and, without a word, we have moved toward our bed. The Aladdin lamp shines light on the page, Kai is snuggled in with us, and Ken continues to read. Kai falls asleep and we carry him to his crib. Ken reads until the Aladdin runs out of kerosene and goes out with a puff. "Gandalf," we say together.

❧

In the morning, Ken's voice is hoarse but with the light we can continue the adventure. After a couple of days, he finishes *The Hobbit*. We fill the stove, get water, make food, feed Kai, feed the chickens and the rabbit, shovel the walk, and climb back into bed where it's warm to begin *The Fellowship of the Ring*. Kai sits in a bouncy chair, plays with toys, and chews on zwieback. He seems to be listening, too.

The next day, with Kai in the baby backpack carrier, Ken and I walk to the mailbox.

My head is still in Middle-Earth as I walk through the balsam trees loaded with snow. I guess Ken's head is, too, because when we get back home, he picks up the book and we are soon in bed under the down sleeping bag traveling with Frodo.

All day Ken reads the book while Kai and I sit together and listen. Ken finishes reading it and starts *The Two Towers*. We aren't sure if we made a decision to keep reading. We just do. What better vacation could there be than going to Middle Earth for a week or two during the coldest days of winter? Especially when the wind sounds like a train outside and the warmest place is in our bed under the down sleeping bag. At the end of two weeks we have been through the whole trilogy. Ken's voice is two octaves lower.

"Wasn't that amazing?" we say to each other. Gollum. The ring. Pocketses. Climbing mountains. Exploring paths. Gollum's cave and lake. The different beings along the way. A two-week magical adventure. Just perfect.

❧

During the spring and summer of 1968, our home in Newark is a very active place. Kai is growing and starts to walk. We are digging a cellar under our house, trying to put a line in to have running water from the brook, and canning and freezing food from our garden. An abundance of friends, usually five or more a day, come to visit or stay or help, and share a meal. When water flows through a pipe from the brook into a tank over the ceiling in our house, we can turn on a faucet, heat water, or take a bath. Stores and galleries send orders for our woven pillows, ponchos, and smell cushions, which we package and mail out. People have stopped calling us beatniks and started using the new word "hippie". We hope that the next winter will be easier.

In August, things change. Dee and Jay, who own the land our house sits on, are upset about our overactive work ethic. We have talked about it with them and it seemed like a question of living our lives differently, but now the problem seems bigger. They feel we are judging them for taking life more slowly and Jay has sent carbon copies of a four page single spaced typed letter condemning us for talking to the townspeople about it. Even though we have support from the community, since the townspeople also have a hard work ethic, the letter opens all kinds of problems we didn't even know about. We don't know if we can be comfortable here and since we still don't have the deed to the eight acres (although we believe they will deed it to us, and they do later), we wonder if it is possible for us to stay. The differences multiplied by the letters to everyone seem irreconcilable.

Even though being here is paradise to us, we have a sick feeling about being around the anger on the land. Ken and I sit on a log in the woods behind the home we built and cry. I pull bark off the log. Ken sits with his elbow on his knee and his hand over his eyes. Kai toddles around picking up sticks, looking up at us. We smell the moss and rich hummus from the forest floor and talk about how much we love this land, our home, the birthplace of our son.

What should we do?

For four days we don't eat, just talk about our options. Together, we slowly accept that we need to let go of our dream place. It can't be paradise if our relationships are not peaceful. Should we leave? We can't stay on the land. We have to move. Where do we want to live? Denmark?

South America? West Coast? Wherever it is, we need to do it before winter.

🖎

Vermont is beautiful. My brother Harry is attending Middlebury College at the other side of the state and working for a building supply company for the summer. We have no money and don't want to get involved with bank mortgages. He offers to ask around at work for run-down empty houses. A house on a ledge in Cornwall seems to be a possibility. With the forest floor covered with leaves from deciduous trees, the land smells of my childhood in Connecticut—different from the evergreen forest in Newark.

We visit the selectman, Mr. Gingras, who tells us that the house has been boarded up for years. The town of Cornwall bought it with four-and-a-half acres for the town dump, but the neighbors campaigned against it. "We've been stuck with it. How much? Let me see, it's just the price we paid for it, plus the taxes since then. Umm. $2296."

Our families offer to help us get the house. My sister Joan has been saving for college and offers a short-term loan and Ken's mother will help us with a longer loan.

We enter the one-hundred-and-twenty-year old building through the basement until we take the boards off the windows and doors. Our shoes make tracks in the dust on the linoleum floors. The stairs to the second floor are so steep we have to climb on our hands and knees. There is no heat, no insulation, and no bathroom. A shallow well has questionable water. An outhouse sits on the ledge in back.

As we head back to Newark to pack our things, I think about the extras—a barn and garage, a stained glass window in the house, and wild onions growing on the property.

In addition to fourteen-month-old Kai and us, our Saab carries the chickens, cats, plants, and belongings inside, and on the roof, our beehive. We look forward to our new house. But feel a big hole in our hearts to have to leave Kai's birthplace, the home we built, and the locals who made us feel so welcome in Newark.

༄

In Cornwall, we are back in civilization—on a dirt road where cars, trucks, and tractors pass. We quickly have the electricity turned on and Kai is mesmerized by light switches. On and off. Off and on. We get a phone—a five-party line with different rings for each family. Our parents are elated. We are three hours closer to them. Dad tells us that Cornwall's Addison County, gets forty more days of growing season than Newark's Caledonia County. Dairy and vegetable farms abound. One is next door. We imagine growing lots of vegetables and having an in-house freezer to preserve them. We're dreaming.

Life will be different from Newark, where we made, produced, built, birthed, or planted everything. Having lived a subsistence life for more than two years, we have learned what is necessary and now can choose the rest from a menu of modern conveniences. Ken's plan is to remodel the house to live in and the barn for his weaving studio.

༄

In the local paper, I see a want ad for substitute teachers. Why not get a little job and make some money? When I call the Superintendent of Schools about subbing, he asks if I would like a full-time teaching job. I am torn. We haven't had any money for so long, and yet, I want to be home with our fourteen-month-old son. Ken says it's my choice. He will be happy to have Kai with him as he rebuilds the house and barn, so I visit the school with the superintendent. Having had three years of college toward an elementary school teaching degree, I needed only one English course and a semester of student teaching to graduate as a teach- er. That's when we moved to Newark. I never finished. This year, 1968, has a teacher shortage, so the school board hires me without a degree.

༄

I go directly from being a back-to-the-land hippie in the Northeast Kingdom to being a full-time teacher in Weybridge. This way I can pay for a freezer, and some building materials while Ken, with Kai, renovates our house. From jeans, no bra, and chambray shirts to miniskirts. From walking in the woods to standing in a classroom. From a town with an old one-room schoolhouse for eight grades to a town with a school that looks like a ski chalet filled with shiny desks and four classrooms. I meet the principal Ella Thompson and even though her face looks like a bulldog and her shape is like a cardboard box, I assume she will have good will. A woman in her fifties, she tells me that for many years she was the teacher of the town's old-fashioned one-room school. Her eyes gleam when she mentions this new school, as if she built it herself brick-by-brick. On the introductory tour, she takes me into a supply closet stuffed with pencils, notebooks, rulers, paints, crayons, and piles of textbooks. Everything smells new. Although in the same state, I never saw an abundance of supplies like this when I visited the musty one-room school in Newark.

Even though classes have been in session for two weeks, Weybridge needs another teacher because the combined first and second grade class is too big, with thirty-one kids. There will be four girls and eleven boys in my second grade class. I am optimistic as I sign the contract at the superintendent's office. I have wanted to be a teacher since I was in second grade myself.

I think it's too good to be true. Of course, it is. A week later, the superintendent contacts me to say Mrs. Thompson is complaining that I haven't been wearing nylon stockings to school. According to her it is obvious teachers are supposed to. I wonder if I would have signed the contract if I had known. In any case, I meet the requirement in my own way. I buy fishnet stockings in blue, green, and yellow and wear them under my miniskirts.

The children and the school are lovely. But Mrs. Thompson? Not a child lover. She uses a butter paddle for discipline and demonstrates the procedure to me, in a closet at the end of the hall. "Put him over your knee, like this," she says, plopping down on a chair already there. She lifts a fifteen-inch-long, four-inch-wide, and half-inch-thick wooden butter paddle, an old tool that was used to form hand-made butter, and demonstrates. "Give him three paddles. Then he will behave."

If her combined fifth and sixth grade class is noisy? Dictionaries for recess. The students sit with elbows bent, wrists back toward shoulders, palms up and flat, fingers splayed, holding thick dictionaries. Twenty minutes. Or the wall punishment where the whole class lines up on their knees facing the multi purpose room wall. Their noses touch it, arms straight over their heads, and hands flat against it. Twenty minutes of recess torture in the all-purpose room.

Corporal punishment. I'd thought it was something done in the past. The students and even the parents seem to accept it. I feel sick.

Or food. Laura can't stomach oatmeal? Mrs. Thompson stands over her until she puts a spoonful in her mouth. When the eight-year-old student vomits into the oatmeal? Mrs. Thompson still stands over her until her bowl is empty. Food torture.

Every day I want to cry. I am twenty-three years old with a son. I would never want Kai in a place like this.

One day I get to school five minutes late and Mrs. Thompson takes me into the teacher's room and yells at me. I start the day with red eyes. One of my second graders looks up from her desk as I walk in. "Mrs. Thompson, right?" she whispers as I walk by, nodding at me in sympathy.

Some days Mrs. Thompson stands in the hall and shakes her finger at me through the glass window in the door. I wonder why she isn't in her own classroom with her fifth and sixth graders. Another time when I'm not in the room, she goes through my desk and admonishes me for not marking attendance for two days.

But, she never catches me in my biggest defiance. The Vietnam War requires patriotism. I am a pacifist. Our country fights and kills people. Even though the Pledge of Allegiance is recited every morning in every classroom, I never speak those words myself. I choose a student to lead the pledge and I stand in the back of the room facing the flag with my hand over my heart, my lips sealed.

One day I describe how we have mistreated Native Americans in such detail that the son of a Vermont State Trooper can't stop crying. I wait for repercussions, but there are none. I need to tell the truth no matter what.

❦

Two second graders who repeated first grade still can't read. They haven't made the connection between the written shape and a spoken word. How can I help them? Ken's degree is in teaching art. He gives me an idea. I get a huge roll of paper, two-inch wide brushes, and mix red tempera paint. I move the desks aside for space, set up the paper on the floor, and ask each boy what word he would like to learn. **Plants. Pictures.** I spread the paper out, pencil the words, and give each a brush and a baby food jar of paint. Their eyes are alive, their lips tight between their teeth as they begin the first stroke. And then one boy knocks his paint over. Immediately, the door flies open. Mrs. Thompson's hands are waving in the air. Her bull-dog face is purple. "I knew this would happen," she says. "Look at what you have done in this brand new classroom. Already you're ruining it." Red paint on linoleum is a sin to her. A much bigger sin than a child who can't read.

At the end of the year when building materials, a new well, and our avocado-colored freezer are paid off, the Weybridge school board offers me a contract for the next year. I am surprised after all the criticism from Mrs. Thompson. I enjoy my class, but I can't possibly spend another year with the principal. I don't sign. I will be home with Kai and Ken and someone else.

Chapter Nineteen

Adoption

Since that day of having my hair combed in Roxbury with Mrs. Roberts and her family, we have wanted diversity in our family. We did not want to add to the overpopulation problem. I was always grateful to have a brother close to my age to play with. We want Kai to have a sister and will adopt her. On April 24, 1969, we sign Vermont Children's Aid Society papers to adopt a biracial (African-American and white) baby girl, even though her mother has not released her in court. We don't know that she was born three days before, but we are told that because of her racial background, she is labeled "hard-to-place." She is just the baby we are looking for.

Soon after we sign the papers, Harry comes back from a visit with Mom and Dad. "They want you to call them—alone. Don't tell Ken," he says.

It is an unusual request and makes me feel uncomfortable, but when I am in town buying groceries, I call from a phone booth. Mom and Dad each get on an extension.

"We think this is a very bad idea for you to adopt a biracial child," Dad begins. Strange. They are ganging up on me. It is rare for Mom to join him against me. My silent answer is, well, we are doing it and she's coming in a few weeks. I can hear Mom crying. I know one extension is upstairs in their bedroom and one in the kitchen downstairs, so they can't give each other signals.

Dad says, "I know a biracial person and he doesn't fit in with the white community or the Black community. It's a sad life. You don't want any part of it. People will boycott your weaving business. They will isolate you."

"There is a lawyer in town who has just adopted a biracial son. They haven't had any problems. His business is very successful," I counter.

"Well, that's a lawyer, not you. You are asking for problems. Black people are not like us. For instance, you will never see a black president."

"This is a baby," I say. "She needs love and we will give it to her."

"If you do this, I will disown you," he says and hangs up.

How could he say this because of a baby? I know my lifestyle is very different from my parents. I know my maternal grandmother lived on a plantation with slaves. Still . . . I sit in the car for a while until I can see clearly enough to drive home.

❦

Meanwhile, our roof in Newark needs repair. Ken, Kai, and I go back to Newark to do the work. We think no one knows where we are so are surprised when our old mailman Ray Walters drives up our road.

"I didn't think you were here, but it says right on the envelope that you are." I look down as he hands me the envelope. Dad's writing. Our old address and then, "Please deliver this. Very important."

My hands shake as I open it. Inside, Dad writes, "I will always be your father and the grandfather of any of your children, biological or adopted."

I ache and yet I am grateful.

❦

On July 24, 1969, Ken, Kai, and I drive to Burlington where we will meet three-month-old Heidi at a playroom outside the Vermont Children's Aid Society office. Her mother has just released her in court. Blue-black or café au lait? I try to envision the color of our new daughter Heidi before I see her. At the moment the social worker carries her into the room, I am already her mother. Small, soft, brown baby with a pink dress. Iris and pupil deep black, curly black hair. Ken places his sun-

123

browned arm beside hers. She matches his tan skin.

After a few minutes, the social worker says, "Why don't you go out to lunch, talk it over, and come back after you eat." Ken and I look at each other, knowing we have been waiting months for our baby, knowing that there is nothing to discuss. Why would we leave our daughter?

"We're ready to take her," I tell the social worker. We sign some papers, change her diaper, and I carry her to the car for the ride home.

I want to nurse her to nurture her, even though I didn't birth her. But at three months she already has a mind of her own. My milk doesn't come fast enough. She has a thirst, a thirst for the world only a bottle can give her now.

❦

The next weekend, my parents come with my sister Joan to meet Heidi. She is napping. When we hear a little peep upstairs, Joan, Mom, and I go to pick her up from her bassinet. I normally would hand her to Mom, but today I am feeling grateful to Joan since she has been supportive of the adoption right from the beginning. I hand Heidi to Joan first. Downstairs, before two minutes are up, Joan, Mom, and Dad are all smitten, holding the baby and kissing her.

No one shuns us. In fact the next day, Mrs. Gill, from the farm next door, brings a yellow gingham and lace dress that she has made for Heidi.

❦

Even though we live on a dirt road, we own a crafts gallery called Kensal Studios. Anyone can stop in and see what we have. One day a New York Times freelance writer comes and interviews us about our reasons for living simply. "Team of Craftsmen Who Try To Keep Their Income Low," appears in the paper September 26, 1972. The story is about how we avoid paying federal taxes to support the Vietnam War.

Heidi is three years old at the time of the interview. By now I am a potter making whimsical animals. The journalist describes a set of candlesticks I have made. "One depicts a figure with a frowning face, mouth drawn down at the corner, the other, with a smiling, beaming face," he wrote. And quotes me, "She explained that the first reflected her father's disapproval of the Mayberger's intention to adopt a racially-mixed child. The second showed how he melted upon seeing the baby for the first time."

❦

Dad loved his grandchildren and died at ninety-one just a month after President Obama was inaugurated. I am grateful that he lived to see that day.

Chapter Twenty

⤙ *Cocoon Breaks*

On the last day of July in 1970, college students riding in the bed of a pick-up truck stop at our Kensal Studios. As soon as they step into the gallery, they start asking questions.

"Do you do the weaving and pottery? How did you get started on this?"

"Yes," Ken says, "I was in the Amazon basin of Peru for a time and saw the indigenous people weaving. Sas makes the clay sculptures."

It's a normal visit to our gallery until the driver introduces himself as a Latin and Greek professor at Middlebury College who lives in a geodesic dome and adds, "Why don't you come with us to the Leicester Quarry? We're going swimming."

"Just a minute," I say, "Let me get my bathing suit."

"Oh, you don't need that," a female student says.

I ignore her comment as we squeeze into the back of the truck with the students. Bill drives us south on Route 30, takes a left at Whiting, turns right onto a dirt road, and parks. We walk along a narrow dirt path around the rim of a quarry to a rock ledge that is about forty feet above the water.

The quarry is a dark jade green with sun reflecting gold. When I mention the unusual color, a male student says, "It is a lime quarry about eighty feet deep." The top rocks are flat and while I look around for a place to change, the students rip their clothes off, leaving them in random piles. Some students immediately jump into the water from where we are, which terrifies me. Other students climb down footholds on the rocks to a jumping place maybe ten feet above the water.

I have never been skinny-dipping, but okay, I think, as I stand beside Ken, both of us with our clothes on. My eyes search Ken's, asking the question. He nods his head. It doesn't seem strange. Not when everyone else is naked. It's natural. I take my clothes off and pile them on the rocks beside my towel and bathing suit. A guy is just climbing back up the rocks and points to the footholds. Naked, I carefully place my feet and hands in the grooves until I am close enough to the water. Then I jump in.

The water is heavenly—a whole new feeling—swimming with warm liquid touching every pore of my skin. I am awake, soft, smooth—moving through velvet. My hair flows behind me. A mermaid.

We take to nakedness. On our property in Cornwall there is a hedge between the road in the garden. We garden naked.

During a physical exam, my doctor, an establishment-type man with a crew cut, looks at the slight sunburn on my side going all the way from my arm to my leg. He asks, "Where did you get that sunburn?"

I say, "Skinny gardening."

He laughs, "I've heard of skinny-dipping, but I've never heard of skinny gardening."

Fifteen years later at a wedding reception, he and I happen to be seated side-by-side. When conversation begins around the table, he turns to me and says, "I've done it."

"Done what?"

"Skinny gardening. It's so much fun. I just work in the garden and run up the hill to the pond and take a dip—it's really terrific. Freeing."

❦

I hum with the vibration of being with Ken. But, soon after going to the Leicester Quarry, Ken and I are talking in bed one morning. We have been married for seven years. When we lived in Newark, we had a cocoon. More closeness than most people ever have—two and a half years, twenty-four hours a day together in our isolated, open-room home. It was bliss. We still live and work together every day, although his studio is in the barn.

On this day in 1970, out of the blue, Ken says, "I don't want to end up being an eighty-year-old man sitting in a rocking chair on a porch, wondering what it would be like to have sex with someone else. I want to experience others—women and men." It felt like an ultimatum.

What? I gasp. We have talked about how precious it is that we are each other's first love. My throat is dry. I can't say anything. My heart and whole being feel like a brick wall crumbling. I always assumed we would stay married, have a monogamous relationship, and grow old together. I picture fifties women whose men liked to keep them barefoot and pregnant in the kitchen. I never wanted to be one of those women. I thought I was a partner to Ken these years—respected and honored. Quickly spinning through my head is, how can I live with someone for seven years and have no clue that he wants something else? And my next thought is: I am not enough.

Ken describes his vision. We will be the main relationship, he says, our marriage stays solid, and we can add other partners.

I will do whatever it takes to keep Ken. I have no idea how this will work, but believe I will lose my marriage if I say no. I think the only way to move forward is to be part of this. "If you do it, I'll do it," I say. There is no road map. I am devastated. Like all other women brought up in the fifties, I was taught that having a husband and family was all that mattered. Now the bottom is falling out. I have never lived alone. I have to hold onto Ken, no matter what it looks like. Or I am a failure. I imagine that I can handle this. Then it begins.

> *First the honeyed southern accent*
> *Of a Middlebury College girl*
> *In our bed*
> *Oh, I won't have sex with her*
> *He explains*
> *So don't worry*
>
> *His energy flips*
> *Like the page of a book*
> *I am invisible*
> *All sweetness of our love*

Focused on her

I am a dead thing
Smell my fear
Displaced from our bed
Where do I sleep?
My bed is not mine

I wander through
The house seeking
A place to lie down
I am a bear
Frantic to find her cave

Ken propositions everyone. The only friends he invites to visit are those interested in being sex partners. I lose some dear friends. He thinks we can come back together and be loving. That I will want to be a part of his life. Ken is with others and is happy to come back to me. I guess to him sex is just sex.

But to me, other relationships change our arrangement, split our energy. I can't focus the same way. I feel fragmented with the energy of love making directed toward someone else. I am not happy. I feel ungrounded. I long for a cocoon. Try to find it somewhere, anywhere. I want to feel needed, all of me. To be enough. To have a full life with someone. I have always expected nothing less than unconditional love from Ken, as I had had from my mother. And gave him the same.

His plan shatters everything. I want to be alone with Ken, but he's not available. Being with Ken has been much more than sex. I had learned about making love from him. To me it had been a way to achieve oneness, not a transient experience. Sex had been something that led to a cocoon, a deep connection of two. Making love to Ken had been the way to come together after the trials of the day. An extension of the love of our family. The way to come home fully. The way to forgive any mistakes and be forgiven. A smoothing of the rough edges of life.

When he comes home now I don't feel the same. I always had had a strong sense of smell and was attracted to his. Something has changed.

Maybe it is his pheromones, but now I feel repelled by it. I don't want to get near him. There is something missing. A room I was in always became full when he entered. Not now. Energetically I have lost the connection. My heart doesn't expand at the sight of him. The openness to each other is different. No cocoon. Our souls used to be accessible to each other through our eyes. The connection is broken. Now our eyes are hooded.

The Swirl

Chapter Twenty-One

~ *Rosemary*

Everyone has been made for some
particular work and the desire for
that work has been placed in every heart.
~Rumi

$\mathcal{N}$ow comes the Swirl when my life changes, spirals, and loses its chronological order. All aspects mix together. It doesn't matter what comes first or second or how things fit together. Life is sometimes like this and for me it is this period. Everything has its own pattern which makes it hard for me to tell, understand, and separate the pieces. My goal is to keep my feet connected to the gazar. But there is no order. Come fly with me. See where I land. See where I touch down lightly. People and places come in and out. Time lines suspend. Things do happen and move toward something. Suspend judgement with me and don't try too hard to make sense of it all. The pieces will spiral together and make sense in the end. I hope.

❦

December 1974. Three years have gone by. It is ten degrees out and I am driving to Boston for the day in a rumbly old Volkswagen bug with no heat. I need to get some guidance and direction for my life. A friend named Carol had gone to a psychic and learned that her karma with her husband was finished. She got divorced. Is my karma with Ken finished? I am traveling to see Rosemary to find out. I feel the lonely, dark, and cold of the car. I am scared about what I will discover. The car is hard, not soft, not in good condition. It putts along as only a VW bug can. I feel close to the ground. This is no fifties big, smooth Buick. I need to focus on getting to Boston. Kai and Heidi are staying with a friend. As I drive along in Vermont, I can feel the thirty-five dollars in my pocket—more than two weeks of our family's groceries—to pay for this session.

I am twenty-nine years old. The last three years have seemed like a blur. My goal has been to re-create a cocoon—if not with Ken—with someone.

❧

We had flown to Europe when Ken got a grant to study Jacquard weaving. We decided to travel as much as we could with our children who were two and four. Our family traveled from Denmark to Italy to Switzerland and Spain, visiting museums and art centers. In France we visited the original Jacquard museum in Lyons and a Jacquard hand-weaver in Bretagne. With no money, we slept overnight on the deck of an icebreaker ship to Finland and learned how the government supports artists and crafts people by providing studios.

By the time we got to Sweden we had travel and language fatigue. Our family circle had been closed for those three months.

But the arrangement of open marriage confused it all. There were no boundaries to relationships. I met Mats in Sweden. He could speak English and it was the easy communication that drew me to him in the first place. It seemed so intimate to be able to talk and be understood by someone besides Ken. When we visited my old friend Kirsten whom I knew from my time as an AFS student in Denmark, Ken and she became a couple. I had hopes of being in a cocoon with Mats since we both wanted monogamy. Ken's and my relationships with Kirsten and Mats had taken a lot of our resources and energy with many trips to and from Sweden and Denmark from spring 1972 to spring 1974. Then the relationships with Kirsten and Mats were over.

Now at the end, I think back to the beginning. What was it about Mats? Mats had eyes like the Swedish sky. With reddish shoulder-length hair and beard, he stood like a tall and mighty spruce tree in a Swedish forest. His eyes invited me in, to dive into his musical soul. I would pause and look up at him and he would stop. Like with music, the stop was more powerful than the sound. Our joy and discovery matched and became an invitation for moments like the sound of crackling ice, the newness of listening deeply. That's what I got uniquely from Mats the drummer. I was a child in the newness of Swedish spark and snow and hills, tasting the harmony and communication of improvisational jazz.

This look between Mats and me was beyond love to awe. We looked at each other as beloved. With Mats, I was enough, a goddess. That moment our eyes met, the sun filled my heart and from the look of him, filled his heart, too. All of the faint, short light of the Swedish winter sun became one beam that we absorbed in that moment. The look included the raw energy of yearning. He smelled right and was a gift that felt like magic. I was his first love. He didn't seek more. I felt like I was enough. He would not leave me.

The VW shudders to a stop at a red light. I watch the light turn green.

In the end I didn't want to live in a tract house in Sweden, even though I had emigrated there with Kai and Heidi to create a life with Mats. Meanwhile, Kirsten who was in Vermont with Ken decided to go home to Denmark. We had been four months in Sweden when we returned to Vermont and Ken. Mats kissed me good-bye at the airport. I had an empty feeling that I might never see him again. When I climbed onto the plane, my main thought was, maybe it will crash. I couldn't imagine being back with Ken. Kai was excited to see his father. Heidi had adjusted well in Sweden and was fluent in the language. On the plane she started a conversation with an American in the seat behind us, but she wouldn't speak English. So the man would ask her a question in English, she would look to me to translate it into Swedish. She answered it in Swedish and I had to translate it to him. It was the only bright light on that flight. Mostly I was confused and grief stricken with no comfort in my relationship with Ken, felt no attraction, had no money, and knew I was headed for a cold house during a fuel shortage. I wanted a divorce but couldn't bear the risk of losing Kai and Heidi from my position of never having been independent. I didn't have money, an income, or a comfortable place to live.

Yet, I was finished and after a few months I told Ken to find someone. Right away he started a relationship with a woman in Middlebury and moved in with her. In December 1974, they left for Guatemala for a month. And I came on this day trip to Boston.

༄

Ever since Ken's announcement that he wanted to have an open marriage, my life has been a swirl. Hard to take hold of. Hard to feel grounded. Hard to feel worthy. Girls in my day were groomed to be wives and mothers. I had already failed the wife part.

From Rosemary I want to find out what she sees about the future of my kids and me. Where could we live? Who will get the house? I desperately want Kai and Heidi with me but how can I afford to support them with money from selling my clay sculptures? I'd quit college after my junior year to move to the Northeast Kingdom, but what can I do with no degree? And what about Mats?

༄

I see the snowbanks on the side of the road. I have arrived. I hadn't imagined that Rosemary would live in a tract house similar to the one Mats offered us in Sweden. As I climb out of the car, I check the address on a slip of paper. Yes, this yellow split-level tract house, not a mansion or hippie house as I had envisioned. A song goes through my head: "Little boxes . . . And they all look just the same." Lace curtains hang in the windows. Small patches of snow dot the grass. I walk through the open garage, knock on the door. A clean-shaven, short-haired, tall man quietly opens the door and seats me in a circle of eight empty chairs. With carpets, soft lights, lace on the table, and sunlight streaming through a skylight and the windows, I am surprised that the house is so normal.

He says, "Rosemary will be with you in a minute. She is meditating between clients," and hands me an instruction sheet. It says, "You may need therapy after this session. Some deep issues may be uncovered that will need further work."

I bet. My stomach hurts and my ears buzz. In my mind swirl thoughts of Mats, of Ken, of cocoons, of children, of life. Confusion. Nothing lines up. Boundaries don't exist. I can feel the questions ready to burst.

A door opens and closes.

Rosemary swishes in with her long red hair and floor-length plaid wool skirt draped with a shawl. She doesn't look at me as she smiles and motions me to sit with her at the dining room table. The tone of her voice is calm and reassuring and we sit quietly as I place my Uher reel-to reel tape recorder (like Nixon's) on the table in front of me and turn it on.

"Green," she says. "You are surrounded by green. You are a healer."

I don't know what a healer is.

"I see you starting an Edgar Cayce study group. Do you know about him? No? Well, I'll give you the address."

"I see a comforter, a rocking chair. These have very good energy and make you feel safe."

"Who is on the beach? I see beach balls, sun, playing, and happiness."

I answer. "That's my husband with his girlfriend in Guatemala. Are we separating? Who will get the kids? He has been a loving father."

"You get them. You have much to teach them. I see a man with a hunched back taking boxes out of a house."

"That's Ken. Are you sure he's leaving? We haven't decided who will get the house."

"I see a past life in Australia where you were a young couple building a log house and you got hit by a log. You went into a coma for six years before you died. You even had a baby without experiencing it." So in this life we moved to the Northeast Kingdom of Vermont, built a house in the woods, had a home birth. Seven years after getting married, he wanted something else. Completed the past. Makes sense.

"And Heidi?" I ask.

"She was your daughter in a past life and her mother took her from you. Now she's given her back."

"What about Mats?"

"Were you comfortable in Sweden?" No, my mind screams. "He will not move here," she adds. And just like that, I know there is no hope in

being with Mats. I need to move on. Actually, I feel relieved. One less
option to think about. I will focus on the children and me.

❦

It hasn't been what I expected. I guess she answered the main question, but what about the rest? I wonder, as I climb back into the frigid
Volkswagen with my wallet empty, hoping I have enough gas to get
home. What is a healer? Who is Edgar Cayce? Will Ken really leave me
the house and the kids? And how did she know about the comforter and
rocking chair?

I am in a fairy tale. I set off for one thing and something completely
different happens. I'd expected her to say that Mats and I were finished,
so I'd be ready to rebel and contradict her in my mind, maybe to go back
to live in Sweden with Mats. It had been pretty smooth of her to ask me
if I was comfortable with him, but I have to trust my strong response that
I'm not. My heart hurts, but my mind feels clearer.

She nearly avoided the whole subject of men. Her first words were
about being a healer. What is that? For the first time, I accept that I am
on my own. What this requires is for me to figure out how to support
myself and my children—how I can create a meaningful life for the three
of us. Maybe something about her guidance for me to be a healer will
help?

❦

When Ken gets back from Guatamala, he tells me that he has decided to give me the house so the kids can continue to live here. He will pay
$50 a month for child support. Even though Rosemary saw this, I never
imagined he would actually do it.

Chapter Twenty-Two

~ *Imaginal Cells*

There is nothing in a caterpillar
that tells you it will be a butterfly.
~Buckminster Fuller

If I just need to learn what a healer is, that would be one thing. I do need to learn, but I have so much more to figure out.

❧

Imaginal cells are the magic that turn a caterpillar into a butterfly. The cells of the caterpillar begin to change and multiply in its chrysalis. The caterpillar resists the change and eats the imaginal cells to get rid of them, but they become stronger and increase in number. Finally the caterpillar completely dissolves—all the organs, tissues, and limbs become goop. Imaginal cells hold the blueprint for all that will be, but the old form has to be completely destroyed before the butterfly can emerge. I am living this. I don't like this new arrangement with Ken and keep trying to recreate the cocoon. I don't eat new cells, I fight the change by having one relationship after another. I retard the process instead of moving on. What is required is a total transformation starting from my lowest point. The goop.

❦

Every part of my life is in chaos. In transition. Before, I knew what to do or was told by Dad or Ken and felt sure of my actions. Now I don't have a nuclear family or a grounded monogamous relationship. No husband. No man. Nothing is enough. I am not enough. I have no idea how to move forward.

Ken has moved out which makes it easier for me, but I see him when he comes to his weaving studio in the barn every day. My heart hurts. I would prefer a clean break so that I can get on with my single life. He still wants to be with me and have other relationships. I can't and I won't. I am repulsed by his scent.

I date but am not in love. It is an isolating experience. Intense vibrations. Deadened awareness. No communication. I am definitely goop.

❦

Mom will visit. That my mom Ann Titsworth was born on Sunday, May 9, 1920, the second Mother's Day ever held, was no accident. She came to this life to be a mother. Her first twenty-five years were preparation for motherhood. The next sixty-seven, she reached a fine-tuned balance between being supportive and giving her children independence. She wanted her children to be best friends with each other and with her. This is a good time to review her hopes for us:

- Be thin
- Don't eat so much
- No chewing gum with your mouth open
- No hair in your eyes or over your face
- Short hair
- Smart
- Sensitive
- Giving
- Achieving
- Never sit still. Knit or sew if you must sit
- Don't waste time
- No smoking
- Be outdoorsy
- Natural

- Healthy
- Traveling is okay, but home is the best
- Cleaning is not so important as long as the kitchen and bathrooms are clean
- Sense of humor
- Pleasant attitude

I look around the house and am embarrassed for her to see my life. Rats nest in the oven in the kitchen where it's warm from the gas pilot. Across from the kitchen is the thin tin heating stove Ken installed during the oil crisis while I was in Sweden. A rat killed in the basement by our cat Licorice, barely bigger than the rat. The rat is fat from eating the chicken grain in the chicken coop. I look at the dead rat and wonder what to do with it. Do I shovel it into something? I certainly can't touch it. Kai is only seven but he says, "I'll take care of it, Mom." I feel horrible for him.

And the living room—I could definitely use more coziness. The floors are bare wood. A rug would be nice, but there's no money. There is a hanging spider plant to appreciate.

How can I come to terms with a divorce? How can I live alone?

I live in the goop of the imaginal cells and I can't see what will happen next. I know the results for the caterpillar. A butterfly. The butterfly's wings are soft at first and it has to pump blood into them. By flapping them and making them stronger, it can fly. But for me, there is no end in sight.

When Mom arrives, she helps with the food and works on her knitting, making an afghan for a friend. Each stitch is love. She is peaceful as she rocks in the chair. She doesn't criticize, but I can tell from her serious expression that she hurts with me.

And when Ken takes Kai and Heidi for a night, the little tin stove becomes too hot, turns red, and roars with a chimney fire. Mom and I grab our coats and run outside in the dark winter night. Chimney fires are known to burn creosote inside the stovepipe, heat the wood around it, and burn a house down. The house is more than 100 years old with wooden siding. Will it burn? Since our phone is on the wall beside the stove, all we can do is stand together and watch, smelling the overheated metal pipe, listening to the fire roar while our hearts pound. Slowly, the glowing pipe cools from the top, fading to orange. The roar gets softer. The white clapboards are still behind the pipe when it turns from red to black. The roar stops. My heart is still drumming when we walk back inside.

If I were a dog, I would put my tail between my legs and climb under the studio couch. Mom doesn't say anything—she gives me a hug. But her face is still. Her cheeks are hollow. The air has been sucked out of her as if she doesn't know whether to breathe or not. Compared to standing out in the snow, I feel cozy in the living room.

This is where I start. My goop. Being called "morally degenerate" by a Quaker woman, being a single mother with two small children, and having a chimney fire with rats in the oven and basement.

Yet, at Christmas, Kai & Heidi wrap their toys in newspaper for me and when I open them I can't help smiling. Three wooden blocks with red letters that spell S-A-S.

Chapter Twenty-Three

━ *Healing 101*

*A*fter psychic Rosemary tells me I am a healer and that I will start an Edgar Cayce study group, I try to figure out what that means. With no Internet in 1977, there are no fast answers. I ask my friends. Whenever I hear about a different kind of spiritual meeting, I look into it.

One meeting I hear about is at the end of a dirt road in a geodesic dome. An open staircase like a ladder crosses above a first floor greenhouse. We file over the staircase to a smoky room with a few chairs. I don't understand anything that is going on. Maybe they don't either. Everyone is stoned on the downstairs foliage. This isn't my group.

I hear about another spiritual group and get directions to a musty cabin. When they finally clear off a place to sit down, I decide to leave before the meeting starts. Doesn't feel right.

Rosemary had given me the address of Edgar Cayce's center, the Association for Research and Enlightenment (ARE) in Virginia Beach, Virginia. When I write them to ask about joining a group, they reply with a list of groups on the other side of Vermont—too far away. In the letter, the ARE also explains that the groups meet once a week studying *A Search for God*, with exercises channeled by Edgar Cayce, the "sleeping prophet".

I learn that I was born in the same year that he died. During his life, he made suggestions from a trance state for healing and staying healthy with herbs and ways to live, exercise, diet, and attitude, as well as intuition and reincarnation.

For six months I try to find an Edgar Cayce study group nearby. Contacting others involves writing letters and because of that, getting answers takes a long time. ARE keeps my letter with the request for a group. And when a couple my parents' age who live half an hour away wants to start a group, ARE gives them my name.

When Frank and Grace contact me, we agree to meet at my house in Cornwall and invite others who might be interested. The night is stormy with lightning and thunder crashing on the ledge under my house, making the twenty or so gathered seekers jump.

Everyone has their own idea of the spirit world and each of the twenty has a different plan for spiritual development. One brings a Ouija board. Jon Shore, owner of the Bead Shop in Middlebury, is a fan of the Seth books channeled by Jane Roberts. He says in a demanding voice, "I invite Jane Roberts to come to me." I play with the board saying I would like to contact Edgar Cayce. "Go home with Jon and stay overnight," says the board.

Jon and I drive to the next town after the meeting ends. Jon has a large waterbed. I carefully lie on one side and he on the other. Waiting. Asking to meet Edgar Cayce.

At about two in the morning, I feel pressure in my feet, as if the space between my cells is filling. Someone or something is trying to take over my body, moving in through my feet, my legs, into my core. Jon is asleep. When it/he/Edgar Cayce (?) gets to my waist, I say, "NO!" And push the energy out. It is at this moment I decide not to be a medium like Edgar Cayce or like a shaman. Both require giving over my body to spirits. I decide not to allow a presence to take over my body. I later grow into being a psychic channeler, but not a medium. That is, I agree to allow spirit energy to coexist with mine, like a mother pregnant with the child, but am not willing to let another energy completely take over my body.

Jane Roberts never comes to Jon.

❦

"Entertain the notion" is a phrase that has moved me to make many important changes in my life.

Around this time when I am a single woman with two young children working as a potter, my friend Judy, with the same family configuration, teaches me this phrase as she speaks about her plans to work at a Rutland Mental Health camp. Her job is to be a crafts director for the summer. I already teach crafts in the schools—I could do that. I ask if there are any more jobs.

"We are still looking for a waterfront director. You swim."

With the possibility comes the presumption that there is no way I can go away for a summer. What would I do with my house? What about my kids? I have no money. My Water Safety Instructor certification is expired.

Judy listens. She doesn't try to explain how I can turn each obstacle around. Instead, she says, "Entertain the notion."

There is something gentle about those words—something that puts the responsibility back on me. Is this important enough for me to keep thinking about? I guess so, because I overcome the obstacles one by one. The camp's staff cabin has two bedrooms upstairs and two down, enough for our four kids and us. My house can be rented. Furthermore, with one call to the camp director, I discover that a water safety instructor class is starting next week at Green Mountain College and I can ride with someone taking the class from Middlebury .

From that time on, whenever there is an option for change, I entertain the notion first to see if the obstacles will move out of the way.

Frank and Grace and I create an Edgar Cayce group and meet every week from 1975-1978. While I work as a part-time women's health counselor, Frank works as an accountant at a hospital. Even though he is a person grounded in numbers, he connects energetically with the spirit of anyone, including someone passed over. As we practice in the Edgar Cayce Study Group, I learn from him to see and feel the energy both from those on the physical dimension and those on the other side.

One day I wake with such severe abdominal pain that I tell Kai and Heidi I have to drive myself to the Emergency Room. The doctor says my appendix is about to burst. I am learning to be a healer and having surgery would make me a failure, I say. The nurse and doctor hand me a phone to call Frank as I am lying on the hospital cot. Frank says there are times when we need to accept allopathic medicine. I know I am not leaving the hospital with this level of pain so I agree to surgery. I also learn that healing and surgery are not mutually exclusive, which later becomes an important factor in my development as a healer.

❦

I get the waterfront director job. Judy, her sons, Kai, Heidi, and I move to the Rutland Mental Health camp for the summer of 1977. Groups such as troubled teenagers, prisoners, and Day Hospital, with its patients in crisis, come each week to enjoy nature, swimming, and canoeing.

I meet Zed when he visits as a patient of Day Hospital. I am still feeling unworthy from Ken pulling the rug out from under me and am flattered by his advances.

Zed I

I am tan and trim
Swim a mile a day at camp
He is broken somehow
Bald longhair fringe
Beer belly at twenty-eight
Dimpled nose lazy eye

I say my name
He steps back and trips
Is head over heels
Stumbles
I want to be needed
He is needy

Stoned child with raspy voice
Sings folk songs and anti-war ballads
Glides down mountains on skis
Grace and harmony

On the slopes
Yet awkward in life

A year later, in 1978, I am still thinking about the spirit, mind, and emotions and realize a healer needs to know how the body works, too. I briefly consider taking a two-year intensive program to be a physician's assistant. I send for brochures about programs all over the country. My favorite one is Hahnemann Medical College in Philadelphia which would start in the fall. I am thinking about moving to Philadelphia to study when I get a brochure from another camp, Farm & Wilderness. A photo of a boy in a coonskin cap is securing a rope around the top tent poles. I jolt with energy and know that Kai has to go to there. He is a nature boy who loves leather, fur, and wood. Kai and Heidi will attend Farm & Wilderness camps. Zed and I take jobs there to help pay for it.

When the time comes for camp to start, Heidi resists going. Leave her friends in Cornwall? Live in a three-sided shed with no windows or doors? With no light at night? In fact with no electricity in the cabin? Her princess self is not attracted to the idea of living there. We all go for the summer so that Kai can get the experience he needs.

Heidi is nine and attends the girls' farm camp for nine to fifteen-year-olds and Kai, who turns eleven while there, goes to the boys' wilderness camp—the one I had seen in the brochure. I am in charge of the waterfront at a teen camp and teach life saving, canoeing, and other classes. Zed is a driver. Kai feels at home living in a tent even though he is the youngest camper. The boys live in the woods, cook over a fire, and get special names. Heidi, being a social person, loves the camp experience—spending her days with girls from different places who become life-long friends.

Every morning each of the Farm and Wilderness camps have a Quaker Meeting outside in a circle—a time of silent reflection to be 100% present in nature with the community. At one such time, surrounded by teenagers, I am thinking about moving to Philadelphia, when a girl reads this poem by Nadine Stair:

"If I had my life to live over, I'd dare to make more mistakes next time. I'd relax, I would limber up. I would be sillier than I have been this trip. I would take fewer things seriously. I would take more chances. I would climb more mountains and swim more rivers. I

*would eat more ice cream and less beans. I would perhaps have more
actual troubles, but I'd have fewer imaginary ones.*

*You see, I'm one of those people who lived sensibly and sanely,
hour after hour, day after day. Oh, I've had my moments, and if
I had to do it over again, I'd have more of them. In fact, I'd try to
have nothing else. Just moments, one after another, instead of living
so many years ahead of each day. I've been one of those persons who
never goes anywhere without a thermometer, a hot water bottle,
a raincoat and a parachute. If I had to do it again, I would travel
lighter than I have. If I had my life to live over, I would start barefoot
earlier in the spring and stay that way later in the fall. I would go to
more dances. I would ride more merry-go-rounds. I would pick more
daisies."*

I sit in silence with this poem. I see problems uprooting Kai and
Heidi, now running half- naked Farm and Wilderness Camps. Taking
my bi-racial daughter and nature-loving son to the city does not make
sense. I know I still need to begin training so that I have grounding in
health care and healing. Instead of training as a physician's assistant, I
decide to look into nursing schools in Vermont.

Chapter Twenty-Four

⟶ *Healing Progression*

*B*efore I make the final decision to apply to nursing school, I keep wondering if I can deal with death. A nurse needs to face death and I have never seen anyone die, not even gone to a funeral. I attend a home birth and sadly, the baby is stillborn. I realize that a baby is beautiful whether it is breathing or not. I can do this. I get accepted at the University of Vermont's Bachelor of Science program in Nursing. The year is 1979. I am thirty-four. Nursing school will require three more years of specialized requirements.

I begin and when we learn about stress factors, I have many: Zed and I have just gotten married, we've moved from Cornwall to Middlebury, Kai and Heidi have changed schools, Zed has graduated from college and gotten a new low-paying job. Not to mention we have no working car and no money. There are days at school I don't have ten cents for a phone call. Yet, I keep moving through the classes.

In name we learn how important it is to balance mind, body, emotions, and spirit to do holistic health. In the classes, we have lectures on the first three but the program only has one lecture on spiritual health— during our senior year. I am not impressed with the small amount of attention to what I believe is a big part of health.

In my last year of nursing school, I get a migraine that will not stop. I go to the school health center for relief and, getting none, go to the local emergency room. Still no change. Finally, after ten days, I tell my psychic friend Mariah. She says something is trying to come through and suggests that I use the liminal time between sleeping and waking to listen to spiritual guidance and record the words that come. This, she says, will allow the spirit to tell me whatever I need to know. After a week, I play a tape to her. Yes, she says, that is the voice of the spirit.

My migraine stops. I listen every morning for the next five years and record messages every day. The experience feels like clearing rust out of pipes connecting me to Spirit. I can ask questions and receive answers. The line is open. Mariah gives me a prayer of attunement to say when I seek spiritual connection: *I ask to be a channel of higher love and higher wisdom. All negativity depart . . .* This is for protection.

❧

In my psychiatric clinical, I wonder what makes these patients sick when I am well. Or am I well?

We work directly with the patients. Grandiosity. A patient thinks he is Jesus. I wonder if he could actually be reincarnated from him. Why not? When is someone over the edge, what puts them there? I don't express my questions out loud, but I might give patients more leeway than other professionals on the psychiatric floor. Why are these patients here? Other students are afraid of them. Not me. The patients are just like me.

Maybe it is that they have taken a step farther? I listen. I hear truth. We students can go into any room and talk with anyone if the patient gives us permission. I visit a psychopath. He closes the door. We have a nice conversation. My teacher is appalled that I let him close the door. Don't you know that a psychopath can hurt you?

I learn that the line is when someone is unable to function in life. Can't eat, sleep, make a living, make decisions, take care, or if they want to hurt themselves or others. The voices and compulsion inside are stronger than life outside. Still, the border between psychic and psychiatric patient is a fuzzy one.

With one patient, I get overzealous about energy healing. I ask her if she would like therapeutic touch, which is not touching but moving my hands in the patient's energy field. She says yes and when she doesn't feel any differently, she blames herself, says she is hopeless. I don't yet know how to articulate that healing is not curing. She feels more depressed.

From that experience I understand that I have more to learn.

❦

After I graduate with a BS in Nursing in 1982, I work one year as a medical-surgical nurse, then in 1983 I take a heart job to work at the Addison County Parent/Child Center, creating and facilitating a program called Alternatives for Teens. I travel to five schools with a six-month grant to prevent teen drug and alcohol use. We get another grant to continue. Together with the teenagers, we create a program of discussion groups and activities. The students ask questions and get answers from their peers and me. They choose the topics—drugs, friends, conflict resolution, positive sexuality, meditation, families, feelings, peer pressure, suicide, spirituality, and leadership and other group roles. From these discussions, the group members set up activities as alternatives to using drugs and alcohol—raft races, roller skating, dances, and once camping for a weekend in the Adirondacks.

❦

As facilitator of the Alternatives for Teens program, I am invited to be on the planning committee for a governor's prevention conference in 1984. At one meeting, a committee member has a splitting headache. I know how migraines feel and can't sit still seeing her so uncomfortable. I ask her if she would like me to give her some energy healing. Her face brightens. The meeting continues with me standing behind her drawing the pain out of her head as if it were taffy. And when she gives a sigh of relief and I feel lightness around her head, I stop. The others stop mid-sentence and ask her what happened. She says that the pain is gone.

❦

Many experiences contribute to my training in healing. A bachelor's degree in nursing grounds me in physical health. Two years as a counselor teach me about mental and emotional health. I learn to connect with Spirit through meditation at Quaker meeting and three years of weekly Edgar Cayce groups. I take some high-powered workshops in therapeutic touch, massage, and energy healing, take a class, study books by Barbara Brennen about healing and Dolores Krieger about Therapeutic Touch.

After receiving a master's degree in education in the eighties I give classes in healing and in the nineties I start Life Energy Healing School. Healing matches the concept of holistic health—balance for mind, body, spirit, and emotions.

☙

The conference committee members turn to me. "You should do a workshop for the conference," someone says. "People need to learn how to do this." We schedule an "alternative" workshop for spiritual readings. Twenty-two sign up.

At the conference, we start with eleven participants who sit in a circle for readings. I tell them the person beside me will be first. When she says her name, I will give a reading or message, and after I say, "Thank you," the next person will say his or her name. I close my eyes. The messages come without effort and seem simple, not dramatic. I forget the interchange right after it happens. A new group of eleven people come. When we finish, it is dinnertime. There is a buzz about the amazing and truthful messages. I don't remember them. My main feeling is tiredness.

Zed II

Our brick house
Comes with a gazebo out back
Built in 1900
Moved from a children's home
In Shelburne
The gazebo and house
Hold us and the kids

When the gazebo platform
Falls into the ground
He creates new pilings
And with Quaker men's group
Builds a new base
Hires a crane to move it

Eight years married
It is my lifestyle

In 1985, after five years of early morning messages, three years of nursing school, working as a medical-surgical nurse, running the teen groups, and the workshop at the prevention conference, word begins to spread. My private practice as a spiritual reader and energy healer begins. Clients come for me to channel energy through my words or hands. What comes through is to focus healing energy and speak guidance for clients to move along their live's paths.

For one specific type of spiritual readings I call relationship healing, a client might ask me to connect with a loved one, alive or passed over. Since a name holds the vibration of the person or entity, when I say the name, the energy of that entity comes to me. I feel a jolt or twitch and allow the other energy to co-exist with mine. The energy does not take me over. I have control. I can be in the energy and also explain it to my client.

A session might go like this. Let's say someone is having trouble with divorce finances. I allow the energy of the client's spouse or partner into me. My client begins a conversation. Since I am in the partner's energy, I can answer in their words. Not my words . . . While the client is speaking and even while I am speaking for the partner, I can feel their emotional response to what the client says. By slipping out of the other energy, I can tell what the other person feels in response to the client's words and ideas. Then the client can reformulate the way to communicate, so the partner can react in a way to resolve the conflict.

When I take on the energy of someone else, I might experience a special quirk that a family member recognizes. I might get up and walk or move in a certain way that matches the energy of the person or spirit entity. To start this process, the client says the name, age, and location of someone. I experience that person's energy as a ball of light attached by a strand from the client. I might get a certain word or phrase that the friend recognizes. I see this type of session as an opportunity for the client to learn something more than what she or he knows already. I don't see it as a test for me. I ask the entity or person we call for permission to connect. Even the act of giving permission can soften a relationship.

We are all connected. This is the reason it works. This type of session could help a client say good-bye or apologize or work out a conflict in a peaceful way.

Sometimes when therapists are stuck in their work with a client, they come for supervision. Through me, the spirit helps the therapist see what it will take to help a client break through by seeing the issues from a spiritual angle. This is Super Vision.

The veil between the earth and spirit world is thin for me. Some call me a "psychic" and it's about this time that Mom begins to introduce me that way. She tells her friends that I can see things. Her friends want sessions and Mom and Dad invite me to see clients in their condo in Connecticut. Meanwhile, Dad introduces me as a nurse.

When clients have physical dis-ease, healing energy is not flowing in their body. Blocks cause stagnation of the energy. A healing encourages thick, static darkness to flow out through the soles of the client's feet so that energy can flow. The chakras move in a circular pattern when they are open and balanced. When chakras are not moving in a spiral, energy is stuck. As I hold my hands above my client's body, I hurt where my client hurts. My hands feels a change in the heat over parts of the body depending on whether it is balanced or not. There are a couple of ways I release any energy I may filter from someone else. Sometimes I automatically jolt as I guide the negativity into the ground under my feet. One of my teachers says to be a good healer, my body needs to be a clean beaker so negative energy will not get stuck. I think of this as burdocks, attaching to anything they get near. To clear myself out, I meditate or stand barefoot on the gazar, put my hands in a river, or swim.

Chapter Twenty-Five

⟶ *Swimming through Life*

If I can see the opposite bank across a body of water, I take it as a challenge to swim across. Just like my life. When I needed to become a healer, I figured out a way to learn it. If I become aware of someone who needs healing, I provide it. On things relating to color, if I get the notion to paint the doors of my house turquoise or buy a turquoise car, I do it. Maybe I have to go out of Vermont to find the right color car. No problem. When a message comes to me that I should do something, I do it. Except in the area of men, this has worked well.

For me, swimming is life. There are tides and currents, white caps, wind, and cold water. There is an expanse of water. New York is on the other side of Lake Champlain from Vermont. Since I swim half a mile every morning at the local college pool, I am always ready. I used to think about how amazing it would be to swim the English Channel, the ultimate accomplishment for a swimmer. Then someone discouraged me by saying that it would be so cold that I would have to grease my body with Vaseline. And I thought of the weather one summer day when I was on the Seven Seas ship crossing the channel—a cold and raw day. Never mind the water temperature. Of course, you couldn't eat or sleep. And I remember a picture I once saw of a woman looking sallow and depleted after doing it.

In 1985 when I am forty years old, I decide to swim across Lake Champlain for the first time. The idea starts when Bob and Linda Waterman, two of the most welcoming and down-to-earth people on the planet, invite the kids of Bridport to use their farm's pool for lessons. I know Linda because Kai and her son Roger are friends in high school. She asks me to be the town's swimming teacher. After classes one day, Linda says in a joking and matter-of-fact tone, "Why don't you train to swim the English Channel?" I tell her Lake Champlain is more my speed. Roger overhears us and says it would be fun to canoe beside me. He would be perfect as my support since he is calm, gentle, and light-hearted. Plus, he knows where to start for the shortest distance across, which is about a mile. The place is just south of the Lake Champlain Bridge in Bridport, just a short jaunt from here.

We discuss the route and its inherent dangers. Along with Champ, the dinosaur-like lake monster, there are risks of cold-water temperatures, undercurrents, unpredictable winds, and bad weather. When we drive there to check it out, the neighbors who live on the shore say that early mornings are calmest. So, we plan to meet at seven in the morning on a day in late August.

The day comes. No clouds. I drive to Roger's house, still half asleep. He and his family have already milked the cows. Without much effort from me, we load the long fiberglass canoe onto his truck and drive to the water's edge. A beach of flat black shale with a rotted dock sticking up from the land is our embarking point. From here, the land on other side of the lake appears to be a thin line. Typical of this part of Lake Champlain, the water looks a little slimy. Bits of algae bob with the waves, which today are tame enough. We have decided to canoe over and I will swim back with Roger in the canoe beside me.

With a beach towel around my shoulders over my bathing suit, I climb into the canoe after Roger slides it into the smooth water. He jumps in. As we paddle, we marvel that we can go to New York directly. Always before we have had to take a ferry or drive across a bridge. Now we are crossing on our own power! As we paddle, the fuzzy line on the New York side becomes houses and rocks. We reach a jetty of blackish boulders. Touch land.

I strip off the towel, leaving it on the seat and roll over the side of the canoe, hold onto the edge and gently lower my feet. Roger gives a smile of encouragement and starts his leisurely paddle. I focus on what is underneath the water and feel some slippery rocks before I push off into swimming position. Now it is just me in my bathing suit. No Vaseline. No bathing cap. No goggles. The water and me.

Soon I am gliding with my crawl rhythm of four kicks and two arm pulls to each breath. Roger paddles on my left, so that when I breathe I can see him and the boat through my blurry eyes.

The rhythm makes me think of learning to swim at six when Coach DeGroat told me to put my face in the water. Maybe I am wishing for a challenge again, so here I am. Today is not that kind of fiery excitement but a sustained effort and feeling. Slow like a turtle.

My father encouraged me to not swim alone, but I often ignored the warning. I didn't know how much fun it would be to have Roger along. He stands straight up in the canoe. We are in the middle of the lake. I change to the breaststroke so I can watch him. He stands up again and looks like Huck Finn conquering the Mississippi. He is trying various antics in his boat. He paddles backwards. Then sits back and stares at the sky until I catch up.

I remember lying on my back in Vermont's Elfin Lake. I had watched a cloud change shape and felt gratitude for the size and color of the trees, when a turquoise dragonfly landed on my nose. I wondered if I should breathe. All four wings had become still. I didn't want to scare it away with any movement. I lay still in the water for as long as I could. The dragonfly stayed. It was a moment of oneness where all of life and spirit connected for me.

Somehow I have always been confident that I will not die in water. I love taking risks. I think of other places I have swum. Like in the ocean at Haystack Mountain School of Crafts in Maine. A large boulder sticking up in the water looked inviting from the beach, so I dove in. As I swam, the boulder got smaller instead of larger. The tide was coming in. Before I reached the rock, it was submerged but I found its tip just below the surface and I touched it. Then I swam back.

I feel a cold pocket of water in the lake as I kick. Maybe Champ is passing under me. Roger asks how I am doing. Fine. I love that my body can do this. I feel alive.

On our family trip out West when I was eighteen, we visited my birthplace Olympia, Washington. Some of the old neighbors were still there and we walked with them past the porch of the house where we had lived onto the shore of Black Lake. What could be more amazing than to swim across the lake where I lived for the first few months of my life? My sister Joan was a strong swimmer even at twelve and we took a swim together. We headed out from the shore, saw the other shore, and kept going. The other side of the lake was farther than we thought. Motorboats and water skiers passed us as we got to the center of the lake. When we arrived at the beach on the other shore, we thought it would be safer to walk back on the road around the lake. It took more than an hour. When we got there, our parents and family were a frenzied clump of people on the shore with binoculars trying to find us. Very upset. My insurance man father thoroughly lectured us about safety, but obviously was relieved that the motorboats hadn't chewed us up.

I feel a vibration in the lake water. A slow, old barge heads south. Roger and I are already past the midpoint, where barges seek their depth. Nothing for us to worry about.

I feel peace. Relaxation. What a sensation to conquer the lake distance! The rhythm, the breathing, the calmness are a meditation. With each breath, the Vermont shoreline becomes more and more in focus as if I am a zoom lens. A farm silo comes into my view. Through my water-filled eyes the dock is appearing. Seaweeds begin to brush my legs. I swim in as far as I can through the shallow water to avoid walking on the slippery rocks and algae. When I stand, I am on the black slate beach in Vermont with water dripping off me, the breeze warming me, and a sense of power. The same feeling I had coming out of the ocean at Haystack or Black Lake in Washington or, as a girl, stepping out of the water after jumping off the rope swing I got to use when I passed my swimming test. Alive.

Roger whips out my towel like a victorious bullfighter and waves it to me. As I wrap it around, he says, "Next year, I think I will swim, too!"

Chapter Twenty-Six

⁓ *From Beyond*

*I*n the early 1990s a friend in Burlington offers to let me rent her office once a week for healing sessions. Church Street is right in the center of Vermont's biggest city, a half- way point between the Northeast Kingdom and Middlebury. Clients from the North can get to a session in half a day instead of taking a whole day. I have prepared the space with a few decorations, some chairs, and a painting.

As I drive north on Route 7, I have no radio on. I am getting centered for the two upcoming sessions. Glancing at the keys dangling from my ignition, I feel expectant. The purple key is the one for my new office. It is my first day and I have clients from Stowe and Cabot, Vermont.

I turn off Route 7 just past Shelburne. The car stops. I pull over and turn the key in the ignition. Nothing happens.

"What?" I ask the air.

Don't go.

"What do you mean?"

No.

"No?"

That office is not for you.

In my work I listen to my inner voice. I guide others to follow theirs. If I don't follow mine or say exactly what I hear, the voice stops.

"All right," I say and car starts. I put it into second gear. That was close. I putter along.

It stops. "Now what?"

Do you understand? Not that office.

"Okay, not that one." The car starts. Stops. Is this a test to see if I am listening?

"I understand, but what about today?" I ask. "I have two clients."

On one condition. You see your clients, take your things, put the key under the door and never return.

"Wow! Okay. Leave the key."

At the word key, the car starts and chugs in second gear all the way to Church Street. I unlock the office door with the purple key. The room is dark in spite of the sun streaming through the windows. I need to get rid of the dark energy so I spread Epsom salts in a Teflon pan, cover it with alcohol, and light it to smudge and clear the energy of the room. Holding the wooden pan handle, I flame each corner. The darkness is absorbed by the flame just as the first client comes. An hour passes. The second client comes and leaves after an hour.

I pack my two red office chairs in the back of my Honda, along with the massage table, leave the painting of the ocean and the chair Mom and I upholstered, lock the door, and pass the key through the letter slot. I don't know why that is not my office. Maybe it is just something wrong with my car, but I don't have any trouble on the way home.

I take the car to Pete's Service Station, telling him what happened. Pete's mechanic checks my car. I watch as he motions Pete over. They look at me. He says, "We checked everything. There is nothing wrong with it, Sas."

The car has no more problems. I never go back to that office. After this experience, I have all meetings, classes, and healing right in my house and gazebo.

❧

While at Rutland Mental Health's camp, I hear about a massage class in close-by Rutland. I am still trying to figure out what a healer is and figure massage is one way to learn about bodies. The class is held upstairs over a restaurant where forty half-naked students sit on the floor in a very large room. The seventies are the hippie days. Clothes optional. Our teacher demonstrates aspects of Japanese shiatsu or pressure points massage, and massage from Native American and Swedish traditions. He teaches an eclectic class of meditation and various practices. We usually start with a circle sitting on the hardwood floor and chant OM. The way we do it, each person takes a different tone and all tones eventually become one harmony.

One day he walks on and cracks my back as I lay on that floor. It feels great and probably sets me up for many years of good health. After class, he asks me why I am so loose. I swim a mile a day.

Every time I walk into that room, I move into an alternative zone. I learn exercises that I will later use for my students. Each week we find a partner and do an hour massage on a different part of the body. It is blissful to have so much attention. My skin, muscles, and even bones become more alive. Our massage teacher emphasizes the importance of male-female balance. His teachings turn out to be important additions to my understanding of healing.

&

After I graduate from nursing school and spend seven years working with teenagers, I write a manual, *Life Skills for Teens: The Group Leaders' Guide to Alternatives for Teens*. In 1990 on a hot, sticky day in Washington DC, I receive one of ten national Exemplary Prevention Programs Awards from the Department of Health and Human Services for the program. An award winner sitting beside me studies the energy of drugs in the laboratory. I tell him I see the energy of drugs. What do you see? He asks. With cocaine, it is a swirling tornado. With alcohol, shaking energy as with delirium tremens. With heroin it is a whole body vibration. He responds that his project researched cocaine and found that it does, in fact, move in a spiral. Sometimes I feel my life is so alternative, I wonder if I can relate to academics and scientists. Nice. I could.

Negative ions are rocks and impediments. Go around rocks? Easy for water. Negative ions? Energy can't move because negativity sticks to itself like burdocks in a field. When the flow stops, stasis creates disease, then vulnerable, sensitive people find openness painful. They might start using an addiction to make the pain stop. As time goes on, the addiction creates a shell, like a nutshell around the soft, vulnerable soul of the person. The shell gets thicker and thicker until it is nearly impossible to break through it.

The person cannot connect with their self or others because now the shell surrounds their soul. The person is sick.

Zed III

My healing doesn't work
Zed needs too much
I need to find myself
Yet the house and gazebo still hold me

In 1989 I give a presentation on energy healing at the United States Dowser's Conference in Danville, Vermont. Hundreds of dowsers of all kinds attend. Some have forked branches and L-rods for dowsing water, minerals, and treasure, and others use a pendulum to assess chakras like I do. The movement of the pendulum over a chakra or energy center shows me what part of the body or psyche is out of balance. I demonstrate the assessment on a volunteer, discuss what imbalance there is, hold my hand over the area to bring it into balance, measure it again, and answer questions from the audience.

As I often do, I close the demonstration with a circle, inviting everyone to hold their left hand palm up and right hand palm down, but not touching. Then to focus on sending energy with their right hand and receiving with their left hand. It is a big circle which stretches around the pews of the church where we are meeting.

There is a commotion across from me. I ask what is happening and hear that a tiny, older woman's feet are lifting off the ground from the energy. I tell her to come stand on my right so I can help ground her. Instead, I learn that the focused energy of one-hundred- fifty people is enough to lift a small woman off the ground, because I can feel her elevate.

She's not the only one. Now that I have stopped trying to find the comfort of a cocoon with a man, I am able to do my real work. The only way for me to be transformed, to become enough as a person, is to flap my wings and let myself lift like the woman beside me.

❦

I am still finding my niche in healing in 1993, when I meet Gregorio, one of twelve psychic surgeons from the Philippines. He is visiting Hans, a Swiss friend and hotel manager, who is interested in working with me to create a healing center. Hans says I need to see how Gregorio works. While I do healing in a person's energy field, Hans tells me that a psychic surgeon works inside a person's body to take negativity and disease away.

I am now running Life Energy Healing School and two of my students want to meet with Gregorio, so they make appointments and we travel there together. As we step through the door of Hans' house, a patient wearing a bathrobe comes out of a bedroom across the hall to change in the bathroom. The woman is peaceful and smiling, as if she has just finished having a massage.

"The balance of energy in the room is delicate," my host explains to me. "Usually no one can watch, but since you do spiritual healing yourself, Gregorio says you can join him. He invites you in now as he prepares." Hans explains the process, saying that Gregorio puts his hand through skin and tissue and removes disease. He works at a juncture where liquid, solid, and gas intersect. Is this possible? East and West, spirit and science, clash in my mind. Is it a sleight-of-hand? What about AIDS? Does he wear gloves? Use sterile techniques?

In the past I have walked through the same bedroom when visiting Hans. It has the same bed, painting, built-in basin, and view of Lake Champlain out glass doors. The only change is a massage table with a stand beside it. On the stand sit plastic cups, cotton, a mirror, antiseptic-type bottles, and jars—for cupping I'm told. The room has the feeling of a makeshift doctor's office.

Gregorio, with short black hair and a crisp short-sleeved shirt, walks in, nods to me, says the Lord's Prayer, and crosses himself. He enters his own alternative space, focused and interior. An invisible fog fills the room. The energy is thick. Already, I can feel a shift in reality. I glance at the painting and it is wavy, not solid any more.

He nods to his assistant who invites my first student in. "What can I help you with?" he asks. She explains her problems. "Change into this bathrobe," he says matter-of-factly, handing it to her.

She lies face-up on the massage table. Gregorio prays again. The energy in the room is light-colored, dense, and peaceful. The assistant hands me a plastic cup with water and some cotton. Gregorio continues to pray, takes the cotton in his bare right hand and places his fingertips on the patient's midriff. It looks like her skin boundary is not solid—it dissolves, becomes another type of matter—because his fingers disappear into her skin. When he brings his fingers out, the cotton is covered in stringy clotted blood. He drops the red cotton into the cup that I am holding. There is definitely blood on that cotton and it was white before he put his hand "into" her middle.

He takes a new cotton ball and repeats the process. I check Gregorio. Does he have something up his sleeve? No, he has short sleeves. The blood is coming from where? He continues to pray out loud as he places his hand palm down on her solar plexus. He is running energy just as I do. When he takes his hand away, the skin is solid. No line. No opening. No mark. Can it be an optical illusion? How can this happen? I am puzzled. The patient gets up and leaves the room.

After observing the same procedure with my second student, after watching his hand disappear, and seeing her intact midriff, Gregorio turns to me. "What about you?"

I tell him I don't have anything wrong and I don't know if I need anything.

"You do healing, don't you? You've probably collected some negative energy around your heart from your patients. I'm here. You should take advantage of my being here."

"Okay," I say and I step out to change.

As I lie on the table, Gregorio prays. I watch and just as before the energy of the room is thick. More cotton balls and cups. Everything is set up and happens as I have watched it twice. When he places his hand through the skin and fat over my solar plexus, I feel tickled on the inside—a fluttering like air bubbles moving around, like Kai moving when I was pregnant. He brings out the same red-clotted blood on the cotton. I not only witness it visually, I feel the sweep inside as he moves his hand.

As I change back into my clothes, I notice a tiny red dot on the skin of my midsection. Was it there before? I feel lighter. I want to dance, like after a massage or healing. But, along with knowing that I am a channeler and not a medium, I can see that I am a nurse and energy healer, not a psychic surgeon. I need to follow my own way.

Chapter Twenty-Seven

～ *Let me Entertain you*

I am paying attention to my daughter. Heidi has an unmatched imagination and intellect. I watch with awe. At three, she reads *Cat in the Hat*. At five, she writes stories. By the time she's ten, the titles are My Mean Long-Lost Uncle, Being a Baby Dove, and Beeblety's Big Secret. All are explorations of imaginary worlds. My Life Story begins: "Hello, my name is Mystery. I am a Rolls Royce. I am long, black, and always shiny." In school she, the sole person of color, imagines herself a black car.

～

At a friend's six-year-old birthday party, she holds the strings to a rainbow of balloons and runs through the town's green with the rest of the kids behind—following her joyful, charismatic happiness. She is so different from me.

At seven, she already struts her little self down the streets of Middlebury and gets used to attention. I hear about it from friends.

One Christmas I am expectant as I give her a heavy, full suitcase long hidden in the attic. It is filled with a high quality boarding school wardrobe from the fifties—wool suits, rayon skirts, and silk blouses. I found the suitcase for a dollar at a moving sale. She is ten, rips the wrapping paper off and seeing a beat-up suitcase with its the gray plastic cover, her face drops. Hope dashed, she says, "Thanks, Mom," and nudges it aside without lifting the lid. This is my best present, but she moves on and I watch her open her "ooh! and ah!" presents. Finally, she peeks under the lid and notices hand-sewn silk gowns and other period pieces. At first she uses these suitcase clothes for dress up. Then for hours and days and years she uses them to become other personae, other styles, other periods, and even acts out stories with her friends.

At fourteen the extra-small outfits match her extra-small body. Clothes conscious and creative, she chooses a silk suitcase gown for her first prom—and for the one the next year. A third year, she shops for a gown with her friends, but, discouraged, she checks and finds another gown of silk still in her suitcase. I alter it and dye it blue. The gown is more exquisite than the ones in the store, she realizes, and I am happy to see her wear something that fits her personality.

Sometimes oblivious to life in Vermont, at sixteen she could be passing a field and ask "who eats all this corn?" (Animals.) Or she dries her new expensive sneakers in the oven. (And ruins them.)

A performer, she hates to be without an audience, hates to share a phone. While it is uncommon for a teenager in the eighties, she has her own line and phone. Using her unstoppable energy, she vacuums the house each week to trade for its monthly charge.

As a teenager at the dinner table, Heidi monopolizes the conversation and fills us in on her day. One monologue describes a girl whose pants are so tight (and before spandex) that she needs to jump out of a tree to get into them. The Queen of Story Telling easily exaggerates and fabricates for the right effect while I literally fall out of my chair laughing.

Her charisma is never invisible. Her challenge during her teen years is to own her beauty. When boys and men eye her, ask for her phone number, whistle, they think because of her looks she belongs to them. I learn from her that being beautiful is challenging.

She has a wild-hair look that I'd love. I'd love to feel my hair springing all over my face, hanging over my ears, wound in a scrunchy and half falling out. I'd love to feel the bounciness, shake it loose, pull it casually out as I put my jacket on, feel it tug and sail in the breeze. But mine is straight and calm hair. Her hair matches her.

Heidi intuitively knows where the earth's power lines are and puts a stake where she thinks the backyard gazebo could be placed at the precise point where these lines cross. She knows where. She just knows.

❦

When the Vermont Probate Judge signed the papers for Heidi Mayberger to become Jasmine Carey, he said, "Well, at least this will get you out of the Alps." She needed to change her identity to being non-white.

"I am the Jane Goodall of white people," she later says. "I have lived among them. I know their ways."

❦

One day recently, Jasmine called me distressed that a young black friend from Brooklyn who has devoted many years to a camp where they both had worked, did not get hired for a leadership position. Even more upsetting to my daughter was that the camp didn't respond quickly to the candidate's post on their Facebook page in which she explained that she was more qualified than the woman who got hired. Her friend spoke of the entrenched systemic nature of racism.

When Jasmine, who was on the camp board of directors for many years, replied with her own deeply felt thoughts in support of the candidate's message, she was dismayed that she herself didn't get any support in the form of "likes" either, even from her closest (white) friends.

While listening, I found myself with familiar feelings of despair and failure to understand, and not knowing how to respond to her or the situation. I realized that even after fifty years of being Jasmine's mother, I really didn't know how to write her a letter of support. I got butterflies in my gut thinking of admitting that. I felt nervous about saying the wrong thing. I thought, I am watching movies, reading, and studying about racism and . . . many clichés came to mind, here's where the rubber hits the road, the metal hits the pedal, push comes to shove. I still don't know how to do this.

What I learned from one book, *Waking up White* by Debby Irving, was that my white privilege is the luxury of not having to be vigilant in my mind and body at every moment. My brain does not have to save a space to be alert to how I might be treated just because of my skin.

Later some people started responding but, even though they might have been trying to say the right thing, their words were still offensive to her. As a white person, can I understand this on a deep level? I am trying.

Then one of Jasmine's friends wrote a Facebook message of support and included something about people of color hurting. My daughter explained loudly, "Everyone is hurting. Not just people of color."

I got my courage up to ask Jasmine what exactly would be helpful for me to write. I texted her to say that I hope I don't say anything wrong. She wrote back that saying something wrong is better than being silent. She explained what she wanted idea by idea. She asked me to write that I am her mother and adopted her, a biracial child, because I want diversity in my life. That I honor the values of the camp and hope the camp will live by them in a way that will make a rich experience for diverse people. All this is true. I didn't have to stretch my truth to say these.

Last summer, when Jasmine visited from Los Angeles, we drove around Addison County and she felt encouraged by Black Lives Matter signs. She has not always felt at ease and acknowledged here and felt that her treatment was the tip of the iceberg for how other folks of color might experience Vermont. By this she meant that she could imagine that if she felt this way, people of color new to Vermont would feel it far more acutely. Since she grew up here, she feels more safe and familiar than many others presumably would. People knew her and her name. Even though she had lots of friends, she lacked a support system as a person of color, she told me as I sunk a Black Lives Matter sign into the front yard.

Chapter Twenty-Eight

⟶ *Kai's Graduation Present*

*If you teach your children to pursue
their dream, be prepared for them to do it.
~Claudia Cooper*

𝓕rom the time he is little, my son Kai loves tools. He gets a mother-of-pearl penknife that had been his grandfather's when he is about four. When he is five or six, he cuts his thumb trying to remove insulation from some electrical wire, but that doesn't deter him. He is careful and well co-ordinated from a young age. He uses matches, starts campfires outside, and creates shavings and scrapings for fire starters with his knife.

He loves making things. His father and I market our pottery and weaving at craft fairs and Kai goes with us. As a craft fair kid, he sits on the floor in our booth, takes a scrap of leather, makes a small pouch or container, and sells it, using the money to buy metal stamps for leather from another booth. Then he stamps a design on his leather and sells it. He is about five.

All through his teen years, he crafts items from leather and wood. At Farm and Wilderness, when he is fifteen, he makes a drum from a tree trunk by carving and burning out the center to make it hollow. He adds leather for the head. Since the log is over three feet high and about nine inches in diameter, it takes him all summer. He still has the drum.

At Goddard College, Kai majors in ecology and Native American studies. He had apprenticed with his uncle making stick furniture as an alternative high school course. In college his advisor teaches him to turn big logs into boards. He makes flutes and drums with wood he mills. I still have one of his early hoop drums and an early flute.

For his graduation presentation, he takes his family and friends into the woods at Goddard. He hands each person an instrument he has made. My mother has a rain stick, which she loves. I have a drum. Kai has a flute. He speaks, thanking us for being with him, for the animals and vegetables being part of the drums and our experience. He describes his senior project making instruments and mentions that both his parents and two of his grandparents are here. He then asks us to be silent and to go inside ourselves. Tears stream down my face as I sit. He is teary, too, and not ashamed of it. When he starts to talk again, he looks at the top of the trees and lifts the wooden flute he made. Kai asks us to play the instrument we have for ourselves. *Just start*, he says. *Maybe we will come together with sound.* I keep getting rushes of energy, especially as we begin, and I can feel the connection playing my drum.

About thirty people are in the forest. After a few minutes, the sounds blend to make one harmony—something tender and loving—the way we feel about Kai and each other. Then, we stop. He talks more about drums and spirits, trances, and shamans. How the drum is a heartbeat. He answers questions, gets moved again, and says, "I'm going to stop." He sits down and sobs. A young woman sits beside him and hugs him. His father Ken, up from Florida, sits down on his other side. I give Kai a tissue. I love him so much, but I know he wants to be grown up and separate from me, so I don't crowd him.

For Kai's college graduation present, he and I camp in the Southwest around the Four Corners area for two weeks. We're driving forty-five degrees up and up in a rented red Pathfinder in Utah. There are twelve-inch rocks and foot-deep holes in the road. Bonnie Raitt is singing.

Kai had met a Diné, Navajo, named Nancy at Goddard College when she was studying for her master's degree. Nancy had invited us to camp on her property in Utah. In fact, the plan had been to help her build a hogan, but the United States government, true to its long history of interference with native land, has decided to put an oil pipe through her planned building site. Her building is on hold.

Nancy drives ahead, leading us to her land. As soon as we arrive at her small trailer, she points out some special rock formations in the distance. Then she gets into her car to drive a hundred miles to teach at the Navajo Community College. Before she leaves, though, she tells Kai there are some Indian caves nearby. Ancient ones like those we just saw at Mesa Verde where Kai's flute sounds had reverberated. His eyes light up. I know he will find them.

We set up our tents near the trailer. As we look at the views, we see the four corners—the rock formations of Monument Valley in Arizona, the snow-capped mountains of Utah, the San Juan Mountains of Colorado and the spires of Shiprock in New Mexico. The land is beautiful in its brown desert colors—ranging from tan to burnt orange to greenish gray. Scrub brush, a few pine trees, and sharp rocks line surrounding canyons. Earth tones are pieced together with textures rough, smooth, gritty, shiny, and matt.

Our plan is to stay for a few days. For supplies, we have brought two gallons of water, some dried and fresh food, tents, sleeping bags, and thermal pads. We had shopped at a health food store, where we bought dried bean flakes, avocados, tomato sauce, pasta, eggs, and more. We have been eating these in different combinations, one of our favorites being spaghetti with tomato sauce, avocados, and dried black bean flakes. Surprisingly delicious. Kai begins to cook, but the wind blows our cook stove out. We consider using the trailer, but when we check inside, we discover that mice have taken it over and it will need a good cleaning.

Kai builds a shelter from the wind outside and continues to cook there. I appreciate him cooking and driving. These feel like a present for me. It is also a bonus to have someone enjoy the same food I do. He is my son, after all.

By the second day, we are already grubby and funky. I meditate in the sun while Kai goes exploring. Dozens of hummingbirds come to the car. They are attracted to the only red color around. Two small lizards play on the ground beside me as I write. In the late afternoon, Kai returns from his discoveries. From far off, I can see the bounce in his step. I know he has succeeded.

"I found a cave. I even sat in it. Lots of energy in there. Plus a cool six-pack of beer. I figure it's an offering. It sure looked tempting, though.

I was so thirsty, but I left it. Come on, Mom, you have to see it. It's incredible."

"Tomorrow," I say.

We make dinner together. "Sun dried tomatoes must have been discovered here," I say. "See that half, nearly dried? It's the other half of the one I had for lunch." I think about the effort we make to dry food in humid Vermont, how I have to use the oven of my gas stove.

After dinner, we hear the hum of a vehicle. Nancy appears in her truck with two Diné, Navajo, men who step down from the passenger side. She introduces one as a medicine man. I stand straighter. From what he has studied and been told, Kai has instructed me not to make eye contact, not to ask bold questions. To respect nature and its ways. I try to be invisible so I won't offend them.

Kai must have told Nancy that I use a pendulum to dowse chakras, because she asks, "Did you dowse for water? Did you find any?" She leads us to a spot she wants me to check. I show her the movement of the pendulum. The two men try it with the same results. "Okay, I guess I'll build near here." Kai tells about the cave and the beer. They nod to each other, "Oh, yah, the place we left Bill's ashes. Jimmy put that six-pack there. You found it, huh?" Kai eyes shine as he nods twice. Watching Kai here on the land, I feel his ease and how at peace he is. He carries his wooden flute in a leather case tied to his belt loop. After his graduation, making wooden flutes will be his work.

As we walk back to the truck, it is getting dark. They still need to drive one hundred miles tonight. Nancy points to the medicine man with her lips. "He hurt his back. Will you do a healing for him?"

"Sure," I say as the other three walk off talking softly. He tells me he hurt his back in Vietnam, that he's been on crutches for years. That a month ago he was at the Grand Canyon and a huge thunderstorm blasted the canyon and when the lightning struck, he laid his crutches down. He could suddenly walk. "Now if I'm walking a lot, my back gets tired."

I hold my hands where the energy is hot at the base of his back, breathe in the dry desert air and the blackness of night. Now that I am quiet, questions come up. *Here? Now? Heal a medicine man? Smelling like this?*

Then I am not nervous any more. I am in my element. Doing my work. Letting energy flow through me. Listening, seeing, feeling, smelling the blackness of the air, the mugwort, seeing abuse and discrimination, feeling his pain of living, hearing the bombs in Vietnam. Running energy through me. The faucet is open. I am letting it into the top of my head, up from this native ground, out my hands, pouring, sucking the pain and darkness with my fingers. Letting it flow continually through my arms, shoulders, down a channel to my legs, out the soles of my feet to be transformed by Mother Earth. Out with the breath. The flow of life, of the earth, of galaxies. In, out. Smoothness in, roughness out. I close his aura with my hands caressing the invisible energy around him. We are standing in the night. Quiet voices come from nearby. The others are waiting for us to finish.

"Thank you," he says. "I don't want to be on crutches again."

We join Nancy, Kai, and her friend. Say good-bye as they climb back into the truck and drive to Navajo Community College.

"They came to see you, Mom," says Kai gently.

I can't believe it. I squat down and pick up some earth with my hands.

Chapter Twenty-Nine

⟶ *Newseum & Spirit*

> ➤ **Correction:** A story on Sally Ann Carey Thursday incorrectly stated that the family of a missing girl came to her for a psychic consultation. Two friends of the girl came to that session, and later Carey talked with the girl's mother. Also, Carey worked for Rutland Mental Health, not the Rutland Regional Medical Center. She taught swimming, not singing, adopted one child, not two, and at times contacts healing guides, not healing gods.

*B*eing home alone I wander through each instant. I feel moments of heart connection, or of losing time and space. Of dreaming. I like real moments when something in the physical world connects my heart. I view energy as the networks of mushrooms underground, I feel the networks of love and energy lines surrounding the globe, connecting people I know and love to people they know and love. On and on. This creates a web of light whose source is spirit. To me, each person to whom I am connected is a source of my place in the universe because it radiates out to Oneness. I am smaller than a dot but connected by my heart to the universe.

I can go anywhere. In my Life Energy Healing School, one of the meditation exercises that we do is to open our spirit to go somewhere in the world that we are needed. We start in Middlebury, expand to all of Vermont, then the US and finally offer to go anywhere. One time I am taken to Sudan in Africa where refugees are lined up with their bright native costumes heading toward a river. The river is the color of coffee. I am spiritually asked to put my hands in the river. When I do, it clears. I get the message that this is what the people need to stay alive.

❦

In Nantucket in 1990 where the ocean's soft air surrounds me, I am doing healing sessions all day long in a gray-shingled cottage with bushes of blue, pink, and purple hydrangea outside. The upstairs room with a slant roof where I am working smells of wood and massage oil. What is the problem the client brings? I don't remember but as I start the healing a light energy comes and I find my hands rising up in a pose for blessing people. The energy is palpable, dense, light, overpowering, comforting and strong. Big. My body is tiny. The room is tiny. The house is tiny. The Presence fills me and becomes a giant light extension, the aura of a giant through and outside me. Light fills the room and the little house as the healing happens. Then the work is done, the energy dissipates, and I am left with a hologram of light as I see the next client.

A healer listens with her heart to life stories, allows them into herself, holds them lovingly. Speaks from her center. As she feels the physicality of another, she holds it in love and light, and transforms it to the brightest light possible. This gives the person a feeling of being the best they can be. In the process, the client learns how to feel a connection to the spirit. I am teaching what I need to learn.

☙

2016. "The Newseum," says Wikipedia, "is an interactive museum that promotes free expression and the First Amendment to the United States Constitution, while tracing the evolution of communication. The seven-level, 250,000-square-foot museum is located in Washington, DC and features fifteen theaters and fifteen galleries." It also features newspaper bloopers, which are tiled on the walls of the restrooms. On a trip to DC, my brother Tom discovers this clipping on one wall.

"Correction: A story on Sally Ann Carey Thursday incorrectly stated that the family of a missing girl came to her for a psychic consultation. Two friends of the girl came to that session and later Carey talked with the girl's mother. Also, Carey worked for Rutland Mental Health, not the Rutland Regional Medical Center. She taught swimming, not singing, adopted one child, not two, and at times contacts healing guides, not healing gods. Rutland (Ver.) Daily Herald 12/17/94"

"Did you ever find the girl?" my friend asks when I show her the blooper.

The facts were that twenty-three year old Karen Sabitini of Brandon,

Vermont disappeared one night in January 1991 with her boyfriend.
The newspapers reported that they left someone's house in Brandon
in the evening and no one heard from them again. The police searched
everywhere, but there were no clues. After a couple of weeks, two of her
friends came to see if I could psychically find them.

When I closed my eyes and said a prayer of attunement, I invited
only healing and positive energy to come through. Then I spoke the name
Karen Sabitini, so that I could be taken to her psychically. Right away, I
saw a couple in a truck under water. I psychically asked Karen if she had
a message for anyone and she did. She had heart-felt messages of love for
her family and messages asking forgiveness. Personalized messages for
her friends in the room as they asked her questions. Then, as I watched,
a light sprang from the woman's center, up through the top of her head,
traveled up through the top of the truck through water and ice, and disappeared. I watched as the same happened to the man on the passenger
side. I described this to her friends, who later told her family.

"Yes," I tell them. "I psychically saw the twenty-something girl in a
truck with her boyfriend under the water of Lake Champlain. I watched
as a light came out from the top of her head and then a light came from
her boyfriend."

About three months after her friends' visit, I noticed a small clipping on the front page of the local Addison Independent newspaper. It
explained that when the ice melted on the lake, authorities found the
bodies of Karen and her boyfriend in his truck under the water. It was a
deep part of the lake, so the truck was hard to find. She and her boyfriend
must have thought the ice was safe and tried to drive on it, the paper said.

How do I explain finding Karen psychically? In spirit, we are all connected by energy and we are especially close to the people we love. We
hold a part of each other inside us. Energetically, each of us is a vibration
of light. Each name contains a unique vibration. When I close my eyes,
focus on the client's light, and state the name of the other person, I am
shown a ball of light containing their energy.

Since there is so much love for Karen from her friends, the distance is
breached immediately and I see her in the truck under water. Somehow,
maybe from the speed of the accident, her light had not left. Now with
the love from her friends, her soul has enough energy to leave her body.

We invite you to our show, Psychic Waves. Every Tuesday 5:15-6. Save your questions, save the time. Call and add to our discussion or ask a question. We talk about energy and that invisible force, the SPIRIT.

Sas Carey is our resident psychic. She will answer your questions using your higher self as her guide.

I, Guanlong Cao, am a junior here from Shanghai China. I am your host.

Listen, call, ask. Your input will make the show.

In 1989 on the Middlebury College radio station WRMC, Cao and I challenge the stereotype that Asians are spiritual and Americans are scientific. With us, it is the opposite.

We have lived for the same number of years but half way around the world from each other. Cao, my radio and home partner, does not believe in psychic ability. I, on the other hand, have a private practice giving spiritual readings and healing. He grew up during the Cultural Revolution where there was only space to be pragmatic and rational. I grew up in New England.

❦

Perry Link, a Princeton professor, "discovered" Guanlong Cao's powerful dissident writing while in China in the early 1980s and John Berninghausen, a Middlebury College professor, translated his stories. The book *Roses and Thorns*, a collection by new young Chinese writers, was published in 1984. During the eighties, Cao was being persecuted for his father's landlord status by the Communist regime and was eager to leave the country. John advocated for Middlebury College to give him a four-year scholarship and he got his visa in 1988, arriving in the United States at the age of forty-two.

I meet Cao at Dance Free at the local elementary school gym. As a single woman, I am always looking for someone. There is hardly anything I do or any place I go where I'm not thinking, maybe this will be the place. I could sit against a tree trunk in some remote forest and still wonder if someone will magically walk by and fall in love with me. Always looking for a fairy tale.

So when Cao dances into the gymnasium, I notice. He has black hair, black-framed glasses, and is a presence. He wears a white tank undershirt and gray sweat pants and moves in perfect rhythm, completely sure of himself.

I keep stepping around the gym, light and free, lost in the music on that cold winter night. When he dances near me, his eyes rest on my bare feet, move up to my breasts, and land on my eyes. I feel a thrill coursing through me. Each time he gets near me, he tells me more about himself. When the music stops, we walk out into the cold. He surveys my Toyota with awe, because, I later learn, he had hardly ever ridden in a car, being poor and from Shanghai. "Why don't you come to my room for a cup of tea?" he asks, instructing me to follow him as he rides his bicycle past snowbanks to a house near Middlebury College. During the short ride, I find it shocking that I could meet an interesting man in our town! Already, he has mentioned that he is a writer, a sculptor, a photographer.

His basement room is cluttered with upholstered chairs with no feet, a VCR and television, plaster sculptures, and photographs. I sit on the low chair and he brings me a cup of tea, which I put on the floor. He touches my leg like he owns it or is measuring it for a sculpture. Then he tries to touch more, but I stand up. "I have to leave."

"Can I see you again?" he asks. "Take this. It will tell you about me." He opens a Middlebury College magazine to the sculptures he makes. Then to another page with a photograph of him standing behind a tripod and camera. "I wrote this story. Read it. How about Friday?"

On Friday, I pick him up and bring him to my house. He says, "I need a pan and a towel. Got any nail polish?" He fills the pan with warm water, sits me down in a living room chair, and places my feet gently into the pan, holding them firmly, yet sensuously. On his knees in front of me, he slowly washes my feet—the tops, the soles, the short stubby toes—and carefully paints each nail pink. He tells me his mother had refused to have her feet bound when it had been expected of women and his father had looked for a woman with normal feet. With this in his background, he has a foot reverence. The feet he touches are not my ugly flat feet with the hairy little hobbit toes. These feet with their newly painted toes are sculptures. And so our relationship starts. He is warm, funny, handsome, talented, brilliant, sexy, and smart. Two 42-year olds from opposite sides of the world who have a lot of distance to travel to learn about each other.

༃

We host a radio show. We start with music, then Cao introduces us. I channel responses to call-in issues from students. The topics range from spiritual to romantic questions.

> Life: What is the point of it? Energy: What is the big picture?
> Heal: How can you be in tune with yourself? Listen: Where are your
>   answers?
> Channel: How do you speak what you perceive? Spirit: Where does spirit
>   fit in?
> Gifts: What do you have to offer? Senses: What is your way of perceiving?
> Relationships: If you avoid them, will they go away? Intuition: Are you
>   born with intuition?
> Reincarnation: What can you learn about your past? Dreams: What can
>   dreams teach you?

Some callers ask about the logistics of connecting with the spirit. Or how do I get my information? How can I find my talents and use them? When someone asks about her new love relationship, it comes through that he is not kind to her. Cao checks with the caller before she hangs up. "Is it true that he's not kind as Sas says?"

She says, "Yes." But he is still skeptical.

Later when Cao hears that my guidance was right about where Karen and her partner had disappeared to, he believes me.

༃

Overall, Cao is fun when he is light and disappears in full sight when he is dark. Over five years, in our connections and his stories that he shares in our bed, I feel the warmth of his attention as if the sun is focused on me alone. Cao's life story draws me in— closer and closer—

until it becomes part of me.

When Cao graduates from Middlebury College and attends the School of the Museum of Fine Arts at Tufts University, he moves to Boston. For two years I trek down there for weekend visits, but eventually, he and I find the distance unwieldy for a relationship. However, he has given me a magical opening—personally and viscerally. From my painted toes to each hair on my head, I have been introduced to a whole new continent. A whole new way to see myself.

IV *Learning Mongolia*

Chapter Thirty

тавтай морилно уу!
Tavtai Morilno oo!
Welcome!

*I*n the summer of 1994, when I am 49 years old, I follow my friend Kathleen Scacciaferro into the heat of Beijing's airport. Kathleen is Italian, sturdy, with dark hair. The bounce to her step creates a path through the crowd. She has a solid, no-nonsense nature, deadpan humor, and the motto "save lives and stamp out disease." Since being in nursing school together, we say this motto often.

Now we head for a sign that says, "Ulaanbaatar" and swim with the crowd like a school of sardines outside to the runway, soaking our clothes with sweat. The temperature and humidity have both hit 100. Barely able to breathe with people pushing on all sides, I climb the plane steps and sit in a window seat. We fly over mountains and long stretches of the Gobi Desert with no cities or roads.

Kathleen and I have spent a week touring China with a delegation of nurses sponsored by the American Holistic Nurses Association. Our group is now going to spend a week in Mongolia with the goal of learning about holistic medicine and how to incorporate Eastern concepts into our practice. Like my visit to Rosemary, what I get is different—and more.

❧

тавтай морипно уу! *Tavtai Morilno oo!* Welcome!

Now I stand on the steps of the plane in front of the airport in Ulaanbaatar. The airport is a small, concrete building. The plane is parked a hundred feet from it. I am waiting for my turn to step down. I watch Mongolians ahead of me step nimbly with ironing boards, boxes of cookies, candy, oil, fruit, and tightly taped bundles in red, white, and blue plastic. I know almost nothing about Mongolia. I am on a treasure hunt, curious, reading clues, living moment to moment.

❦

In the spring of 1994 sixty-eight year old Jean Arrowsmith limps into my healing room wearing a hummingbird sweatshirt and tan corduroy pants with a book under her arm. After she asks how I am, she dramatically unveils the book: *Encounters with Qi* by David Eisenberg.

"This book is about you, Sas. You need to go to China."

"I've read it. Pretty interesting, huh?" I say, looking at the book and ignoring the part about me going to China. She reads voraciously, but usually not about energy.

"You need to go to China, " she repeats. "You need to learn about energy from the masters with centuries of practice."

"Sure," I say. "That's what Cao says, too." Cao and I had seen Bill Moyer's *Healing and the Mind* on television the year before and when it showed David Eisenberg in China, his reaction was immediate, "You need to go there!"

"Yes," Jean continues. "You are a nurse using energy healing in this country where the modalities are separate. You talk about the need to integrate traditional and modern medicine and, as we see from this book, the Chinese practice them side-by-side."

"Strange. Just this past week I got two invitations from the American Holistic Nurses' Association for a tour to China and Mongolia, but I never imagined going myself."

I am resistant.

"You are going, right?"

"How can I go? It costs $5000. I have no money."

"Borrow it," she suggests, as strong and sure of herself as I have ever seen her.

"I can't borrow it. My life is guided by spirit—by guidance I understand from meditation and dreams. I never know where I am needed or what I'll be doing. I have to be free to do whatever is asked. How can I take money when I don't know if I can pay it back?"

It never crosses my mind that this whole idea could be guided.

"All right." She exhales loudly. "How many sessions will $5000 be?" I sit up straighter and get a pencil. We multiply and divide.

"Let's see—sessions every other week for half an hour? Seven years."

"Seven years? Okay. Sign up. You're going!"

"Yes," I say, finally accepting the most important spiritual leading of my life.

❧

It's my turn to go down the plane steps. There is no tarmac. My feet land on Mongolian earth. The gazar. A bolt of energy like electricity, runs from the ground through the soles of my feet, through my legs to my heart and head. When I inhale, the air is fresh, not humid. My skin feels like it is breathing with the space. Green mountains surround the airport and I feel held in the bowl they create. Immediately I am at home.

Now, like a herd of sheep, we migrate to the airport door. There are no lines, no signs, no arrows, no directions. When the immigration officer, a short, stocky man in a black leather cap sitting in an outside kiosk, reaches for my passport, I smell alcohol. It's one in the afternoon.

No one is telling us what to do, like they did in Beijing. I suppose wait. Kathleen makes a side comment to Marsha, a nurse from western US, and me about watching the men. We sit on our bags inside an airport with no lights on, surrounded by the mound of luggage brought by our tour group of thirty-eight American holistic nurses and observe.

The men physically have more in common with indigenous communities in the Southwest than with Chinese. Bronze-gold smooth skin, high cheekbones, and big smiles. Many of them have straight, black, shiny hair, cowboy hats, black boots, and wear silk deels, traditional robes, with orange sashes. Their energy, not diluted with the feminine, says, *I've been here forever. I belong.* Energy that makes their whispery voices sound like they are speaking words of love. Our blood rushes.

Waiting is no problem today.

Eventually, our guide, with the nickname Gan, a tall, thin man with a bass voice and good English, motions us to climb into a new, shiny, white and red Julchiin Tourist Bus for the ride to Ulaanbaatar. Gan speaks into a microphone, telling us that we are the first large tour group to visit Mongolia since the country's transition from socialism to democracy four years ago.

My heart beats with the newness as we pass pasture land with sheep stretching so far into the distance that they look like white rocks. Near them are white mushroom structures, gers, or yurts, herder's dwellings. Mountains are green and bald, with no trees. We cross a bridge over the Tuul River into the capital Ulaanbaatar with a population of 600,000 and see signs in Cyrillic which we can't read.

The bus stops when we pull into a dirt parking lot. Gan points at the highest building and says, "The Bayangol Hotel. This is where you'll stay. I'll call from the hotel lobby around ten in the morning and let you know what we'll be doing." This is a change from our regimented days in Beijing starting at seven in the morning.

In my room on the eighth floor, I step out onto the balcony and look down. Many of the five and six story grey Soviet buildings look like drab boxes, yet the sidewalk is a riot of color from men and women in gold, red, green, blue, and purple silk deels who walk arm in arm.

The day before from the hotel window in Beijing, bicycles made the streets busy ant hills. Today, two horses are tethered to a streetlamp beside the hotel entrance. Three girls sit in a circle on the dirt ground and play a game. I watch dark-haired, dollhouse-sized people step out of a bus and disperse in all directions. More swarm onto the bus and the door closes. Below me is a round white ger and someone ducking to go inside.

What's inside? It looks mysterious. I long to follow, to touch the ground, the people, feel the energy. Learn the secret life.

I have arrived in Mongolia, a place I never in my forty-nine years imagined that I would ever be.

❧

Mongolia is desert, steppe, and taiga. Mongolia is city and countryside. Shamanism and Buddhism, Mongolian medicine, folk medicine, and Western medicine. Nomads and city dwellers. Welcome to Mongolia.

All my life I had hardly thought of Mongolia as a country—more like a metaphor for the farthest, most unusual, most foreign place in the world. My mother sometimes said, "She would go to Outer Mongolia to find him, she cares so much."

As evidence of it being unlike home, to be culturally appropriate in Mongolia, I need to ignore many of Mom's admonitions:

- Knock before entering
- Be on time
- Don't click your gum or chew with your mouth open
- Eat slowly
- Don't slurp your soup
- Carry on a conversation during a meal
- Don't lick your plate or bowl
- Don't slam the door
- Look people in the eye when you speak
- Enunciate your words
- Say "thank you"
- Don't go into crowds
- Stay away from cities
- Stand a certain distance from someone in a line
- Don't scuff your feet, pick them up when you walk
- Driving: Don't pass while turning
- Don't drive in the break-down lane
- Don't show any cleavage
- Don't dance like the sexy dancers on American Bandstand

And to survive in Mongolia even obvious, engrained, unspoken ones will have to be ignored:

- Don't go in a car over wobbly bridges with boards missing
- Don't ride on a motorcycle or in a car with a drunk driver
- Don't drive into rivers
- Go behind a tree to pee outside

I have a whole new learning curve ahead of me.

Chapter Thirty-one

— Seduction

After days of touring hospitals and monasteries, meeting nurses, doctors, and government officials, learning that 44.5% of the Mongolian population is under 15, and buying velvet hats, silk clothes, and cashmere socks, we travel by bus to the countryside for a Naadam Tourist Festival. Buses, wrestlers' tents, chairs, and a military band with speakers on buses form a bright circle in the middle of the open Mongolian steppes or plains. Mongolia seduces me starting with the omnipresent scent of Sweet Annie (Artemesia or mugwort).

We have just walked onto the festival ground for the day's "three manly sports" of horse racing, wrestling, and archery, when Gan says, "Come back on the bus. We are going to a restaurant so we can use the toilets. It is only five kilometers away." Around me horses gallop, the band plays, camels move like royalty with their long straight necks, and Mongolians flow by wearing brightly colored silk deels. Blue and red banners top tents. Bright colors contrast with the sparse vegetation of the open plains. Each step releases the fragrant scent of wormwood and mugwort from the plants. Shadows of large birds of prey—condors, eagles, vultures, and kites—glide over. I've just landed in heaven, down from the eighth floor tower.

I am not leaving. I had noticed while traveling along the mud tracks of the countryside that there are no gas stations, stores, or motels and only a few trees, bushes, or even tall grasses. In Vermont, I am used to spending time in nature. When we went camping as kids, Dad explained the use of brush and trees and even carried a shovel for that purpose. Peeing in the woods is really no problem. But, land without woods is a new experience.

Sweeping my arms around at the hundreds of people at the festival I ask Gan, "Where do all these Mongolians go?"

"They do it naturally."

"What is naturally?"

"Just go."

"Where?"

"Anywhere."

"How?"

Mongolian women can squat anywhere because their *deels* easily become their outside toilet. I see an elderly woman completely covered by hers as she squats at the edge of the crowd. We are the only women wearing pants.

Five of us will stay and manage, even without a deel. Harriet, a large, warm-hearted, red-haired nurse from California, says, "I have a rain poncho."

Gan says, "That will do," turns abruptly, and leaves with the bus. We huddle together, like football players, and take turns putting the red poncho on for privacy. It is a little awkward seeing hundreds of people as I pee, but definitely better than leaving the blue-sky paradise.

Now we five have a head start on the festivities. Close by a man beckons us to take a ride on his two-humped Bactrian camel. For one dollar, I climb on, sitting between the humps with the owner holding the reins. The camel unfolds his back legs and I lurch forward, gasping. I have never been on a camel. Then he straightens his front legs and I jerk back. I feel a buzz of excitement in my chest as I sway with the camel underneath me. I try not to look down to see the long distance to the ground.

After the ride, we pass bulky men the size of sumo wrestlers wearing traditional Mongolian wrestling costumes of blue or red bikinis and open-front tops with knee-high, leather-inlaid boots. Kathleen keeps saying, "Oooh, nice boots!" I don't think she means the boots. I think it's the exposed skin.

In a match, the wrestler tries to get a good grip on his opponent's reinforced clothing. To win, he maneuvers his opponent until he is off balance and a knee or elbow touches the ground. The burly winner then does an "eagle dance" waving his arms gracefully like eagles' wings and tosses *aaruul*, cheese curds, into the air to honor the land. Here even wrestling has a natural spiritual component.

I videotape women's archery. Women in bright deels aim their arrows at a wall of eight centimeter sheep gut baskets piled under a rope one meter above the ground. When someone hits the target seventy meters (seventy-six yards) away, the referees sing the results of each shot in a traditional melody that sounds very much like a Native American chant I heard the previous summer in Arizona. It vibrates in my heart.

Erotic art is spread out on the ground—not hidden. In it, couples make love on or behind herd animals like goats, sheep, yaks, horses. I learn that there is not much privacy living in a ger. In fact, there is no word in Mongolian for privacy. The closest word means "personal rights" or *khoviin*, personal and *noosh*, secret.

A young man watches me video him on his horse and motions me to join him on it. When I smile and walk to him, he helps me up onto an orange-painted wooden saddle inlaid with silver. He goes bareback, riding behind the saddle and holds the reins around me. Just yesterday I was in my hotel room, longing to touch Mongolia and now a young man smelling of lanolin, horse sweat, and smoke is sitting behind me on his horse. We ride to a line of other horses and squeeze in with the audience to watch riders finish the horserace. A comforting, earthy smell embraces me while eagles glide overhead in the wind.

When I arrived, I was a white foreigner at a tourist festival who had never ridden a camel or horse. Now I feel included and welcome.

༂

My body is still vibrating from the festival the next day when we thirty-eight nurses file through a dirt courtyard and climb through a fence entering the Institute of Traditional Medicine. In Ulaanbaatar animals are fenced out, not in. When Gan gently opens an inside door without knocking, we meet Dr. Boldsaikhan in his office. Sage, cinnamon, mugwort, and sandalwood scents greet us. As often happens when I shift from or to the spirit realm, I jolt. I recognize this as my body's signal to be alert.

Dressed in khakis and a blue plaid shirt, Dr. Boldsaikhan is a serious Buddha-shaped man with a moon face until he explodes with laughter. About five years younger and a few inches taller than I am, his eyes are humble and calm, surprising for such an accomplished man who practices Mongolian medicine as well as allopathic (Western) medicine.

On a table is the first computer I have seen in Mongolia. He explains that from a Sanskrit sacred *sutra*, holy text, he is creating a database of herbs and minerals used in Tibetan-Buddhist medicinal recipes. So far, he has uploaded the names of four thousand ingredients. Dr. Boldsaikhan tells us that traditional Mongolian medicine comes from Ayurvedic and Tibetan practice. He holds up a book he has written with sketches of the herbs, animal parts, minerals, and gems used as medicines. For years, I have talked about holistic medicine combining many different beliefs, techniques, and procedures from all over the world—how ancient wisdom could blend with modern thought—but this is the first time I have seen such a clear example. I can feel a quiver in the air from those disciplines meeting here.

Dr. Boldsaikhan takes us on a tour of the Traditional Medicine Institute buildings, centers for research and making medicines. When he opens one door, we see squares of paper being folded into packaging for powdered medicines. Behind another, one doctor gives chiropractic treatments to a young boy while another gives energy healing to a blind woman. In a third room, a patient receives an acupuncture treatment. In this one institute I see techniques it has taken me years to find in the US.

My heart suddenly beats as if I am in Quaker Meeting being led to speak and I blurt out to Dr. Boldsaikhan, "Would you take an American disciple?" The words come from beyond me.

"Yes," he says.

I don't know it then, but when he says, "Yes," my life's real work begins.

❦

1994. We still have one night! I'd thought I wouldn't go out at night in Ulaanbaatar because, according to *The Lonely Planet*, it's dangerous. Yet, I am determined to have every experience I can with Mongolians while I am here. After dinner, we nurses in the tour group dance at the Bayangol Hotel bar. My body moves with the flow of music and life. When a Mongolian performs the horse dance and shimmies his shoulders, he is so sensuous that Kathleen and I look at each other and at the same time say, "Whew!" Then the dance floor and bar close.

Kathleen, Harriet, and I climb into a taxi with Gan to find another place because we want to dance. When the place Gan has in mind is closed, we stop to ask directions for somewhere else. A woman points to the majestic Cultural Palace. "There, in a little bar." In the US, I never, ever go to bars since I don't drink, but if that's where the dancing is? Okay. Through a dark alley, we come upon a grand entrance, with marble steps and marble columns. Built by Russians, Gan tells us. Through a heavy door, dark, unlit corridors and stairways, we find a cone of light, hear loud pop music in Mongolian, and find a cozy bar with ten tables. Red and white checked tablecloths give a homey feeling. While the others ask for a full meal with a bottle of vodka, I order a Sprite.

A tall, slight man in black from his hair to his clothes and knee-high, shiny, leather boots politely asks me to dance, flirting with his eyes. I never catch his name, but then Mongolian names are very difficult for us, with whispery sounds we can't distinguish and written in Cyrillic. His moves are gentle and flowing. It is my first time dancing with a Mongolian and his first with an American. We step onto the floor for every song.

I have such rose-colored glasses on that I am not noticing other men with shifty eyes and wandering hands. Gan follows us down the hall when we go to the bathroom "so that nothing bad will happen" to us. My money, ticket, and passport are safely in my money belt under my shirt. Since I got married at nineteen, I missed the college dating scene. Just being in a bar is a challenge.

The vodka bottle is empty. Harriet, the big redhead, is engrossed—kissing a short, thin Mongolian who is nearly on her lap. Kathleen and Gan dance and talk, become oblivious to their surroundings. Harriet sways with her little partner and drinks straight vodka shots every time she sits down. A second bottle of vodka appears and disappears. Harriet dances with a man and woman at the same time. Gan, still on duty to protect us, says, "Don't have anything to do with those girls, they have diseases."

The Mongolian men we saw at the Naadam Festival and the men here have the energy of indigenous warriors, of power, earth, and horse riding. They seem connected in a way that crosses the boundaries between spirit and physical, sensual, and sexual energy.

The very peaceful man is still dancing with me, each of us gliding separately yet together in harmony as long as a song has a beat. He is not drunk like the others. On and on we dance, smoothly, flowing around the whole floor. Harriet weaves around hanging onto her small man who has left and come back. At 2:30 Gan gives the bartender some money to stay open for another hour. At 3:30, even though the dancing is thrilling, I mention that we fly to Beijing tomorrow and maybe need some sleep. "Pooooohhhhh!" they sneer. "Let's dance for another hour."

A new group of six men sits at a table, talking and drinking. How they found out the bar is open, I don't know. "Come join us. Your partner here has bought some special wine just for you. Drink some," says one man in English who wears a leather jacket and white scarf.

"Sure, I'll sit but I don't drink," I say. Gan introduces us to Chuluun, the giant man who is translating, as his English teacher from the university. I watch the professor take command of those around the table.

At the same time, my partner and I say, "You are a very good dancer." We get up and dance some more. It is five in the morning. I get Harriet and Kathleen's jackets and hand them to them.

"One more dance," slurs Harriet.

"Okay and then we go." I feel like a mother hen gathering her chicks.

At the end of the song, my dance partner gives me a gentle kiss and hug and goes down the stairs. The rest of us walk through the corridor and out the front door. Harriet moves off to the side with her man. Kathleen walks ahead with Gan. I stop for a moment to look up at the stars, wondering if they are in the same position as they are at home in Vermont.

Wham! The professor grabs me and forcefully kisses me. I gasp and try to draw away, but he holds on and pulls me back. I am resisting, but he leads me to the steps at the front of the building. This can't be happening, I think, he's an English teacher, harmless. Yet, he is pulling at me. Harriet has ducked around a column with the small Mongolian, too drunk to be any help. I feel Chuluun's big hands on me. Tug, pull. I have never been raped. Yet, I could be. I exhale, trying to make a sound. I try to pull away, but he is too big and I can't move. I'm thinking, Is it too much to ask to pause for a moment and look at the stars? Why would an

English professor do something like this? Does he think I like it? He is forcefully kissing me and touching my breasts and thighs. It doesn't feel like spiritual energy at all.

I want to yell, but my voice catches. Finally some words come out, "KATHLEEEEN, HEEELLLP, I MEAN IT." She turns reluctantly from swooning over Gan, not want to be disturbed with the few hours she has left.

"Come here. I am being attacked," I shout.

With hands on her hips and our guide behind, she comes running. Kathleen explodes, "STOP IT. Leave her alone. SHOO," she motions with one arm and grabs my arm with her other one, pulling me away. Gan is slow to react, following Kathleen. Maybe he doesn't think I am serious since he doesn't know me as Kathleen does. Or maybe since the man was his professor, he won't interfere.

"Where is Harriet?" Kathleen asks in her no-nonsense tone.

"Over on the steps with that guy."

 Kathleen marches over to the red head.

"Put your clothes in order, Harriet. NOW. Get up. We are walking to the hotel." Kathleen brushes the small man away. Gan does nothing. We three women with our guide walk slowly toward the hotel. We need to watch out for Harriet who is trying to lag behind—sneak around planted shrubs with the guy—while Gan and Kathleen try to finish their important conversation. I just walk, glad for safety in numbers.

It has been a (nearly) perfect night.

Chapter Thirty-two

~ *Arriving to Begin*

*W*hen I get back in Vermont, I have a lump in my throat thinking about Mongolia. I have to get back somehow. I feel incomplete. Kathleen finds a movie that takes place in Mongolia called *Close to Eden*. I cry to see the faces and want to be the one to sleep in the ger, wrap the deel around me, and have a tryst on the steppes.

Letters to Mongolia take two weeks each way, with no email in those days. Dr. Boldsaikhan offers to teach us traditional Mongolian medicine. Kathleen and I start planning even though we have no idea how to do this logistically. Mongolia isn't so keen on individuals traveling there, having changed from being a socialist country only four years before. To enter Mongolia, we need a formal invitation, a visa, health forms, somewhere to live, and funding.

A Quaker Friend Honey Knopp comes to my house with envelopes and copies of a fundraising letter. She tells me I need to send it to everyone I know. Going to Mongolia to study traditional Mongolian medicine is a spiritual leading and others will help me. She, her husband Burt, other Quakers, and I address a lot of envelopes.

For my fiftieth birthday, friends and family rally to create a back yard event with a band donating their music for dancing in the gazebo. Kai's wife Julie makes and donates two delicious cakes—one shaped and decorated as a Mongolian ger and one with traditional Mongolian designs. On the deck is a basket for donations. With this early method of crowdfunding, I have enough for a plane ticket, housing, Dr. Boldsaikhan, food, and a tight budget for extras.

❦

Gan will arrange our stay for one thousand dollars and a large suitcase full of hundreds of dollars worth of goods not available in Mongolia. This includes jeans of specific sizes, classical music tapes my Dad donates, and English language books. His requests are out of line, but we don't discover this until we learn that Mongolians in 1995 are happy to make three dollars a day. Kathleen and I don't know that we are giving him a year's salary or that the money will buy him an apartment for his family. We only know that we will do whatever it takes to get to Mongolia.

Халтар царайт. Dirty Face. On May 24, 1995 Kathleen, her medium tall, strapping, blonde husband Bruce, their kids, timid blonde Jenna (seven), deep-voiced dark-haired Noah (four), and I fly to Ulaanbaatar. Gan meets us with a hired Russian van. While riding to our apartments from the airport, there is no traffic. The streets are empty. It's a little eerie. Our driver goes the wrong way around a round-about. "Where are the police?" I ask.

"Халтар царайт, *Dirty Face*. It's our first soap opera. The whole country watches it every weekend."

"What about horses hitched to a post at the Bayangol Hotel last year? It will change everything!" We pass three trolleys parked in a line on the side of the road. Gan points to a shed behind the trolleys where the glow from a screen shines off the faces of uniformed men.

"Even the police watch it."

Gan directs the van driver to stop at a dusty courtyard outside a Russian-style concrete building. "Yours is the only six-story building around here," says Gan, lifting a suitcase. I look around. Bland, grey, Soviet apartment blocks surround bare, dirt ground. Two large cranes tower over unfinished cellar holes.

Russians had left the cranes and other equipment after Mongolia's peaceful sit-in for independence in 1990. They had been a presence in the country since 1921 when they had helped to protect Mongolia from China, but Russian support had been mixed. A Mongolian version of the

Stalinist repressions from 1936 to 1952 had killed Buddhist monks and forbidden shamanism. On the other hand, the socialist government had constructed schools, hospitals, and apartment buildings until they left in 1990.

"For garbage," Gan says, bringing me back, pointing to a ten-foot square three-sided brick enclosure in the middle of the courtyard.

We each grab a suitcase and follow Gan. Up one flight of stairs. Two. Three. Four. Five. Six. "Oh, my God! I will never be able to do that again," I pant to Kathleen at the top. Her face is beet red, and she can't even talk. The kids are whining.

When Gan motions to Bruce and says, "Let's get the rest," I catch my first glimpse of sexism, but I feel relieved. The men will carry the luggage up. Men's work is different from women's here. I always wanted to be able to do what my brother did. Get Lincoln Logs instead of dolls. Ride Harry's tricycle with a red wagon attached to learn to back up a trailer. Learn to sail from Dad like he did. Go to Middlebury College or Williams College like my brothers instead of a state school. But, if being a woman means that I don't have to help lug seventeen heavy bags up six flights after thirty-four hours of traveling, I'll take it. I smile at how it feels like a different kind of liberation.

Meanwhile, Kathleen and I explore her family's apartment—bedroom, kitchen, living room, bathroom. The more we look, the more I feel like Goldilocks in someone's home. Soup bubbles on a low hotplate. Slippers line the hall with coats hanging above them. "Someone lives here," I say.

"Nah," says Kathleen.

"Your room is over here," says Gan to me, pointing to a door adjacent to Kathleen's after he and Bruce deposit the last piece of luggage. "Let me get the key." He walks out the entry door to the hall, and knocks twice on a metal, locked door. When it opens, I see a crowd of people in the dark facing in one direction, lit from the front. A young woman, who turns out to be Gan's wife, hesitates and steps out, walking sideways to keep her eyes on the television. The sound from the soap opera pours out the door. She runs to a jacket hanging on "our" wall, fishes in the pocket, and, without a word, drops some keys in Gan's hands, runs back through the door, closing it.

"She doesn't want to miss a single minute of *Dirty Face*," says Gan seriously. He tries to open my door with the key, pushing and pulling, squeezing and shouldering it. Finally, it opens. "We call this a pocket apartment," he says waving his arm at the small space. He gestures behind him at the new wooden panel and door entryway in the hall. "Safety for your apartments. Three doors. Be sure to lock them all. And don't let anyone in." I don't say anything, but if Gan can't open my apartment door, I am sure I can't. I don't lock my door in Vermont for fear that I will lock myself out.

I step into the "pocket" and find a living room with two day-beds and a table with two chairs. On the wall above one couch is an earth-colored Oriental carpet. Over the other, portraits of an elderly man and woman, whom I assume to be the owners of the apartment who are renting it to me for the summer. The bathroom has a deep tub, a basin, and a toilet, but no toilet seat or paper. The tiny kitchen has a dorm-sized refrigerator, small sink, two-burner hotplate, and a small shelf with a couple of Chinese rice bowls, unmatched mugs, a teakettle, odd pieces of silverware, and a saucepan. Home sweet home for the summer. This will do fine.

As I begin to unpack I hear rhythmic pounding outside. On the ground below a dozen kids dribble basketballs on the packed earth and shoot them into the metal frame of a fire escape. It is ten o'clock at night. Still light. Inside, Gan's wife Oyuna is ladling mutton stew into bowls. *Dirty Face* is over.

Oyuna and their daughter Shishgainaa come to my apartment, open one of the daybeds and get blankets from underneath, preparing a bed.

"The buses stop running at ten," Gan explains, meaning they are all sleeping here. Good thing I brought a nightgown.

The next day Kathleen and I ride a red and white city bus with standing room only, returning from a day at *zakh*, the market, where I'd bought necessities like a light bulb, toilet paper, and a toilet seat. The dilapidated bus lurches and when I look up, a Mongolian woman is shaking hands with Kathleen. I think someone is introducing herself, so I reach over to shake hands, too. The woman looks at me a bit strangely because, I later learn, if you step on someone's foot or touch their leg with your foot, you need to shake hands to give the person's soul back.

Chapter Thirty-three

~ *Dr. Boldsaikhan*

I have come to Mongolia to study with Dr. Boldsaikhan. To learn about health and balance. I don't know what will happen or exactly what I need to learn. I do know that am where I am meant to be. I am open to whatever comes.

On the second day of this, our second visit, Gan takes Kathleen, Bruce, and me to plan our studies with Dr. Boldsaikhan. The outside of the large three-storied L-shaped Institute of Traditional Medicine does not look like a doctors' building or a hospital. Once elegant, it is now faded yellow stucco. Inside, patients sit on benches in the dark halls waiting to see doctors. The glossy mustard-yellow doors and floors remind me of a clubhouse.

His office does not smell antiseptic like a hospital or a doctor's office in the US. In his room, the same as the previous year, the rich smells of Artemisia, cardamom, and sandalwood draw me to the mystery of Mongolian medicine.

His room is not bright because the city's electricity is off. In front of the window is the same table we saw last year with the computer and Buddhist sutras open to a certain page of holy text. With peacock feathers for long life and a ten-foot-high Medicine Buddha *thangka*, god-painting, I feel like I'm in a secret cave for mysterious learning. Dr. Boldsaikhan will not disappoint me. Kathleen and I will spend three months in this office-classroom-examining room sitting at a shiny table, learning from our teacher.

To plan our studies, the men take over. Our teacher and guide have made it clear that women are not to be a part of the discussion. We are trying to be culturally appropriate. Gan, Bruce, and Dr. Boldsaikhan discuss the finances and scheduling for our training. Kathleen and I, who have planned everything up to now, and will be the recipients of the studies, sit quietly while the men hash things out. After we roll our eyes at each other, I use the time to attune myself to the space. On the wall hang plaques that say *Mongolian Society of Yoga and Parapsychology* and *President of the Union of Mongolian Medicine*. Being in the presence of Dr. Boldsaikhan, I feel a jolt as his powerful energy bounces around the room and inside me. I have dreamed of this for a year and now I am living my dream.

Children's voices ring in through the window. The florescent light flickers on. Test-tube-shaped containers with metal tops sit in a tray on the windowsill. Variously shaped roots, powders, and dried flowers fill other test tubes on his desk.

The men turn to us, "Do you agree with the plan, five days a week, ten to five every day?"

Yes.

I give the doctor a handful of mint from my Vermont garden. He places the Mentha x piperita with the other herbs on his medicine tray. A shadow is cast on it, as an eagle flies overhead. The leaves of a tall tree rustle against the window. I already love this room. Mongolia. The smells. I am floating.

☙

Okay! Monday! Our first day of class! We get off the bus near the Ulaanbaatar Hotel, cross a tiny spur, and a car slams on its brakes. The driver has hit an older man who is lying on the road. His shoe has flown off exposing a hole in his blue sock. Kathleen's eyebrows go up. She presses her lips tightly together inside her mouth, as she does when she is thinking. The driver gets out of his car, collects the shoe, helps the man put it on, walks him to the sidewalk, and drives on as the man hobbles away. Our first city lesson: Drivers don't stop for pedestrians. The next time we need to cross a street, we lock arms, look both ways, and stand still. When a Mongolian couple starts to cross, we step up to them on the side away from the traffic and make it across.

As we get to the Institute, we notice that the building has six entrances and they all look alike. Since we followed Gan here when we were jet-lagged and disoriented, we don't know which entrance leads to our classroom. The first entrance has a padded yellow-brown door. We nod to each other and step inside. No white coats. No herbal smell. People walk in and out, like they do in our apartment building. When we look up, we see a clothesline hanging out a balcony window. Apartments, not medical offices. We leave and step into the entryway of the next four doors and shake our heads. At the last entrance, the herbal scents hit us.

"This is the one," I say. "But, which room?" All the inside doors are mustard colored, closed, not marked with names. We say, "Dr. Boldsaikhan" to a man with a white coat. He cocks his head, listening. We repeat Bold sai' khan" in our American accent which makes the "h" silent and puts the accent on the last syllable.

"Oh, Bold"sai'khan," he says with a gutteral "kh" like "heh" emphasizing the first syllable. He leads us to Dr. Boldsaikhan's office, motions to the door. We knock before we remember not to.

"How is your apartment? Is everything okay?" Dr. Boldsaikhan asks. "You have the directions? Any trouble getting here?"

We show him what Gan has written in Mongolian in my tiny black notebook:

Bus: Улаанбаатар 1р зам
Buses have Route No.1 on front and 3-011 on the side
Address: 53 Орх Оолуг
16 Хороо 27 Байшийн
71 Тоот
Б. Ганбаатарорих
Phone: 53140 GEEGEE

54547 Явли РГ
Bus stop to institute:
Байшийн дээ
Bus stop to market:
7г Гуанз Цирк

Gan says if we get lost, we can show someone this. The only thing we recognize is Kathleen's apartment number—71.

"Any trouble getting here?" He repeats. "How did you come? Past the Ulaanbaatar Hotel? Oh, that's the long way. Let me tell you a better way. Tell your taxi driver *'Huuchin gemtliin emneleg'*." We write it phonetically. "It means 'old hospital for crippled people,'" he says. "You need to use the front door, not the way you came."

I feel like I am spitting when I try to hold my tongue flat for the "l" and repeat *Huuchin gemtliin emneleg* to practice.

Our classroom work table is covered with books—medicine books in Mongolian and Tibetan, a Russian-Mongolian Dictionary, a Tibetan-Mongolian Dictionary, and a Mongolian-English Dictionary. An American herb book and the mint that I had brought. Our teacher gives us each a signed copy of his Mongolian translation from Tibetan of the Blue Beryl Treatise, the foundation of Tibetan-Mongolian medicine. He uses this textbook with his Mongolian students, he says. It contains theory and sketches of medicinal ingredients. We leaf through pages, including sketches and at the end find a Table of Contents in English. The rest is in Mongolian Cyrillic.

As the light reflects on the wooden table, he begins to lecture with his back to the window. "Mongolian Medicine is a synthesis of Chinese, Ayurvedic-Indian, and Tibetan Medicine." The scent of herbs hangs in the air. I write every word. "My father rescued Tibetan medical sutras from Buddhist monasteries before the Russians burned them down in the forties. Some of the information is very secret, but I will share it all with you."

Dr. Boldsaikhan is teaching a culture, a way of seeing health. Mongolian medicine, he says, has a cosmo-physical view. Everything is related and a part of that view. I listen, noting down facts. Everything he tells us is different from what we have learned in nursing school. I don't understand, but stay with the unknowing. I hope I will eventually understand this by osmosis as the summer goes along. Diseases are divided into wind, bile, and phlegm, into hot and cold disease. We are stepping into a whole new paradigm.

When we stop for lunch, he takes us to a restaurant for foreigners saying, "Mongolian food is too greasy for you." We walk along a corridor, up steps to a cafeteria- type restaurant in the same huge Cultural Palace where we danced last year. German and French are spoken at other tables. We eat soup. Dr. Boldsaikhan tells us that hot food is easier for the body to digest than cold food.

After lunch, he teaches us our first Mongolian medicine formula. Medical raw materials are made of combinations of plants, animals, and minerals. The medicine Barmehorlo is for cold wind disease. In our notebooks, we list thirteen ingredients for Barmehorlo in Mongolian, Tibetan, and Latin and later learn the English names. This recipe is made from dried pomegranate, turmeric, large and small cardamom, clematis, saffron, coriander, nutmeg, red and black pepper, resin of the Pokka tree, black Sanchal salt, and three-year-aged yak butter. Most of these are familiar to us and all are natural ingredients. Being for cold disease, Barmehorlo has hot components like peppers and salt for balance.

Dr. Boldsaikhan lectures for seven hours. I am shocked that I can sit and listen this long. I usually take a nap around two and I am wide awake here. I must be in an altered state. In nursing school, I had to chew Chiclets gum to stay awake during afternoon lectures. Maybe Kathleen is keeping me awake. She gives me grief for using whiteout instead of crossing out my mistakes and for using a ruler to box-in the herbal recipe.

Maybe I am straining to understand Dr. Boldsaikhan's English or keeping active by looking up ingredients. But I secretly think it's the sacred energy of our teacher and his room with its potent herbal smells.

Between Ulaanbaatar's altitude of five thousand feet and living on the sixth floor, Kathleen and I are floating on top of the world. There is a bounce to each step. Even though the magical paradise has a lot of dirt and not much green, I still feel a bursting in my heart. As summer arrives, mountains surrounding the city become green. Everything is new to us. Everything amuses us even when the smell of mutton is overwhelming or the air is so dry we feel like we are breathing dust. Even when we get respiratory distress from not drinking enough in this desert, the medicines Dr. Boldsaikhan gives us don't cure us fast enough, and we spend a week lying in the apartment's day beds across from each other reading instead of going to our class, we still know we are in paradise. Exactly where we want to be.

Chapter Thirty-four

Хөдөө
Countryside

𝒲hen my family camped in the US, we took our food with us. Mom would make a batch of chili to heat after setting up camp. The rest of the food ingredients, pans, and utensils for the trip were packed in the car or trailer.

❧

After studying in the classroom in the city for a month, we are leaving on a five-day camping trip to the **Хөдөө**, khuduu, the Mongolian countryside. Even though there are no stores or restaurants where we are going, Dr. Boldsaikhan doesn't take food. Instead, he takes a sharp knife, a fishing pole, a kerosene torch, a kerosene stove, and some newspaper. He, his sixteen-year-old son Enkhe, Kathleen, and I will be gone five days. We're eager to leave the city and breathe country air. Dr. Boldsaikhan will show us medicinal herbs in their natural setting. Now that it's July, sparse steppe grasses stand about a foot high along the sides of the bumpy, dirt track paths where we travel. When the tires of the Russian jeep brush against plant growth, the wonderful scent of Artemesia raises up along with the dust from the tires. We pass gers and herds of sheep, goats, horses, and yaks, which look like cows in skirts.

Every time Dr. Boldsaikhan sees a flower along side of the road, he slams on the brakes, gets out with his camera, and takes pictures.

"*Tumsnii ulaan*," he says, shooting a delicate red lily for his new book, "balances the thyroid."

After five hours, we arrive in Bulgan Aimag, Province, at the home of Dr. Boldsaikhan's friend Batsuuri. People use one name in Mongolia. As the director of the sum, county, he now leads us along more dirt roads and through rivers with the water sloshing along the sides of the jeeps until we reach a fork of two waterways. Batsuuri says we will camp here, where the president of Mongolia recently camped. I look around. I would never know anyone had camped here. There are no people, no tracks, and no bent grass. We smell green and moist earth. Dwarf willows and cotton trees grow beside the fast-flowing rivers. The grass is thick. Walking around, we notice a board on each side of a hole, hidden behind a cotton tree—a squat toilet. Since Mongolian land is not privatized, we can stay anywhere in the countryside. This is a prime sacred spot, being at a river fork.

Kathleen and I are experienced campers, so we set up our tent, but when Dr. Boldsaikhan and Batsuuri see it, they shake their heads. Don't we know that men set up tents? Don't we know that a tent always faces south? They take our tent down and put it up again. We laugh because being experienced in the US doesn't mean we are experienced in Mongolia.

Next they grab their fishing poles and say, "We'll catch some fish for your dinner."

In the US I once asked a fishermen, "How's the fishing?" He said, "The fishing is great but the catching is a little sIow." When I fished with Dad and Harry, I could have answered that way. I wonder if there will be any supper.

But, half an hour later, the men arrive with smiles along with two fifteen-inch trout. "Here," says Dr. Boldsaikhan handing us the two fish.

"Aren't you going to clean them?" Kathleen asks, wide-eyed that they could actually catch two gorgeous fish in such a short time.

"Oh, no, you are the ones who eat fish. Mongolians don't eat fish. We eat meat. Here," he repeats. Fortunately, Kathleen and I know how to clean and gut fish. It's dark out and after Dr. Boldsaikhan turns his kerosene hot plate on, they leave us. I don't know what our teacher, his son, and his friend eat. Mongolians don't eat vegetables, though. Maybe they drink *airag*, fermented mare's milk. Kathleen and I have a delicious meal of fresh fish and sleep to the sound of gurgling water.

The next day, as we travel from ger to ger, Dr. Boldsaikhan teaches culture and behaviors specific to the countryside:

- How to set up a ger
- What direction to walk into it
- How ger doors must face south
- How to not step on a door sill
- Where to put my feet
- Who feeds the fire
- Where the garbage goes
- How to pass food with my right hand
- How and what food is made in the middle of the ger
- How to not hesitate at the opening
- How not to touch the stove or pillars
- How to address people inside
- When to sit and stand
- Where to sleep
- How to fold my legs underneath me
- Who is in charge
- Where guests walk
- How the saddle and the gun go on the men's side
- How the wood, water, fire, and kitchen goods are on the woman's side
- How the clothes and bedding go around the outside wall

Dr. Boldsaikhan identifies more flowering herbs—Monk's Hood, Dianthus, and buttercups. Enkhe tells us there will be a *boodog*, Mongolian barbecue, tonight. We don't know what this is and realize by now that we'll just have to wait and find out. In the afternoon, Dr. Boldsaikhan and Batsuuri stop and duck into a ger. We suppose the nomads are welcoming them by drinking bowls of fermented mare's milk. Our teacher needs to check at each ger for the best quality *airag*, fermented mare's milk, in preparation for filling the two ten-gallon plastic containers waiting in the jeep.

The men stoop as they come out of the low ger door and mill around the field with goats and sheep and herders, catch a goat, pat the rump, let it go, catch another. Kathleen and I lean against Dr. Boldsaikhan's Russian jeep watching. We have no idea what's happening but we trust our teacher and go with the flow.

The herder grabs the horns of a black goat. The director feels the back and rump. Dr. Boldsaikhan nods. They drag and push it to the car. One lifts the goat by the horns and the other two men push his rump onto the floor of the back seat. Kathleen and I exchange a quizzical look and then can't stop laughing. A dog is one thing, but a goat? We climb in. I am fine in the front but Kathleen and Enkhe have to hike their feet onto the seat because a goat stands where their feet usually go.

Dr. Boldsaikhan drives us to a former classmate's ger. This time he takes us inside where his friends gather in honor of his visit. Thirty people sit in half of the twenty-foot diameter space. Most are dressed in deels. Each one tucks himself or herself into a tiny floor space so that there is room for everyone. The old school buddies tell jokes, drink vodka, laugh, and share. Kathleen and I sit in the family side of the ger (east) and, although we don't understand the language, we don't feel excluded.

A handsome, friendly man in a tan wool deel, a local teacher, offers to build me a ger if I come back to visit. At that moment, I get a tiny glimmer, a vision, that I could actually come to Mongolia again. I thought my first trip was "once in a lifetime" but here I am a second time. Until now, I assumed there wouldn't be another trip. Yet, with this invitation, inclusion, these people living on the land, I get a whiff of living in Northeast Kingdom of Vermont. It feels familiar and I begin to entertain the notion of coming back to Mongolia.

Then Dr. Boldsaikhan says that to be polite we need to drink three shots of vodka and three bowls of airag. Fermented mare's milk is 2% alcohol. I don't ever drink alcohol and can't drink milk since I am lactose intolerant. Dr. Boldsaikhan teaches us not only medicine but traditional culture. I don't know what to do. I want to be culturally appropriate. In fact, in Mongolian medicine, the student must follow the teacher in any instruction, but I am fifty years old. Does that rule still count? It was my choice to be his disciple. Do I have to do this? Well, I compromise by drinking the vodka shots but not the airag. They push me to drink more, but then don't seem to mind when I stop.

After many toasts, the men and their wives pile into four Russian jeeps—a caravan of six—and we follow Batsuuri along more dirt ruts. As usual, Kathleen and I have no idea what to expect. We are getting used to not knowing. Enkhe mentions a party. The goat is still in the car with a little pile of droppings on the floor. After an hour's drive, we stop at some woods bordered by a stream.

The men pull the goat out of the car and walk him to the edge of the forest while the women head for the trees, return with fallen wood, and start a fire on the ground. I am videotaping the men with the goat until a man holds a large knife pointed at the back of the goat's neck. When he sees the camera, he motions it away. I put it down as the goat is lying on the ground surrounded by medicinal herbs and flowers with a knife in its neck. The men carry the goat with the knife to the forest.

A fire burns as Kathleen and I walk to the river with the women to gather round stones, which have to fit into the palm of a hand and be very smooth. As we place the rocks among the embers of the fire, the sun is beginning to sink in the sky. My stomach is growling with hunger as I witness this beautifully choreographed event.

When the men return, one carries a pile of meat and bones on some newspaper, one the rinsed and cleaned skin, and another the organs, which he gives to the women to clean, prepare, and cook. Nothing is wasted. When the holes in the goat skin from the legs and butt are closed with thin leather cord, it is time to pack the meat into the skin through the neck hole, alternating meat with hot rocks. When the skin is full, the neck hole is tied. For a boodog, the skin, all in one piece, is the roasting pan. The men lay the now-filled skin on the embers of the fire. Dr. Bold-saikhan fires up his kerosene blowtorch and aims it at the boodog. The men scrape the hair from the goat skin as the torch fire singes it. One of the men holds the point of a knife over a small hole that has been nicked during the preparation.

After cleaning all the organs and intestines in the frigid river, the Mongolian women crowd into a car to gossip. Kathleen and I keep watching the fire. The meat requires hours more of cooking so men take turns with the blowtorch and turning the full goat skin on the fire. The skin is a pressure cooker and the blowtorch roars in the night air. A kerosene smell joins the smell of singed hair, wood smoke, and cooking meat. Kathleen and I stay by the fire and shiver.

Stars fill the sky, black with a new moon. As I step into the darkness beyond the light of the fire, the familiar smells of Artemisia and other herbs waft up from the ground. The sound of rushing water gives me shivers. When I step back into the firelight, Dr. Boldsaikhan hands the roaring torch to another man. "It should be ready soon," he says, and walks out of the circle of light. We stay to watch the goat cooking until we are numb with cold and only then climb into the car to bundle up, pulling our sleeping bags over us as we doze off.

Silence wakes us as the kerosene torch is turned off. My camcorder batteries are used up. It must be past midnight. The women come out of the car and the men roll the stuffed skin off the fire. Batsuuri slits the skin open and rich meat smells stream out. Mouth watering smells, even to a vegetarian, well, a hungry vegetarian. Dr. Boldsaikhan dips a plastic jar cap I brought into the skin container, filling it with meat juice. He passes it around as everyone has a sip. The meat and knife go from one person to the next. Each holds up a meat bone in their left hand, lifts it to the front of their face, draws the knife toward them, cutting a slice of meat right into their mouth.

Now the plastic top is a shot glass for vodka. Dr. Boldsaikhan fills it, tugs the material of his sleeves over the wrists, puts his left hand under his right elbow, and hands the container with his open right hand to Batsuuri, who receives it with his right hand and, holding it, starts a song. After one line, his friends join in.

Then Batsuuri drinks with his friends encouraging him to drink the straight vodka— more, more—to finish the three-inch wide capful. He hands the empty cap back to Dr. Boldsaikhan, the vodka host, to refill it for the next person. Tradition dictates who is served first, first the sum director, the rest of the men, the women in order of importance, age, and respect. When handed the cap, each person pauses holding the vodka and starts a song. Soon the others join. After the song is finished, Dr. Boldsaikhan fills it again. When the vodka comes to Kathleen and me, we sing "Country Road" and "America the Beautiful". No one knows our songs, but they nod. More Mongolian songs come, telling about mother, nature, nomads, and horses. We sit in the circle around the fire until we are stuffed with meat and three bottles of vodka are empty.

At two or three in the morning when the wood is running out and the fire is fading, guests begin to leave. We walk them to their Russian jeeps, as is polite, and they drive off. Batsuuri douses the fire. There are no pans, plates, or utensils to wash. Our teacher wraps the remaining goat meat in newspaper and places it on the ground under his jeep to keep it cool during the night. We climb into our tents, which we put up facing south while the goat was cooking, and quickly fall asleep.

ༀ

In the morning Dr. Boldsaikhan says it is time for a medicine tour. We walk through tall plants, a riot of purple, red, yellow, and pink flowers as he names each one in Mongolian and Latin and tells us how it is used to create balance in Mongolian medicine. My notes list the Mongolian name, Latin designation, and English common name:

Shudag. *Acorus calamus L*. Flag Iris. Good for digestion
Bashig. *Dianthus versicolor Fisch*. Sweet William. Removes pain
Serjmyadog. *Hemerocallis flava L*. Red lily. For bile disease and
                female disorders
Bongar. *Aconitum*. Monkshood. Cooling
Banboi. *Valeriana officinalis L*. Valerian. For spleen
Jamba. *Malva neglects Wabr*. Hollyhock Mallow. Diuretic

I recognize these flowers, but had not known they were medicines. In this Buddhist system, every plant and flower, even the fungi on the trees, has its use as a medicine.

ༀ

As we are getting ready to leave, some nomads ride to us by horse for a health assessment with Dr. Boldsaikhan.

After traveling for a while in the car, we realize that unless we want to eat goat wrapped in fly-infested newspaper, we will need more food.

"Marmot," says Batsuuri.

We are familiar with marmots. They look like tan ground hogs and are fast and agile like prairie dogs. Bubonic plague comes from marmots. Dr. Boldsaikhan says. "It is illegal to hunt and eat them. Actually, there is no harm in eating a marmot. The bubonic plague is from a flea on their skin," he laughs. Kathleen and I look at each other, wide- eyed. He's our teacher and of course we trust him. He loves marmot meat, considers it a delicacy, which we will be able to try, if we are lucky.

Sure, lucky, I think.

When we see a marmot on the side of the road, the two jeeps stop. Quietly, Batsuuri sneaks out of the car wearing a furry marmot hat while cradling his rifle. A marmot pokes his head out. Batsuuri waits. Ping-whoo. Two minutes later, a dead marmot is lying on newspaper on the floor beside my feet. When the car dips, sways, and bumps up and down, I have to be careful to keep my feet near the door so that the dead furry thing doesn't touch me. The metallic smell of blood, fear, and fur linger. When we have three sprawled marmots, we stop in a wooded area close to a stream. Batsuuri hangs a dead marmot from a branch. It spins around while he removes the skin in one piece with intestines hanging out. He separates the meat from the organs and ties the neck and leg holes with leather strips.

Dr. Boldsaikhan, Kathleen, Enkhe, and I collect dry wood and smooth river rocks. We build a fire and put the rocks on the coals to heat, just like last night. By the time Batsuuri has the marmot meat ready to pack back into its skin, we have hot rocks to alternate with the meat. Meat, hot rock, meat, hot rock, though the headless neck hole until the skin is bulging like a bloated woodchuck. He lifts the package onto the coals. The loud hissing sound of Dr. Boldsaikhan's blow torch fills the otherwise quiet nature. The smell is burned hair and then gamey meat. As he turns the round package, the leather becomes smooth and dark and the meat becomes roasted inside.

Finally, the skin is slit open. They scoop the greasy juice for all to share, toss the hot rocks to each other. I place one on my face so I can be young again, then on my belly to clear up any indigestion. The heat penetrates my cheeks, warms me in the cold air. I toss the rock from hand to hand like a hot potato. Being a vegetarian, most meat smells are unappealing, but marmot meat's gamy smell is beyond unappetizing for me. "The oil heals AIDS," says Dr. Boldsaikhan as he cuts the meat. We have been out five days and are hungry. Our choice is to eat marmot or go without food. When I take a bite, it's a stringy pot roast, only more oily and metallic.

"You have to drink vodka, too," says Dr. Boldsaikhan. "To cut the grease." Our local Mongolian dinner is vodka, marmot, vodka.

❧

Two days later, when we arrive at the outskirts of Ulaanbaatar, with its apartment buildings and paved roads, I glance at the newspaper-wrapped, left-over marmot. Dr. Boldsaikhan throws his leather jacket over it as we pass through the city guard. Eating marmot is illegal. Airag, still fermenting, sloshes inside his ten-gallon plastic jugs. He shows his papers and we pass through into the city traffic.

With a friend, a sharp knife, fishing pole, kerosene stove, and some newspaper, we survived for five days. Хөдөө аж амдрал, *Khuduu aj amdral.* Countryside living.

Chapter Thirty-five

⟶ Хот *City*

$\mathcal{T}$rolley Ride. I am the only woman standing among Mongolian men. The ticket lady on the Ulaanbaatar trolley with her stack of limp, worthless bills motions me farther toward the front of the trolley at each stop. I breathe in the energy, try to resist holding the bar so that my arm will not touch the bare, marble-smooth one of the man beside me.

I close my eyes listening to the throaty Mongolian utterances, whispery like pillow talk. My senses are enveloped in pure ecstasy . . . until the trolley driver says something I don't understand. He slams on the brakes. I am rammed against the front wall behind the driver into the man whose arm I was so carefully avoiding.

A soldier is pointing at my feet. I am standing on his hat.

❧

After being in Mongolia for a couple of months, when the weather turns colder and the wind bites, Kathleen and I decide to shop for black leather jackets. We want to be more like Mongolians. Leather protects against the wind. Dr. Boldsaikhan says the quality of leather is very high here. The prices must be reasonable, we figure, since everyone from women in fancy dresses and spike heels to policemen, wears a leather jacket. Of course, the women are slim and nearly half of the population is under fifteen years old, so we won't match exactly. Still it will improve our wardrobe of tee shirts, jeans, and sneakers.

Gan's wife Oyuna and her sister Somiya offer to take us to zakh. They will be our guards for the shopping trip since we are foreigners and targets for pickpockets. The last time at zakh, someone slit Kathleen's hip pack and her camera dropped into their hands.

We hail a taxi, which is any car, as we know from getting to our class every morning. There are no seatbelts or inspections. Cars have broken windows, broken door handles, grinding gears, bad brakes, some without turn signals or mufflers. All taxi drivers have driven less than five years, since regular people couldn't drive during the socialist period which ended then. And Mongolians drive the way they ride a horse—they disregard lanes, double up when another car is turning, pass on the right or left, and inch-up close to the car in front. Every ride is wild and thrilling.

The car that stops today has a cracked windshield. The driver leans across the front seat to pull on a piece of cloth to open the door. When we get in he avoids the numerous unmarked potholes by driving in the breakdown lane.

Traffic gets tighter and tighter. Outside zakh, vehicles park randomly at all angles to each other. Horse-drawn carts sit beside cars, trucks, and half-full micro-minivans. Our driver takes us as far as possible, until there is no opening for a car to get through. Then we walk.

Zakh is a feast of smells—*buuz*, steamed dumplings, fresh wood, incense, plastic, new clothes, dust, packed bodies, sour milk, horses, horse dung, mutton, vodka, canvas, felt, lead paint, cigarette smoke, and leather. Goods are folded and placed on canvas ground covers. There are no booths, tables, or tent coverings.

Mongolian voices shout, "Airag for sale."

"Buy a bag!" says a vender with bags lined up on both arms.

A man's voice shouts something. I don't understand and Oyuna grabs me just in time to avoid my being mowed down by a heavy metal cart. I realize he is saying, "Watch out, I am coming through."

Everything I love in Mongolia is here for sale. I can buy, build, and equip a ger—the felt, framework, orange hand-painted furniture, stoves, linoleum, and woolen carpets. I can clothe myself in silk and cashmere. Or buy animal parts like *shagat*, sheep anklebones used for games, from a booth beside antique jewelry. Another section holds horse supplies and equipment—saddles of orange painted wood with inlaid silver, leather reins, bridles, whips, chaps, stirrups, and spurs. Near a selection of award medals from the soviet period, drunken men are rolling on the ground fighting. Close-by someone is someone playing such beautiful music on the *morin huur*, horse head fiddle, that it makes my heart leap and brings tears to my eyes.

Yet, with an omnipresent sense of danger, we stay alert.

Oyuna and Somiya lead us to the leather section. When Kathleen and I show an interest in black leather, every salesperson in the area hurries over with coats and jackets in our size. The sellers seem to have a code. Maybe all the venders work together. Maybe they give a bonus to someone who gives them a customer. I don't know exactly how it works, but we are surrounded with offers.

"Try this on." "Try this one." When I point to a long coat, they dress me, helping with the sleeves, the buttons, and the belt. They pat me all over to make sure it fits. Even when my grandmother made my wedding dress, I never got more patting. I buy the coat, pulling the bills from deep within my pocket. Kathleen buys a leather jacket. As we walk away with our purchases, we shiver thinking about the Mongolian men selling to us. If we ever actually wear these in Vermont, we will remember those many hands patting and checking.

My leather coat covers all of me but my sneakers and face. If I cover those, could I be a Mongolian?

⁂

I am riding home one evening in a public micro-minivan. The van's back seats are replaced by planks to make room for more riders. The slim Mongolians have a special way of sitting to fit more passengers. One person balances on the edge of the seat and the next person scooches all the way back. This accommodates nearly twice as many people.

Micro-minivans are a cheap and basic transport for regular Mongolians and that's what I want to be—a regular Mongolian. So I climb in. Perfume from the women floats over me, then sweat, stale cigarette smoke, and alcohol breath. Two men are working the van ride, the driver and the money collector, whose job it is to drum up business by yelling the destination out the window. The point is to fit twenty-five people in a space, which in the US would be considered big enough for five or six people. The money collector sticks his head out the door as the driver slows. *"Gandan, Gandan,"* he shouts to advertise our destination and when the van stops, the door slides opens wider.

A man staggers into the van. Cuffs frayed. Jacket elbows muddy. Black leather boots dusty. Smells of unwashed clothes dowsed in alcohol. He falls into a seat near the door as the van starts forward. Fifteen passengers move, as if choreographed, along the plank seats to make room. Thank God, I am not sitting near the door. But now I can't move— passengers are touching me on both sides. Personal space is close. The smells of alcohol and urine are filling up the van. Its newest passenger is struggling to pull a bottle out of his jacket pocket, but the lining is holding it. Three more stops before mine.

As the van comes to the next stop, the man tries to stand, but instead, falls out the door bumping the collector on his way. He loses his balance, falls backwards, and he and his money fan out on the sidewalk. Arms and legs are pushing, shoving, punching, kicking, and hitting. I try to be invisible, my way of dealing with a tense situation. I hear my heart pounding over the loud guttural male voices shouting outside. I look around. Some of the passengers have blank faces, like this happens every night on their way home. Others stare out the street side of the van. My eyes are drawn back to the scuffle. The drunken man is attempting to get himself up from the sidewalk, the bottle still hanging from the inverted lining of his jacket pocket. The money collector gets up and gathers the paper tugriks. When he has the pile of money back in his hands, he folds it in half and puts both the money and his hand into his pants pocket. He takes his place near the door.

The van starts up. He swings the door closed and we're off. Everyone moves in unison to fill the vacant space. When I lower my eyes I see fifteen pairs of feet in women's high-heeled shoes and men's polished leather boots. Above them, Mongolian hands—all thirty of them— placed lightly on knees. After that, I make it to my stop quickly—but in the future, I take a taxi.

Chapter Thirty-six

 *Bold Blood*

*I*n my quest to expand my healing practice, I'm looking for new methods to use in the US, like massage, simple adjustments, herbal medicines, or more healing techniques. I am always ready to learn, even though I don't think our next subject, bloodletting, will be one that I will use.

At lunch, Kathleen and I discuss the spread of AIDS in the US and how, now in the mid-nineties, sanitary measures in relation to body fluids, like gloves, sterile techniques, barriers, and disposal of items, are carefully regulated by OSHA. Blood requires elevated precautions. To be admitted into Mongolia, we had to give the authorities a clean bill of health, including a negative HIV test. Yet, traditional Mongolian medicine says that body fluids are normal, sacred even, and the doctor must not have any compunction about dealing with them. Dr. Boldsaikhan has intimated that he will demonstrate bloodletting this afternoon without any precautions.

The patient, a solid policeman with sideburns to below his ears, wears a navy-colored uniform jacket with epaulettes, creased pants, and shiny black shoes. His hat has a badge on the front just over the narrow brim.

According to Mongolian medicine practice, Dr. Boldsaikhan first checks the patient's twelve wrist pulses, which correlate with the health of twelve organs. We notice that the patient's skin is yellow-red. His face is wet with perspiration. Our teacher says he has hot disease which is yang in Chinese medicine and often depicts acute disease, whereas yin or cold disease relates to chronic illness. Health is balance. The policeman is out of balance and one of his symptoms is high blood pressure, which comes from too much unhealthy blood. The treatment is bloodletting.

To prepare, Dr. Boldsaikhan dons a white lab coat and spreads a few sheets of newspaper on the orange-painted, wood floorboards. "He's a policeman. All policemen drink too much and have hot disease," our teacher comments in English, laying down more papers. He takes out some strong smelling antiseptic that takes me back to a time I burned my arm at three years old. He puts gauze on his desk and checks the sharpness of his scalpel by flicking his thumb over it. He tells the standing policeman to roll up the right sleeve of his uniform and bend his elbow. Dr. Boldsaikhan palpates the patient's forearm with his bare hands, finds the right point, and douses it with antiseptic. He wraps a rubber tube around the policeman's upper arm. Then with the smooth, strong movement of a martial arts master, he stabs the point of the scalpel into a vein, grabbing a glass jar to catch the dark blood as it spurts out in an arc. Dark blood causes illness, he tells us. After the first strong spurt, he puts the jar on newspapers he has spread out on the floor. The stream of blood continues to flow, some hitting the jar. "Black blood," Dr. Boldsaikhan reports. "See, it's still black? See, it's getting lighter? Okay." Smack! He places a gauze pad on the spot, pressing it. Then wraps a length of gauze around the policeman's arm tightly to hold the pad on and stop the flow. Nothing is gentle about Mongolian treatments.

Kathleen and I glance at each other wide-eyed. We can almost hear what the other is saying inside. If we weren't professionals, we'd gasp. Of course, we have spent time as student nurses in the operating room. Seeing blood is not a problem. It is more the setting and lack of precautions that we are trying to come to peace with.

"Now your left leg, for balance" the doctor is saying. The policeman, still standing, rolls up his creased pant leg and turns around with his back to us. Our doctor performs the same palpation, placement of the tube tourniquet, fast karate movement to jab with the scalpel, and a new stream of blood spurts out. The blood splatters on the newspaper and the floor as Dr. Boldsaikhan places the bloody jar somewhat under the trajectory. The blood begins black red and continues flowing out until it turns lighter red. Finished, Dr. Boldsaikhan covers the spot on the man's leg with a gauze pad and wraps it with more gauze. The policeman pulls his pant leg down, puts his jacket and hat back on, says a few words, and goes back to work.

We look at the floor. Dr. Boldsaikhan makes a few swipes at it with a wet cloth in his bare hands, rolls up the newspaper, puts it in the wastebasket, and carries the jar across the hall to the bathroom, where he puts it, half full of blood, on the floor under the bathtub beside the toilet we use and leaves it there. "Phew!" says Kathleen when he is out of the room.

The office floor has a red pattern of spots and splashes for the next few days. When the cleaning lady comes, she squeezes water from a cloth in her pail, puts her wooden mop with its flat bottom on the cloth, and pushes it around the floor, then lifts the cloth and rinses it, leaving the water in the pail dark brown and the floor a darker shade of orange than it used to be.

Sometimes we don't understand Dr. Boldsaikhan. It's not only the language. We know how to convert his "v" sound to "b" or "w" and the "p" sound to "f" and we know that in Mongolian all letters are pronounced. For instance, saying wind, bile, and phlegm, the three diseases of Mongolian medicine, our teacher says vind, vile, and fleg-em. Or if he talks about a phone he calls it a pone. But, even now when we can decipher the sounds, there is content that is we don't understand. For instance, a powerful medicine called Bargashun took us a long time to figure out. When he described it as, "Resin made of rat droppings from the north side of a mountain," we thought we must be missing something, but that's what it is.

A person is whole when there is balance. Dr. Boldsaikhan uses the word *balanceruu* to describe the process of healing. In Mongolian the suffix "-ruu" means moving toward something. Balance is peaceful, centered, and the absence of polarities, like hot and cold, happy and sad, etc. Energy healing helps the patient move toward balance. Dr. Boldsaikhan also calls energy healing "psychic massage" and explains that when the positive energy ions of a healer's hands are joined with the negative energy ions of disease, the area becomes neutral, healthy, balanced.

When the spirit within me asked Dr. Boldsaikhan if he would take an American disciple, I had no idea what I was asking nor what kind of a person he was. As he teaches, I learn that Mongolian medicine has a completely different approach and belief system. Before I would have talked about integrating the systems. Now I use the word harmonizing. Patients carry their own medical records, own their x-rays negatives, and have copies of their prescriptions, so all treatments can be harmonized for health.

A male patient comes to see Dr. Boldsaikhan with his arm in a sling. The doctor tells him to go to the hospital and get x-rays and bring them back so that he can prescribe traditional herbs for balancing. When care targets the system as well as the symptom, a person has double the chance for health and balance.

ॐ

As the head of the Union of Traditional Mongolian Medicine, Dr. Boldsaikhan could be very serious, but when he asks us to identify various Mongolian medicinal herbs, he adds my garden mint to the others and looks at me. I am about to open my mouth when Kathleen scratches her head. He gives a belly laugh and tells her it is mint from Vermont. I snicker when I think of him. Feel an amused smile on my face. He is a world genius. Works on security for the Japanese space program. Is an expert on systems. Brilliant. Even with his Buddha body, I can't keep up with him walking. When he teaches yoga breathing and movement, even younger athletic students can't keep up. When he comes to the US to teach my students, he never has jet lag or looks tired, even with the twelve-hour time change and the thirty-four hour trip. Dr. Boldsaikhan is magic and also very human.

When a woman patient comes into the room, Dr. Boldsaikhan sits with her, asks her questions, takes her pulses, checks her tongue and pulls down her lower eyelids to check the color of her "eye beds". Not having paper, he rips three inches off the corner of a newspaper on his desk and writes a prescription for herbal medicine that she can get filled at the Institute's pharmacy. "She has cold disease and will take hot medicine to balance it," he teaches.

From listening and watching the practice of this system of medicine,

I discover a whole different paradigm. It takes me five years to find words to describe what I learned. Western medicine targets the symptom and assumes the system will heal while Eastern medicine targets the system and assumes the symptom will heal.

Chapter Thirty-seven

⌐ *Personal Ad*

*T*he first two weeks in Mongolia in 1995, I am doing exactly what I am supposed to be doing, something just for me, with no children and no husband. It is a time of integrity and wholeness. But it seems a little quiet. I want to "change things up" as my niece Lapde would say.

I ask Gan if they have personal ads in Mongolia and when he says yes, I decide to put one in the newspaper. With the sensuousness of Mongolia, I can't resist seeking a man to help me experience everything in a closer way. While I am not taking care of anyone, I feel like a fifth wheel going everywhere with Kathleen, Bruce, and their children Jena, and Noah. I would like the freedom of doing some things without little kids. I am also seeking someone to pay attention to me, maybe to give me that early look of caring I got as a baby from Dad. All I can see is my fizzy vibration of excitement being in Mongolia. I am oblivious to consequences, sort of like going down the expert trail on my first day of skiing.

I write: "Fifty-year old American woman, who is happy with her life, seeks a single, non-smoking, non-drinking, spiritual man who is ambitious and happy." Gan translates the message and gives the return address as Ulaanbaatar Post Office 51, Box 18.

"Where is the post office?" I ask.

"Oh, don't worry," he answers. "My wife Oyuna and I will pick up the responses." He adds, "There are about fifty newspapers now that Mongolia is a democracy, but Ardiin Erkh, People's Right, is the most popular.

I'll put the ad in there."

When I get home from class two days later, there are several responses. I didn't realize "picking up" mail in Mongolia means "opening,"
but Oyuna has already opened and read them. Now I need someone to
translate. I think of our third floor neighbor whom Kathleen and I met
as we were walking up to our apartment one day. We'd heard a voice say,
"Hi," in English. It was seventeen-year-old Sugar.

I am just about to walk out the door to ask Sugar, when a striking
young man appears. He is a friend of Bruce's named Battur. Bruce says he
was waiting at our local bus stop when Battur spoke to him in English,
asking if he was an American. Since Battur turned out to be so sweet,
Bruce asked him to hang out during the day while Kathleen and I studied with Dr. Boldsaikhan.

Right away, I am impressed with Battur's eyes, alive with vibrant
energy. There is a soft feeling in his face. He has short, black hair and is
dressed in a gray silk shirt and carefully ironed, creased pants. His smile
is as wide as his face. Bruce tells him that I have some letters that I need
translated. Battur answers in polite English, "Of course, I would be happy
to translate." The gentleness of his voice is like a cushiony beach among
the guttural-sounding, rough rocks in the Mongolian language. He ex-
tends his hand and a look of gentle kindness.

We sit on the couch. "Okay, for the first letter."

"Hello, I wish you health. I want to make your acquaintance. Maybe
we'll get married. I don't belong to anyone. I am intelligent and have a
mild temper. I want to marry a woman who is good and intelligent. I was
born in 1969 in Ulaanbaatar."

"Stop," I say. "My daughter was born in 1969. I can't meet him. He's
younger than my son." I find it interesting that he would write that
he has a mild temper. Maybe it could be translated as mild-tempered.
Would anyone say that answering a personal ad in the US?

"Next one. 'I wish you good luck. I was born in 1957. I love truth. I
believe in true friendship. It isn't a game. I hope you have a good heart. It
is not a joke. We must spend a little of our lifetime very happy. It depends
on you. Meet me on the 9th of July at the post office. See you around.'"

"An unpolished person," says Oyuna. I have no clue why she says
that, which shows me how little I know about this culture. I give Battur a
nod to keep reading.

"Greetings to you, American. I saw your advertisement and decided to write to you. In Mongolia or America, all people want to find a partner. They want to see for themselves and talk and then decide if they want to be friends. So I want to meet with you. I am forty- nine years old, a simple Mongolian man. I've had a lot of life experiences. I had a wife and children but now I am divorced. If you want to see me and talk to me please come July 9th from nine to ten in the morning in front of the Jukov Museum. There's a bench in the park and garden. I'll be reading the newspaper. I wish you happiness."

Well, he sounds nice enough, but I am studying Mongolian medicine every day from ten to five. There are no phones, so we can't call to tell him.

Actually, Bruce has already discovered that there is one phone—only one—in our complex of eight, five-and six-story apartment buildings. That phone is at the police station. But the man hasn't left a number, so that wouldn't have worked anyway.

A few days later, Sugar and I go to the police station to call a man named Lhasarang, who does leave a number. Inside is a picnic-type table with a bench on either side. We sit on the bench with four men who are waiting while their friend shouts into the phone. Finally, we get our turn, call, and invite Lhasarang to the apartment.

He is a 46-year-old thick-set driver with a beer belly. "I'll show you the countryside and teach you how to ride a horse," he offers. When Gan's wife Oyuna tells him I am a healer, he immediately opens up his shirt to show me a ten-inch scar and asks me to heal it. Oyuna is trying not to laugh. After he leaves, she asks, "Why do you want someone like this?" gesturing circles around her belly as if she were overweight.

I don't know it yet, but I will have a problem with this one. We are at Dr. Boldsaikhan's office the next day and he walks in. Dr. Boldsaikhan sits on the couch beside him and they talk quietly for a while. He looks up. "Is this your friend?"

"Yes."

"He knows you want to go to the countryside, so he found a trip leaving tomorrow morning. You will be gone for a week and visit monasteries. It will be very cheap because there are so many people going and they want you to go with them." Dr. Boldsaikhan and Lhasarag have arranged everything.

"Wait a minute," I say. "I'm here to study Mongolian medicine. I'm not going away for a week. We have a certain number of days to study with you and we need them all."

"Yeah," says Kathleen.

Dr. Boldsaikhan says, "This is a great opportunity. We can just study longer in August. You should do it."

Lhasarang has driven his car to the institute so we three leave the classroom and drive to our apartment to talk to Bruce, because, as we know, men make the decisions here. When the two men ask Bruce if he wants to go, he says, "No." Now they believe us.

It is lunchtime and we invite Dr. Boldsaikhan and Lhasarang for a bowl of split pea soup. Lhasarang eats slowly. He looks up and says, "I don't think I could go to America, because I need to have meat in my soup." As we close the door and hear his receding footsteps on the stairs, Kathleen and I giggle about the meat comment. We don't see him again and now know how to discourage a Mongolian man.

The personal ad is beginning to taste like a cultural, historical, and anthropological study. Only five years ago, the country was connected to the Soviet Union. Very few Westerners were allowed here. For a Mongolian, the stereotype is that Americans are very rich and meeting one puts you on a path to not only live in the US as Lhasarang thought, but will also solve all your financial problems.

Chokhlabaatar replies next. Without mentioning it to me, Oyuna meets him and his small red car at the post office at ten in the morning while we are at class. The place and time are those he set up to meet me when he responded to my personal ad. She met him instead. It looks like there is chemistry between them.

"He is forty-five. Very nice," she says. He comes to meet me wearing a paisley silk shirt.

"Tomorrow we will go to the countryside," he says, through an English-speaking friend he's brought.

Tomorrow is Saturday, so I agree to go.

I get packed and ready but they never show up.

A couple of weeks later, though, his English-speaking friend climbs the six flights to our apartment to tell me that Chokhlabaatar wants to talk to me.

"Let's take Oyuna and go to the Ulaanbaatar Hotel for dinner," he suggests. When Oyuna and I get into the car, I can see by the looks she and Chokhlabaatar give each other that they have been meeting each other since the last time he was here. Every time I look at them, I snicker.

On the way back in the car after dinner, I find out why they have come this time. "Chokhlabaatar loves you," says the translator.

Oh, really.

"My parents got into an accident with their car and need $1000," Chokhlabaatar tells me through the translator. "Will you loan us the money? We will pay you back on August 1."

"No," I say and that ends my time with Chokhlabaatar.

A man named Sukhbaatar, like the great hero of Mongolia, writes a letter in English! Great, I think, I can read it myself. I write back immediately. When Kathleen and I meet him after our class, I am not attracted to his energy or to him. He's missing what charms me about Mongolians—their moon-shaped faces.

Kathleen and I are really tired from our day at class and want to go home. He begins to talk as soon as he sees us. We say we need to go home. He keeps talking. When he won't stop talking and we are worn down, she invites him to dinner. Tomorrow is our weekly meal with our Peace Corps friends Deb and Betsy. I guess Kathleen figures that with so many people, it will be safe. We give him our address.

As we prepare the dinner, he follows me from one end of the table to the other, explaining that he is an engineering consultant for a gold mine. Do you want to invest in the mine? he asks. He says he has been to Bulgaria where you nod your head for "no" and shake your head for "yes". Confused, his head bobbles in all directions.

Now that he knows where I live, he stops in every weekend, but we are usually in the countryside studying herbs. He leaves a note each week.

"What can I do for you?" "What would you like to do?"

"I want to do whatever you need. Just tell me."

"I can make one day a week for you. I will take you anywhere. Where do you want to go?"

Enough! One weekend, we happen to be home when he comes. I have to figure out how to tell him that I am not interested. I give him tea and *aaruul*, cheese curds, the polite thing to do. I imagine him a needy client and am very kind to him. Finally, I say, "I am not really interested. There is nothing I want to do. I want to study now."

As he leaves, he asks, "If I were a traditional doctor, would you be more interested?"

❧

In all, there are thirty-four responses, two from women who want an American friend and probably more that Oyuna intercepted at the post office. With her husband Gan now in the Gobi Desert working for a mining company, responses to the ad seem to be her main entertainment. It's fine with me.

As nineteen-year-old Battur translates more letters, I know that none of the men can be as lovely as he is. He comes in the evening to teach me Mongolian words while I help with his English pronunciation for a competition called English Olympics. A folktale about a bear that he practices becomes perfect. He wins the first round and the second one. Nationally, there are eight students left for the final round. The winner gets to study in the United States, the biggest prize imaginable for any Mongolian. The next time I see him, he walks in with his head down.

"What happened?"

"One of the eight finalists is a girl who chose the same folktale I have been practicing. One of us had to change our story at the last minute or drop out. I dropped out." Just like that, Battur let go of his dream to study in the US, choosing to be kind to that girl instead. I want to cry.

At the end of evening, Battur murmurs, "I should write you a letter, but you wouldn't read it, I know, because I am younger than your son."

But I have already imagined a cocoon with the two of us in it.

Chapter Thirty-eight

～ *Tumurbaatar*

$\mathcal{P}$art of the reason I am sitting in an office-classroom in Mongolia with Kathleen is to study traditional Mongolian medicine. The real reason is to learn magic. Dr. Boldsaikhan begins to introduce The Eight Higher Accomplishments, seemingly related to magic, when the door from the hall squeaks opens a crack. An eye peers in. The door gapes wider and a gaunt, young man with a moon-shaped face a few shades darker than our teacher's sidles into the room, slipping onto the couch. Out of the corner of my eye, I see a white baseball cap and jeans. He doesn't make a sound, demand attention, or move. His energy becomes invisible and our teacher doesn't pause in his lecture.

Invisibility is one of the eight higher accomplishments, along with using the sword, ointment for the eyes, swiftness of foot, extracting essence or elixir, walking in the sky, and traveling underground. All magic acts. Dr. Boldsaikhan doesn't stop with the lesson until he finishes the section on traveling underground. Then he calmly slides onto the couch beside the man and they speak the whispery sounds of Mongolian. There are no introductions nor any examination, just a conversation.

While Dr. Boldsaikhan is softly talking to the visitor, Kathleen writes the word "Chicklets" on her notebook and taps her front teeth. I try to keep a straight face and not look over at our visitor's teeth, but when I do, I see they are shaped perfectly like my favorite gum Chicklets. The man is in his twenties, with a not-too-white tee shirt under a black leather jacket, jeans, and shiny, formal, brown shoes. After a few minutes, our teacher goes back to the white board without any comment and moves on to the next accomplishment—flying. Chicklets slips out the door.

We become used to Chicklets walking into our classroom. After a number of visits over the next weeks, Dr. Boldsaikhan turns to us and says, "This is Tumurbaatar. He and I had the same Buddhist master. He is a monk, a lama, and a yogi and usually lives alone in the Gobi Desert where he meditates for weeks at a time. He can survive eating one egg a day and do magic. He knows about mind over matter, like how to meditate deeply and put molten metal on his tongue."

We swallow, totally embarrassed about calling him Chicklets. This is just the kind of magic that we are here for. We ask for something, get it, and are oblivious. Can Tumurbaatar really do magic?

♜

Kathleen, her husband Bruce, and I are interested in learning from a Buddhist lama so one day Dr. Boldsaikhan takes the five of us up a steep, gravely road to a "beautiful place" in the countryside. Tumurbaatar will teach us meditation. We arrive at a green, wooded area where red, purple, and white flowers of medicine herbs bloom in the soft grass. The sun peeks through tamarack tree branches stretching above us. Dr. Boldsaikhan unwraps newspaper with bread, fried dough, and mutton and opens a soda bottle filled with airag for lunch. He translates while Bruce plies Tumurbaatar with questions, oblivious to the lama's lack of response. I watch Tumurbaatar avoid Bruce's questions as if in an aikido match. Maybe it's another kind of magic. He nods his head, which I understand as, "Yes, we'll get to that." After eating, Dr. Boldsaikhan puts the food in his car.

Now to sit in a sacred spot where grazing cows won't disturb us, we each find a tree and settle against its trunk. I close my eyes. Smell the earth and larch needles. Feel the wind. Breathe. Wait . . . Wait . . . I peek with one eye to see what's happening.

Tumurbaatar is looking at the sky just as a big drop hits him in the eye. He wipes it off, laughing. Then more drops and then a wall of rain, as we all, including Tumurbaatar, run to the car to wait it out. The sound is deafening as it bangs on the metal, making it too noisy to talk. The rain doesn't let up. Dr. Boldsaikhan finally starts his car and turns on the windshield wiper motor for a swipe every few minutes as we wobble and jolt down the mountain back to our home.

❦

Bruce invites Tumurbaatar to our apartments to "teach us meditation." Tumurbaatar has no way to let us know when he is coming and we have no way of knowing that he plans to spend the day.

One morning just after Bruce and Kathleen leave with their kids to go to a museum, Tumurbaatar knocks on our locked door. I invite him in, excited to hang out with a Buddhist monk-lama-yogi all by myself. We don't have a common language so I get the Mongolian-English dictionary out and we take turns looking up words. *Meditation. Breath. Earth. Fire. Wind. Water. Sinus. Snake. Husband. Yellow. Tongue. Soar up into the atmosphere.* I show him photographs of my family, friends, and home. After some hours, I begin to run out of ideas for entertaining him. And I am tired—it's my normal nap time. I show him a photo of my car with its license plate SPIRIT.

"What is SPIRIT?"

"Setgel." I translate for him.

"Oh, that's a nice word," says the lama.

He gives me Tibetan Buddhist lessons, drawing the paths of the breath, writing pictures, words, and sounds in Tibetan and Mongolian in my school notebook. He draws himself as a monk in the desert, mimes the five poisons—ignorance, hatred, jealousy, desire, and anger and explains the lunar points.

❦

My brain is on overload when the apartment door opens and Battur comes in with Kathleen, Bruce, and the kids. We move into their living room so we can "learn meditation."

"Sas, what do you do for work?" asks Tumurbaatar now that he has an interpreter.

"I teach meditation and spiritual healing."

"Okay, let's begin. First, hold your breath for three minutes." He comes over to me and lays his hand on my diaphragm. "What's wrong? How come you're breathing?"

What? I can't do that. Who can hold their breath for three minutes? A yogi maybe. Not me.

Tumurbaatar explains, with Battur translating, what Dr. Boldsaikhan has already taught us. The only way to open chakras is to hold the breath. In stillness the knotted red and white channels or meridians straighten out and open the chakras. I remember that lesson, but still, as Tumurbaatar can see, none of us can hold our breath for three minutes. He laughs his hearty laugh, sits down, and gives up on teaching us.

But, he is curious about us. Before he leaves, he walks into the kitchen, opens the refrigerator, and holds the door open, looking in. "Are you hungry?" Kathleen asks, standing near-by.

"No," says the lama-yogi, "I just want to see what Americans keep in their refrigerator."

❧

Since that day, I have been practicing holding my breath. The most I can manage is about thirty-six seconds swimming underwater from one side of the pool to the other.

❧

Tomorrow's lesson will be on mind over matter. Tumurbaatar will place a piece of hot glowing iron on his tongue, our teacher tells us.

"Bring Bruce with you," he says.

When we get to the office, Dr. Boldsaikhan and a couple of other men, who are not introduced, rush in and out. Tumurbaatar sits peacefully on the couch. Bruce asks what he will do but, as usual, the yogi doesn't answer, just smiles. On the table beside my video camera, our teacher places his kerosene torch and some pieces of metal.

Tumurbaatar glances at the metal and speaks. Dr. Boldsaikhan quickly sends a man out to the street—where you can find many things including random pieces of metal. He comes in with a bar two-and-a-half feet long by three-inches wide by half-an-inch thick.

Tumurbaatar nods that this will do. He takes his shirt off and sits cross-legged on the floor in front of Dr. Boldsaikhan's ten-foot Medicine Buddha thangka. He closes his eyes and breathes slowly. The roar of the torch fills the room. The flame flashes out a distance of nearly two feet—blue, white, pink, yellow. I can barely breathe from the mixture of the kerosene smell, the crowded room—and excitement. Dr. Boldsaikhan holds one end of the metal and directs the flame to the other end. We watch it turn red like my overheated chimney pipe when Mom was visiting. Tumurbaatar gives a single nod and reaches out for the dark end of the metal, takes a deep breath, opens his mouth, sticks his tongue out, and places the red metal directly onto his tongue. When I move in with my video camera, I nearly get singed by the torch flames.

As Tumurbaatar hands the metal to Dr. Boldsaikhan, he says softly, "Make it colder." He makes the molten iron an ice cream cone in his mind, which convinces his body to feel cold not hot. The torch roars as our teacher re-heats the metal. Tumurbaatar takes the dark end in his hand again and places the cherry colored metal end on his tongue. We hear a loud SIZZLE. Kathleen gasps. The sizzle sound is on the video.

"Is that enough?" He asks in Mongolian and our teacher asks us in English. He takes the metal from Tumurbaatar.

"Yes, I'll just get a close-up of your tongue." I zoom in as he sticks his tongue out. No mark, no injury. A normal pink tongue. Tumurbaatar curls his tongue to the roof of his mouth, swallows his saliva, sticks his tongue out again, and laughs out loud. Magic.

༄

On a trip ten years after witnessing Tumurbaatar's mind over matter demonstration, I am spending a hot day with Dr. Boldsaikhan at Shambala, a sacred place on a sacred day for a sacred ceremony in the Gobi Desert. We are near the Khamar Monastery but it's not open, so we are in the full sun. Shambala is where a number of earth's ley lines intersect so the earth radiates out energy. Dr. Boldsaikhan explains that ley lines are to the earth what meridians and chakras are to the human body. I am familiar with straight ley lines in my back yard, but here they radiate out from the ground in circular patterns. Mongolian people flock here for healing and balance.

The temperature is well over one hundred degrees. There is no shade.

Hot gravely sand heats my feet, especially through the cast on the foot that I had broken in Ulaanbaatar two days before. "Tumurbaatar is now a high lama," says Dr. Boldsaikhan. He points with his chin." He is in that car—the shiny, black one with a driver."

Dr. Boldsaikhan drives us closer. A group of disciples waits outside the car for a chance to meet with Tumurbaatar.

I limp over to peek into the air-conditioned space. His cluster of followers watch me. Inside I see a rotund lama with a familiar round face and Chicklet teeth now wearing robes of saffron and gold holding court. I wonder if this elegant man will remember me.

"Sas? Come in. Come in. Sit down in the car with me." As I climb in, the energy of his followers seem to ask why is a foreigner invited into the car with the high lama?

"Tell me everything. How are Kathleen and Bruce? What are you doing here?"

I say that Dr. Boldsaikhan has invited me to Shambala for a ceremony. Then catch him up on events of the past ten years. His translator mentions that Tumurbaatar is now so esteemed that the Dalai Lama has invited him to India to teach meditation. Thinking about it later, I missed the perfect moment to ask him how long he can hold his breath.

Before I step out of the car, he asks why I have a cast on my leg. I tell him I broke my foot two days ago.

"Let me come to your apartment next week when we both get back to Ulaanbaatar and I will do a healing."

I have heard there are caves here at Shambala where lamas teach and meditate. According to the doctor who put the cast on my foot, I'm not supposed to walk on uneven ground. Yet, all the ground here is uneven. Plus the caves are up a rocky mountain. I can barely walk two feet out of the car but I am at the Khamar Monastery. I have to see this. I start walking. Every tweak of my foot hurts and the sun is blazing hot. A lama invites us into a cave decorated with brightly colored banners. It is amazingly cool and peaceful and worth the past discomfort.

❧

A short distance from the cave and the Shambala hill, eighteen Mongolians, including Dr. Boldsaikhan, Tumurbaatar, my interpreter Zula, cameraman Mende, and I, gather. We sit on the scalding ground in a circle for the sacred ceremony.

"We will walk up the Shambala rise later," Tumurbaatar says has he starts the ritual. I look toward the hill. I won't be walking up there.

The lama chants. Dr. Boldsaikhan opens a bottle of Chinggis Khan vodka and fills a silver bowl, offering it to each person while Tumurbaatar gives spiritual blessings. Zula whispers to me that she has never been hotter in her entire life. At Shambala sitting in a circle with my teacher and Tumurbaatar, the consistency of reality changes. The air feels charged. For me, there is no heat.

But when I leave Shambala to go back to East Gobi's capital Sainshand, I feel it, even with the Russian jeep's doors half-folded down. At night in the hotel, I have to soak a towel in cold water every hour and place it on top of me as I lie on my back. Otherwise, I can't sleep at all. It is the hottest night of my life.

❧

In the city when Tumurbaatar arrives at my apartment, he is dressed like the person I used to know, wearing jeans and a tee shirt. The only difference is that he has an entourage of young monks with him, one a translator. I ask him if he would hold his hand near my foot, which is the way I offer healing. As he does that, I can feel the bone beginning to knit together. But after a minute or two, he says, "I need to do a ceremony." He gives instructions to his apprentices. They leave and come back with sacred Buddhist objects—incense, vodka, a brass *dorj*, thunderbolt, a bell, and bowls made of small skulls. His assistant mixes flour and water to the consistency of clay and puts it on a plate on the coffee table.

I am still a Quaker. I believe in simplicity. We sit in a plain room in silence for our Meeting. Most Quaker Meetings don't have any decorations, not even flowers. I think about how senses are awakened in Buddhist monasteries. The smell of incense. The sound of ringing bells and the traditional long horn. Bright silk banners and wall hangings. Golden sculptures and god paintings. All very busy for a Quaker, yet I can feel the powerful energy . . . and the chants never ceases to open my heart.

Tummurbaatar adds a two-headed drum called *damaru*, along with *khatags*, turquoise blue prayer scarves. He chants, lights candles, rings a bell, and asks me to make a clay figure. Then motions to the candle and blows with his mouth. I blow the candle out. As Tumurbaater calmly re-lights the candle, his assistant explains that he actually was telling me to breathe on the clay figure. I need to exhale the negative energy of my broken foot onto the clay form. I laugh silently in embarrassment. It is amazing how many mistakes I can make. Again, he motions me to breathe on the clay. As soon as I do, his assistant takes the clay outside to destroy it.

Tumurbaatar is reading chants from the sutras. I can feel the healing vibration. To finish, he sprinkles blessed vodka on my foot and into the air over me. He and his assistant wrap the skull bowls in blue cloth khadags and pack the sacred objects into a bag. He tells his assistant to pour the vodka back into the bottle for me to take to America and gives instructions to sprinkle some on my foot every day. Then we have tea and talk for a couple of hours, as is the custom in Mongolia.

❦

I can't tell if the ceremony helps, but when I get home to Vermont, my doctor says the break is at a joint and could cause a lot of problems if it isn't healing properly. She orders an x-ray. I should have known what the x-ray results would show. My foot is healing perfectly. Healing is natural for a yogi who can make red molten metal into ice cream.

Chapter Thirty-nine

~ *Rain & Rock*

Adopt expedition behavior, inhale fresh
air, wonder and be curious with a splash
of love, care and respect each other and all things
~Sunniva Sorby, a Wing's Flag Carrier and Arctic Explorer,
  on the value of embracing expedition behavior as
  a way of navigating one's life

*W*e learn about more than traditional medicine in 1995. In Ulaan-baatar, during the national Naadam Festival of the three manly sports in July, Gan's wife Oyuna invites me to join her for a concert. She and I wander around the outside of the Naadam Stadium with twelve thousand other people, trying to find a way through the gates. Since I don't speak the language and am still learning the culture, I just follow her as she looks for someone who will help. I think we need tickets but I don't see any ticket booths. She has a plan. With her limited English vocabulary, she tells me that her brother had been a policeman and gotten killed this year so now a police friend will help her. I take that to mean she deserves free entrance. I'm not sure of the connection, but there must be one because then magically we are inside.

We sit in a section with hundreds of high cheek-boned, black-haired, honey-colored young policemen in black leather jackets. Oyuna is in flirting heaven.

I understand we have come to the stadium for a traditional Mongolian music and dance concert. A policeman sidles up to me and by sign language asks my name, age, country.

In the middle of a sentence, he jumps up, along with the other policemen. They leap to the grass over the wall separating the bottom stadium tier from the field. Like a swarm of blackbirds, they resettle in another row of seats a few stadium blocks away.

I feel someone else beside me. Oyuna addresses him in a sharp voice. He leaves. "A pickpocket," she says. As a white foreigner I am a target. Check your pockets, she motions. I'm not worried. My money is safe. I happen to be wearing tight jeans. A pickpocket couldn't possibly get his hand into my pocket. I can hardly get my own hand in there when I'm fully standing.

At eleven o'clock when it is dark and one hour after we thought the concert would begin, the musicians file onto the stage with their instruments. Everyone cheers. They play a few notes, and, without warning, the sky opens and rain gushes down. I don't have my umbrella, so stand to leave. Oyuna sits calmly. My hair and shoulders are getting soggy.

Oyuna still doesn't move. The musicians slide as they leave the stage, try to protect their instruments, which glisten with water in the stage lights. The bass and drum players are trying to get a foothold when I turn to exit. No one is moving.

"What's the problem?" I ask.

"They have locked the exits," she says. "No one can leave."

"What do you mean? They can't do that!"

She can't understand my English. I look around, an animal in a cage. I want out. My parents' old warnings play in my head. I shouldn't be in Mongolia. I shouldn't be in crowds. Should be more like my parents. Avoid danger. Avoid risks. This is a perfect example of what they were trying to teach me.

My gut contracts under the skin-tight jeans. I wonder, will there be a riot? Will I live? How long will they lock us up? Hey, I'm an American. They can't lock me in. They can't . . . but they have. My heart pounds and my throat is the only part of me that is dry. My jeans stick to my legs. I could wring my shirt out. I shiver as a chill runs through me.

Sheets of water keep blasting us. The black hair of the Mongolians reflects the spotlights, but nothing is moving. I try looking around. People are sitting calmly, as if the concert is in the middle of the first piece.

As if being locked up doesn't matter. Oyuna is looking for someone to flirt with. I am just trying to breathe. I wiggle in my seat and there's a squishy sound. Now every pore of my body is wet. My jeans are heavy, cold. As I breathe in water, I smell the wet Mongolian earth under the bleachers. Streams of water are still hitting me.

Am I the only one panicked? Did socialism teach the others to sit still while being locked in? That everyone must obey? That no one asks questions? What will we do if we get out of here? Everyone will need a car or bus ride. We will never get one. We will never get home. What, walk the eight kilometers at this time of night in the rain?

The rain slows. A few dancers appear on stage, test it, and end up gliding like Olympic skaters. One falls. And then, the rain starts full blast again. An announcement comes over the speaker. Black hair reflections begin to move. Oyuna says they are rescheduling for tomorrow after a rock concert that will end at three in the morning.

Everyone is standing now, walking toward the exit. People press me from behind, from the sides, and I am pushed into the person ahead of me. We move like crowded wet ants on a mission. The exits are open and we pour into them, squeeze through, into shadows of buses, taxis, and vans. Oyuna grabs my hand as we run from one bus to another. She asks for our home Ulaankhuaran until she finds the bus with our destination. We pack in with the other dripping bodies, so wet and so close that moisture coats the windows. The bus moves.

❦

Soon after being locked in the Naadam stadium, Dr. Boldsaikhan says he wants to take us on a field trip to see *Eej Khad*, Mother Rock. He says that it will be an all-day trip to one of the most sacred sites in Mongolia, but he doesn't give us any details. In any case, our teacher is in charge and we are happy to leave the dusty city for a day.

Kathleen and I can't imagine what Mother Rock might be. Maybe Dr. Boldsaikhan is taking us because we are studying Mongolian medicine, which is Buddhist medicine and we need to see this, just like he had abruptly taken us from our class to see the Dalai Lama a few days before.

The Mongolian way of thinking and understanding is different from ours. In the US, asking questions is encouraged. In Mongolia, we are expected to wait for our teacher to tell us without asking. Kathleen and I wonder what Eej Khad is, where it is, why we are going to see it, and what we are going to do when we get there. All we know is that our teacher is taking us and we need to go with the flow.

Kathleen, Bruce, Jena and Noah, and I cram into the back seat of Dr. Boldsaikhan's waiting UAZ Russian jeep. In the passenger seat sits his wife with their four-year-old boy on her lap. In the way back sits his sister-in-law with the food, gas, and tools. Dr. Boldsaikhan in the driver's seat is the only person with any space.

While we bounce over pitted dirt tracks for two hours, the kids play games, squealing each time they see a marmot run into its hole, laughing when the road is blocked with yaks, and counting how many rivers we ford.

We stop for a picnic at Manjusri, formerly an active religious community, now thickly wooded hills and grassy land with ruins. Here twenty monasteries housed three hundred and fifty resident monks. They ate meals cooked in a two-ton bronze vat, which holds a place in the Guinness World Records as the biggest cauldron. Ten complete sheep and two cows could be cooked at once, a sign says. In 1939 the socialist government destroyed the twenty temples of the monastery and killed the monks. The cauldron and the Buddhist gods painted on the rocks inside mountain cave walls are all that remain. The paint is faded and dusty but the deities are still visible.

Back in the Russian jeep for four more hours, we all get tired of jouncing around. Dr. Boldsaikhan calls Mother Rock a power vortex, a center of energy. I later understand that "Eej Khad is a focal point where all three types of spirits—land, water, and sky—are combined."[2] In the Soviet period before 1990, people knew of its existence, but it was a crime to visit because that would show respect for religion. Five years ago when the Russians left and Mongolians got freedom of religion, they started to visit the holy spot.

We splash through another river as the kids say, "Twenty-one."

Dr. Boldsaikhan stops at a ger along a non-road where men and women wear colorful traditional silk clothing. He gets out to ask directions. I feel a juxtaposition—he speaks the same language as these nomads who look like they could be living at the time of Chingghis Khan. I

[2] The Legend of Eej Khad can be found at https://digitalcollections.sit.edu/cgi/viewcontent.cgi?article=1144&context=isp_collection

feel like I am in a movie. I am fascinated by Mongolian traditional life. Since lunch, we haven't seen a single car, truck, motorcycle, or even a horse, but now we pass two cars and five riders on horseback. Maybe we are getting closer.

As we pass over a rise with a three hundred-sixty degree view of green steppes, we can see six cars and fifteen horses clumped together. Dr. Boldsaikhan stops when we are among them. The horses are nickering. Otherwise, there is no sound. We are at the sacred site of Eej Khad.

The ground is full of offerings—milk, broken bowls, rice, crutches, birdseed, money, broken vodka bottles, blue prayer scarves, incense, and tea. Tea bricks—eighteen-by-six-by-two-inch blocks—are stacked and form a round wall that is a yard thick and higher than my head. We follow a line of people around the outside wall, walking clockwise in single file. Paper money, bottles, and other treasures are stuffed into the crevices of the tea bricks. The ubiquitous scent of sour milk fills my nostrils. Juniper incense smolders, its smoke blending with the milk smell. A woman in front of me scatters rice with a spoon as she walks. A man in front of her sprinkles water. We step under an arch with khadags. The blue, white, and yellow scarves blow in the wind as we continue around inside the wall, circling three times.

At the center of the circular wall, there is a form six-feet high, four-feet wide, and two feet deep. Mother Rock has been decorated with silk clothing and prayer scarves which cover her curves in the shape of a head, shoulders, hips, and body. In fact, the rock is not visible except for a six-inch granite patch near her forehead, which is the point of attention for all the pilgrims. A woman touches the rock with her forehead. A student touches his school notebook to the spot. An older woman sprinkles a drop of milk there. Our teacher's sister-in-law touches it with her wallet, fanning the bills. They are making wishes, I figure out. As I add small rocks to the sacred pile around Eej Khad, a vague thought of meeting a man is on my mind.

Dr. Boldsaikhan's wife Oyuntsetseg and her sister sprinkle lama-blessed water on the rock. They carefully avoid stepping on bowls of rice and fermented mare's milk as we move outside of the circle. I am astonished by the number of broken containers and amount of spilled food covering the ground. When I lift my video camera to shoot, Dr. Boldsaikhan shakes his head, saying it's too sacred.

Then he brushes his hands together and says, "Well, that's it. Let's go."

We have been here for all of five minutes. I walk through the years worth of broken, evaporated, and ripped offerings toward the car. A horse snorts. The steppe plants release their scents as we pile back in and drive a bouncy shortcut for four hours back to Ulaanbaatar.

Later we ask our teacher what he thinks of Mother Rock. "I haven't been there in a long time. I am amazed at how many offerings have been left. It just shows how much people want something to venerate."

❧

Over the years, Mother Rock had remained a mystery to me. It had seemed strange to have driven so far and found so many broken offerings.

Twenty-four years after this first time, I visit Mother Rock again. On the way there, we stop at the Manjusri site where the monasteries are being rebuilt. We are not the only ones visiting, as we were last time. Some Korean tourists are hiking up the mountain path to the Buddha cave paintings. A museum of local animals has been built and there is a caretaker ready to explain what we see. When Anuka, our translator, her husband Baggii, and Jen climb the mountain, I sit on a rock surrounded by a wooded area and hear cuckoo birds sing.

As we get close to Eej Khad, there is a little sign, then lots of cars and buildings. The site has been totally renovated. The Mother Rock, a powerful symbol of the connection between land and spirit, is now in the center of a round concrete wall forty-feet in diameter, ten-feet high, and open to the sky. She is dressed in a reddish silk brocade deel and has a black and gold hat with long braids down her back. Her face and upper sides are not covered, making the dark granite visible. Blue, white, and gold prayer scarves hang from her belt. In front of her is an organized table with a metal bowl for offerings like candies, cookies, and aaruul. Visitors pour their milk blessings into a clean lavender plastic pail. There are booths around the site to buy offerings in case you forgot to bring your own. On the grounds, two wooden teahouses and a number of gers sell visitors tea.

Ovoo, cairn

Dukha encampmen[t]
Photo: Fred Thod[e]

Wild taiga blueberrie[s].

Tsend, Shaman

Shaman altar

Kharkhorin

Gobi couple

Ts. Khandaa

M. Solonge, G. Monkhoo, M.Dalaijargal, T. Sodbayar

Shaman hat and costume, Jura

Rice and meat

Ch. Taivan and M. Dalaijargal's Wedding with T. Maralmaa

P. Erdenchimeg, G. Otgonjarg

B. Baasankhuu

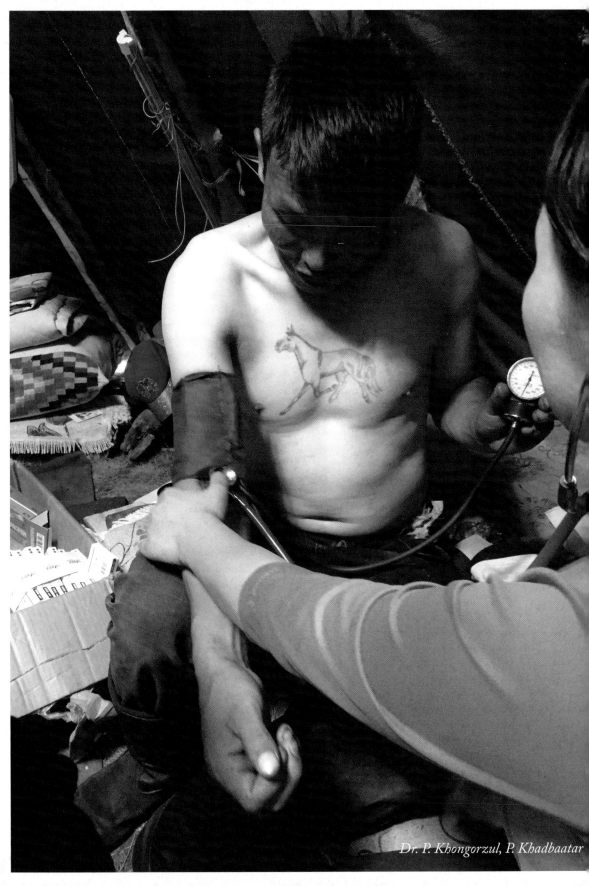

B. Narantuya

Kh. Urankhelkhee Photo: Fred Thodal

Ts. Khandaa, G.Vezeski

Ger District of Mörön

Mother Rock has become a tourist destination.

While Eej Khad is the same shape with more of the rock exposed, the ground around it is very changed. It is hard to believe it is the same place I visited twenty-four years before, yet when I glance down I see earth embedded with pottery shards and I know for certain that it is.

Chapter Forty

⟶ *Battur*

*B*attur and I walk to my apartment for a Mongolian lesson.
I sigh.

"*Sanal-adakh*. What? What's the matter?"

The sigh gives me away. We are walking across the dirt courtyard
from his parent's apartment to mine. The stars are full. The sky is clear.
The smell is burning trash. The dogs are barking. Usual night in Ulaanbaatar. I walk with my young teacher. Why doesn't my heart distinguish
age? He is holding my hand in the darkness, making sure I avoid bones,
dung, and sharp metal objects.

In our closeness, I breathe in the scents of ironed clothes and lanolin.
His hand-holding only lasts until the light of the stairwell. Only for safety. Like when we went camping with his family and had fourteen people
in a Russian jeep with all our equipment. Four people across the back seat
and another layer of four on top. I had to sit on his lap. What a treat to
be that close to him for the whole ride. Wedged in so well, there was no
chance of a concussion from slamming my head into the jeep window on
the rough road. Delicious memory.

We climb the six flights of stairs.

He says, "You are fifteen, not fifty."

As we sit at the table in my apartment, I only wish. I watch his
mouth move for pronunciation, but instead of tasting the sound, I taste
the fuzz of his upper lip. As he moves his arm to explain, I feel the press

of grey silk on smooth skin. I spend every minute of my two-hour Mongolian lesson mentally pulling my feet back, my hands back, my head back, my body back, my heart back.

※

Battur and I plan to do something together. We will go to the movies. Just the two of us.

He shows up on time. We walk through the courtyards following tiny spike heel prints in hardened mud on the way to the bus stop. We get on Bus #3. The bus smells of sheep, meat, sweat, cigarettes, and alcohol. I feel a pulse of life, as if I am Rapunzel down from my 6th floor tower.

In the city, Battur holds my hand as we walk along the empty sidewalks. This is for safety as he guides me around open manholes and pitted concrete. My face feels flushed from pure joy when we arrive at the movie theater. Taking the bus with Battur, getting off at the right stop, and walking to the theater is easy. When I am alone, I can't even read letters of the place names on the bus.

The theater is locked—not a single person in sight.

"Strange. Let's go to another theater. We can walk." Again, walking together along the sidewalk, holding hands, I am thinking, life doesn't get better than this. When we arrive at the other theater, it is closed too.

"Oh, *Dirty Face*," he remembers.

"What?"

"It's *Dirty Face* time. Everything is closed. Everyone is home watching the soap opera."

"So we the only ones in the city not watching television right now?"

"That's right. Oh, well. Why don't we see if the Children's Park is open?" As we walk along, I describe the greenness of Vermont and how recycling keeps it green. His mind is working overtime, but he doesn't get it. I can see why. There is no one-use plastic packaging in Mongolia. The only plastic bag I have seen here a child was using for a kite yesterday, I tell him. I know that the city's sewer system can't handle toilet paper. So along with animal bones, paper is the only garbage here. Shopping bags are cloth, items are wrapped in newspaper, and meat is fresh. Nothing needs packaging. I wish Mongolia could ban plastic before it gets here, I say. It would keep the country beautiful. But, like in other countries, that

243

doesn't happen.

He tells me about traditions. Цаган сар, *Tsagaan Sar,* Lunar New Year, when families gather in the cold winter to give presents. "When we get back to my house, I will show you a video," he says.

Having these conversations breaks down our stereotypes of life in the US and Mongolia. We both grew up during the Cold War, so what we heard about each other up until now has been negative propaganda.

When we get to the Children's Park, we climb up the long, steep dragon's tongue slide. Battur whips down. I step onto the slide, sit, and immediately I'm at the bottom of the dragon's tongue, holding my hand. I wasn't prepared for the fastest and longest slide ever and smashed my fingers against the side. When we take the bus home, my fingers are in pain but my heart feels a lot lighter.

I'm really not fifteen.

❧

When I look out my sixth floor window, I see dozens of soviet-type apartment buildings. Cellar holes for new apartments started by soviets before they left five years ago still have cranes suspended over them. We've been here nearly three months and Bruce has just discovered a sauna out there somewhere. As a past hippie, I am used to sitting naked in saunas. Kathleen and Bruce even had a sauna at their New Year's Eve party last year. But that's in the US. I wonder about sauna protocol here—Mongolians seem modest.

Bruce has rented the sauna for an hour and invited Kathleen, Battur, and me to join him. I am looking forward to it and a little jittery about being there with Battur. I think it will be fine with Kathleen and Bruce there, too. But when the day comes, they don't have childcare and Bruce and Battur go ahead. I wait with Kathleen until she says, "Go ahead. I guess the babysitters aren't coming."

I walk across the courtyard until I find a door with a sauna picture on it, so I know I'm in the right place. Inside I cross a large waiting area to another door—the changing room. Bruce calls out a welcome. I take my clothes off and pass the showers. The wooden benches in the hot room look like bleachers. When my eyes adjust I see the steaming stove and Bruce and Battur sitting naked on the fourth tier.

My heart and my body want to be closer to Battur. I have to control myself. Battur is so dear. He is a bright light in my life. Sharing this is going to be fine, I think, as I sit on a towel on a lower bleacher. But, as soon as I sit, Bruce says, "I guess I'll take a shower and get back to Kathleen and the kids."

"Stay," I implore. I have looked forward to this time, but alone and naked with Battur could be dangerous and too delicious.

"No, we're meeting someone to visit a museum in half an hour," he says as he dresses in the changing area and walks out the door.

Now Battur and I are left alone in a hot, steamy room. I have to practice breathing to be calm. Battur immediately rushes to take a cold shower. Nineteen, I say to myself. I watch the back of his smooth-as-silk body as he climbs down the benches and goes out of the room. Gorgeous. He comes back looking like amber and sits two benches behind me. I don't dare turn around. He is too close. Both of us avert our eyes and yet see everything. He pours beer on the stove to bring a hop-smelling mist into the space. I take a shower, sweat, and take a shower. He seems to take more showers, coming back with goose bumps.

When he mentions the time is up, we dress in separate rooms. I am shaking a little from the intensity. I take more deep breaths.

The two of us now have to walk through the waiting room where the next group, a family of about twenty people, is wrapped in towels. They stare at us, just the two of us—a young guy and an older white foreigner—as we walk through the room and out the door. I feel like I am walking a parade of shame, my hot face turns redder with each step. This will give them something to talk about. Or will it? I don't understand Mongolian culture well enough to know.

Then we are out the door stepping on brown desert ground walking home together—the smell of hops dissipating behind us.

For my next Mongolian lesson, I choose a sentence.
"I love Mongolia," I suggest.
"*Bi Mongold khairtai,*" he teaches me.
Then Battur suggests two sentences, seemingly from nowhere. "*Chi khaloon osand orokh oo?*" He translates, "Do you want a hot shower?"

I repeat, "*Chi khaloon osand orokh oo?*"

Next the negative response, "*Ugui, bi khuiten osand orno.* No, I will take a cold shower."

Seems like he is remembering something.

"*Bi chumd hairtai.*"

"*Bi chumd hairtai.*" I repeat.

"I love you. Really," he says.

When Battur and his parents invite me to dinner, he meets me at my apartment and we walk across the dirt courtyard. Inside his family's apartment, his mother, who is younger than I am, and I exchange greetings, "*Sain baina uu*". She sits at a low, small table rolling dough and folding *buuz*, dumplings, in her compact kitchen. Buuz is a food Mongolians often serve guests. Battur leaves me alone in the living room to get milk tea for me.

While he is gone, I am thinking about a time Dr. Boldsaikhan left me in the living room as he answered the doorbell. He took his friends into the kitchen, a separate room off the hallway, and stayed and talked to them. He never brought them into the room I was in or introduced me to them. After a while he came back to visit with me. A Mongolian custom, I guess, but I don't get any farther figuring it out because Battur returns with tea and a plate piled with candies and aaruul.

"Want to see my photograph album?" he asks as he walks toward a bookshelf. This is the way Mongolians introduce themselves to a guest. At the age of seven I asked for and received a Brownie Hawkeye Camera because Dad taught us about his life through his photographs. I love to learn this way. Battur hands me his personal album, which starts when he is a baby, then onto his school pictures and awards, and ends with him at a Mongolian Tsagaan Sar celebration. In this picture, he is wearing a big fur hat and thick coat. I wonder how it would feel to walk outside in minus forty degree weather. He explains the customs to me. I wonder how it feels to meet your whole family inside a ger, sit in a circle, and give presents honoring the eldest down to the youngest. I want to cry it is so beautiful. The family. The ger. The closeness.

Next we go through his family albums. And, when dinner still isn't ready, Battur brings me a dark burgundy album. "This is my father's military album." I swallow. As a Quaker pacifist, I don't quite know how to respond. When he opens it, he shows me his father's officer training group at military school in Moscow. Now I am breathing deeply. So many thoughts run through my mind at once. Growing up in the fifties, Moscow was the place of our enemies. Moscow—just the idea of military and Moscow—had given me butterflies in my stomach from the Cold War propaganda.

Yet, here I am in my dear friend's home. I pull myself together, just as Battur turns the page and recites the countries of the members of his father's fellow officers. He points to one after another, reciting North Korea, North Vietnam, Albania, Yugoslavia, East Germany, and Russia. My first horrific thought is that these people had been learning to kill us. These are the countries whose very names had made me shudder. My next thought is I have to put this into perspective. I look at their faces. They are people. The Cold War has been over for years, well, five years. We are living here in Ulaankhuaran, Red Army's Quarters, a district eight kilometers east of the center of Ulaanbaatar. Battur's father's rank had been colonel. And here is gentle Battur the son of a Red Army officer, showing me an album. I tell myself, stay in the present moment.

The buuz are ready. His father Battulga comes in and his mother Oyunchimeg serves us all. With his wide smile and crinkly eyes nearly closed from smiling so much, his father sits with us. "Been looking at the albums? Yah, those are my old buddies. We had a lot of fun together."

Fun. Red Army officers? I am still struggling with this. On one hand, I had always wondered what our enemies looked like. When I was a teenager, media and school classes were full of negative propaganda, which I internalized like everyone else. Yet, on a spiritual level, a part of me always knew Russians were people like us and I hoped to go to the Soviet Union to find out. I never did go to Russia, but making friends with this family reminds me that people are, in fact, very much alike.

After dinner, Battur and I sit side-by-side on his bed looking at more albums. His mother steps in. She gets a strange look on her face, says something to Battur, turns abruptly and leaves. He says gently that he will walk me home now.

The next day, I hear that Battur has left to help his grandparents gather hay for their herds.

Chapter Forty-one

— *Marrying Mongolia*

Perhaps, in lives that compressed many
life-times into one, it was necessary to have many mates.
~Erika Jong

The Sources of Perception or the six powers—to hear, smell,
taste, feel, see, and think— form our basis for understanding
the world and its elements: earth, water, fire, wind.
~Dr. B. Boldsaikhan

𝒲hen human hearts connect, they are forever. My life changes, but inside there is always an essence of each person I have been close to. I do not forget past husbands and partners. I saved some letters sent to me many years after those relationships ended.

❧

Ken. When Ken and I were living in the Northeast Kingdom and he wanted to buy another loom, I gave him my life savings from small jobs and babysitting as a teenager. I thought it was natural—we shared everything. We got divorced in 1975, after eleven years officially married. When he moved from Florida where he had lived for about forty years, he sent this letter.

Dear Sas,

Please find check enclosed. In the dull recesses of my mem-
ory I believe you had some money saved which you contributed to
buy my first loom. The particulars evade me, the emotions of your
confidence and love are still with me.

It makes no sense to me to say I wish it had turned out
differently. I think both of us are happy with the persons we have
become.

Hugs my love hugs . . .thanks so much for all the good
years . . .

Ken

Mats. For some years after I left Sweden in 1974, Mats and I shared
letters and phone calls. He sent me signed records and CDs of his jazz
and folk music. Mats died of a heart attack at the age of fifty-four.

❧

Zed. Zed and I married in 1979 and divorced in 1987. When he left
he moved to Burlington, Vermont. For my birthday many years later, he
sent this letter.

Dear Sas,

All I need to do today is to wish you my best: to thank you
in the best way I know how, and to tell you that my life with you
. . .was, beyond doubt, the best and most important thing hap-
pening for me. As painful and disappointing as my living with
you was for you and your family, I thank you for all the love and
tolerance you extended to me.

And, as little as I have contributed towards your destiny, I
am profoundly proud of you and in awe that I had the opportuni-
ty to know you.

Love, Zed

It's 1995 and these men are in my heart, but not part of my life any more. Now that I am exploring my purpose to learn Mongolian medicine and culture, the searching for a man might have been finished, but it isn't. It's hard to explain how being in love/longing with Battur is. I am obsessed. But Battur is with his grandparents for most of the time I have left in Mongolia—time that had seemed so precious. Our classes are over. Kathleen, Bruce, and I have ten days to do whatever we want in Mongolia. I want the impossible—to share time with Battur.

I am home alone when a woman artist, Tuya, comes to visit Kathleen and Bruce. They have taken the kids to the Children's Park. Tuya says, "Are you alone? I will find someone for you. No one can be alone in Mongolia."

I take it as a joke and don't even bother to say, "This is not how we do it in my country."

Yet, a couple of days later she visits to say she has found a husband for me. I can meet him at Tuya's art exhibit at the Zanabazar Museum of Fine Arts later in the afternoon.

The man I meet is young and small with a missing tooth—also animated, bright-eyed, and knows a few words in English. We talk for a short time with Tuya translating. He asks me to dinner the following evening and I say yes.

We meet at a restaurant called The White House, order chicken, talk through a dictionary, and get a taxi to Zaisan, a Russian-Mongolian peace monument, which overlooks Ulaanbaatar. The taxi takes us to a landing about half way up to where the monument is. After climbing the remaining two hundred stairs, we look over the view of the city and he says through charades that he is small because his parents are small. I find it endearing.

❧

My deep yearning and caring for Battur has electrified me. I want to hold on to Mongolia—the faces, the people, the energy. I also can't hold myself back from my longing to be with a Mongolian who is more than nineteen.

❧

Without a taxi at Zaisan, we walk down all of the six hundred and twelve steps and then five miles to Peace Avenue and get a taxi to my apartment. There are no buses this late, so he stays and we spend a romantic night together in my apartment. Within a few days, I am engaged to him. I don't know him. I can't speak the language, but the only way to see him again is to get a fiancé visa. For him to stay in Vermont, we would have to get married within six months of his arrival. I am actually in love with Mongolia, not him, but I don't admit it to myself. My rational mind is not functioning.

At first it's exciting. He gets off the plane in full traditional dress. He is happy to live in such a nice house. I am happy to share with someone. We get married in the back yard in June 1996 after he is here three months. For a while, I serve him in every way as a Mongolian wife would. For instance, he lets his hair grow and I braid it for him each day.

One year after the wedding in Vermont, we fly to Mongolia and his family organizes a traditional Mongolian wedding. With his brother, he picks me up in a car taxi at the apartment. We ride for an hour to the family's *khashaa*, some fenced land at the outskirts of the city. Inside the fence, there is a garden with vegetables from seeds I had given them. A red carpet is laid on dirt ground. As the bride, I am led over it into a shed where his parents live in the summer, guided to light a fire in the stove, and make milk tea. Forty-three family members are milling around the khashaa. The men build a fire and hover near the live sheep which they then butcher for the wedding feast. Inside a larger shed women are making potato salad, coleslaw, dumplings, and arranging fruit.

When everything is ready, he and I sit at the head of the long, long table which stretches from one wall to the door outside. All the adults sit. His father gives a speech, my husband giving me a word of explanation every few sentences. We eat the mutton, salads, fruit, vegetables, and sweets. After the feast in the yard we sing songs, and take photos. I am full of hope that this will make me a part of Mongolia.

We get back to Vermont in the fall. He has learned some English but he has no motivation to work. I have trouble working because he won't let me out of his sight, won't let me travel to see clients, and stands behind my back when I do computer work. He assaults me with demanding, pressured talk that goes on for hours. I tell him how I feel, how hard it is for me. He has selective listening.

Every time I wonder if I can take any more, I think of Mongolia, the wedding, being a part of life there. I wonder if I can be a part of it alone. I am unraveling and wonder what will happen next. Finally, I go to a lawyer and fill out an intake form. The last question on the paper is if there is anything else you want the lawyer to know. I can hardly write the truth, but I know this is my chance. Eventually I file for divorce.

Coincidently, about four years after the first wedding, Dr. Boldsaikhan comes to teach my students. I am driving my teacher and husband in my car when my husband starts ranting and yelling at me. Dr. Boldsaikhan says, "With all the men in Mongolia, you have to choose one who is mentally ill?" I thought I was finished being yelled at many years before when I left my father's house. But my addiction to have a cocoon with a man, my conflagration of Mongolia and my husband, and my yearning for a man have brought me full circle back to anger. I have spent three years figuring out how to get out of the marriage.

The plan is for Dr. Boldsaikhan to return to Mongolia in a month. My husband has a ticket on the same flight to visit his sick father and spend time in Mongolia. I tell him before he leaves that he can't come back here, that I can't live with him, and why doesn't he stay in Mongolia, but three months later, he's back. I tell him he needs to find a place to live. I get a restraining order from his control and abuse, and get voice mail so I can stop listening to his long rants.

Our divorce is in court—he doesn't agree to an earlier settlement. The judge rules that I give him a lump sum. I remortgage my house for the money and add what it costs for a trip to Mongolia for me to make the movie. I had waited three years while taking care of him. I am finished with him and with men.

Before leaving to travel alone to Mongolia in 2001, I wonder what I might say to people who ask me where my husband is. Then it comes: Монгол улс миний нөхөр.

Mongol uls minii nukhur. Mongolia is my husband. My relationship is with the country, not a person.

Би монголтой гэрлэж байна. I am marrying Mongolia.

V

Marrying Mongolia

Chapter Forty-two

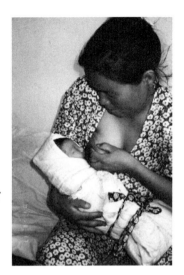

— With a little
help from my friends

There is such a special sweetness in being
able to participate in creation.
~Pamela S. Nadav

 *E*verything I have learned as a wife, mother, teacher, medical-surgical nurse, potter, teen discussion group facilitator, psychic, and energy healer is all needed in my marriage to Mongolia.

      🌿

 While meditating some years after working on a water study with the United Nations Development Programme in 1997, I remember the desert women had said they used five liters of water a day—for cooking, cleaning, and drinking. In the US, we use nearly that much for one flush of a toilet.

 I get a leading to document their lives and show how they do this.

 I haven't had any training for making a documentary.

      🌿

 In the summer of 2001, I travel with cameraman Joseph Spaid and translator Khaliuna to the Gobi Desert in the south of Mongolia to film nomadic women. My former sister-in-law Oyuntungalag and her husband Nyama find a driver and arrange a ger for us in Manlai Sum, South Gobi so we can make a film.

❦

A nomadic herder named Dulma has given us permission to be with her for the birth of her baby. Joseph, Khaliuna, and I are living next door to the local hospital when we are contacted to witness and film the birth. We talk with Ariuna, a sturdy nurse with a low-pitched voice. She is a matter-of-fact, outspoken, funny, big-hearted woman who can't do enough for others while being deadpan with her comments. She makes the nearly bare labor and delivery room into a welcoming space, reminding me of Kai's home birth.

Dulma delivers a baby girl with five women in attendance and Joseph behind the camera filming it. Nineteen-year-old Khaliuna, who had been horrified at the idea of seeing a birth, is now holding the minutes-old baby close to her mother, trying to get her to nurse, and spooning mutton broth into Dulma's mouth. I hold my hands over Dulma focusing healing energy. She is still lying on the table because the placenta has not detached.

"It is better to be born a boy," says Ariuna, as we wait. Even though this is a tense moment we laugh and relax a bit. No bells ring, no voices make announcements over an intercom. The electricity is not on. There is no computer, phone, indoor toilet. No running water. No help.

We watch the doctor pull a glove on that goes beyond her elbows. She is preparing to remove the placenta manually. She safely extracts it and we see that Dulma and her daughter are fine. Everyone takes a breath.

"What we have," says Ariuna, "is women power."

Dulma and her daughter are so fine that three days later she and her swaddled baby climb on their motorcycle behind her husband and three-year old son and ride over rough desert ground back to their nomadic settlement.

Yes, it is possible to live with five liters of water a day.

Our documentary *Gobi Women's Song* tells the story.

❦

2003. On my first trip to the taiga in northern Mongolia, it is October and winter already. We have driven over frozen ground to the East and West Taiga, home of Dukha reindeer herders. I am asking about their health as I meet the women in a small, heavily insulated log cabin with a central fire. It is very hot inside. The women are sharing.

One says, "No one speaks to us like this. Why don't we find you a taiga husband?"

I can't explain that I am married to Mongolia. I do tell them I would like to meet a shaman.

"Gosta," says Erdenechimeg. "He is my brother-in-law. An hour away from here by horse."

I don't have a horse or an hour, yet know that I need to find them for another trip. I will also need to learn to ride a horse.

❦

The next year is 2004, when I break my foot. In Ulaanbaatar I change from the large cast I wore in the Gobi to a splint. With it on, I can barely squeeze into a friend's riding boots for my first long horse ride. It turns out to be a scary eight-hour horse ride to the summer settlement of Meng Bulag. A New York man, Dan Plumley, heads our team and has introduced me to the West Taiga people who are crowded into an urts for a meeting. A man with a baby tucked into his deel breast pocket arrives and sits inside the door of the urts. A guest would not normally be in this area of the home, but I am filming and can see everyone better from the door area. The man motions me to slide over. I motion to him to slide over, pointing to my camera. He does. Gosta.

After the meeting, I ask if I can interview him. He agrees and I find a translator as we go into the urts of Soyan, famous one-hundred-year old shaman. She speaks Tuvan, her ethnic language, not Mongolian. Yet, I begin by questioning Soyan. Getting an answer requires double translations from English to Mongolian to Tuvan and back. Soyan says that I should interview Gosta. "He's younger. I am too old. You will understand this someday." She gives me some reindeer cheese and incense when I leave. The incense is "so you will always have something good to smell."

Gosta and I talk and the conversation begins as an interview. As soon as I turn off the camera, it shifts and he asks, "How old are you?"

I say, "Fifty-nine. How old are you?"

"Fifty-eight," he says, with the broad smile of a little boy who has found a playmate.

❦

From that time on, I try to learn from Gosta. Three years later, my cameraman, translator, and I stay at the urts where he lives with his niece Khandaa and her three year old son, but Gosta is away. Where we stay, Gosta's altar hangs from the poles of the urts. For nearly two weeks, Khandaa lets us stay. We talk and spend a day inside when rain turns to eight inches of snow in July. I try to imagine if someone showed up at my house with two friends and asked to stay for two weeks how I would have felt, especially if I lived in one room. But Khandaa? She welcomes us. Her only caveat is to not walk near the altar. We don't, but the first evening a male reindeer is missing and she wonders. We are vindicated when the reindeer shows up. "You must be very powerful," she says.

During this stay, I'm invited to attend my first shaman ceremony with Gosta's brother Shaman Ganzorig. I describe it in *Reindeer Herders in My Heart*. It whets my appetite for more.

❦

In the years that follow, Gosta asks for healings from me. I ask for information on shamans, which he avoids until one day he says, "You keep coming back. I will answer your questions." I never get to see his drum or witness him giving a ceremony, but he explains things and does impersonations that make me laugh. We become friends.

Later Gosta has had a number of strokes and can't get to the taiga any more. He is in a ger in the local sum Tsagaannuur. Khandaa is helping him slowly sit up. She holds a cup of milk tea for him to drink. I sit on a chair beside him. A tourist, excited to meet the famous shaman, asks questions. I don't ask questions any more. Khandaa hands me her baby daughter to hold. She sits near the foreigner. Gosta can hardly talk. There is no need for talking now in my opinion. Mostly we sit, connecting with our eyes. Then I am leaving and I know I won't see him again. I stand and blow him a kiss as I did with Mom. Gosta can barely move, but slowly, slowly he lifts his hand to his lips and returns the air kiss.

Chapter Forty-three

— *Go with the flow*

This life that we have inherited from our
forefathers is a beautiful life for us. But media
comes up to the taiga, sees it briefly with their own eyes,
and shows life that is ugly. We want the true image, the
beauty of the environment and nature, the beauty of the
reindeer, the special taiga life, every day life. We love reindeer—
that's why we live in the taiga. Our life is not based every
day with shamanism, but when we need it, we have it.
It is very important for us to be portrayed honestly.
Our fathers came to Mongolia [from Tuva, part of Russia]
for the first time during World War II. Life wasn't easy.
They had no common language, difficult communication,
but maintained the lifestyle and tradition.
We are not going to give up.
~Dukha Reindeer Herders Statement to Media 2004

2014. We are returning from a magical shoot of our documentary *Migration*, where I was invited to ride a reindeer, like everyone else. As "jeeps of the taiga," reindeer can go anywhere, even with us riding and the Dukha's household goods packed on them. I follow a family's two days plodding procession through rivers and over rock mountains to Meng Bulag, their summer camp. After arriving, we watch the family set up their urts, make bread, travel to get fire wood, and prepare a new shaman costume by softening a hide for the lining and embroidering the deel with reindeer hairs.

Our driver Ganbat draws me a sketch of how to remove bark from a tree in one piece as we climb into his black Korean Musso van to begin our trip back to the city, south along the west side of the Beltag River. He is an artist, the creative builder of his family's guest house, our base in Tsagaannuur. He's a person who's always interested in our work in the taiga.

Chimedee, my cheerful, never-complaining interpreter and assistant, explains to me that rocks miss their home when they are carried away and I drop some quartz I had found on the ground from the SUV window. She smiles.

We drive for five or six hours over bumps and stony track. Short, wiry Battulga comes with us to the city. He and Fred, our cinematographer this year, sit in the back seat with Chimedee. Ganbat says we are ahead of schedule and will get to Mörön, the *aimag*, province capital, this afternoon with plenty of time to meet our Ulaanbaatar flight at nine in the morning.

Now we are not sure at all.

Typical of rivers in the northern area of Mongolia, the Belteg River has ten-foot eroded banks on one side and a gradual stone beach on the other. Mountains rise beyond the banks with a patch of green steppes and mud tracks between the mountains and us.

The river is usually shallow, narrow, and easy to drive through—the only way across since the bridge has rotted. With the previous day's rain, though, the river is brown, so high that the other bank is about twice as far as usual with rapids in between. Because of the conditions, Ganbat has checked with a driver coming from the opposite direction about the best crossing place.

When we come to a crossing place, Ganbat steers the car slowly down the bank, enters the water, and travels downstream in the river for a couple of car lengths. When he sees a track on the opposite bank, he starts to turn. Before reaching the bank, his wheels spin and the car stops. We are stuck. Water spurts under the door onto my bare feet on the passenger side. I'm not alarmed but I move my sandals onto the dashboard. The Mongolian countryside is so remote that car problems are frequent. Water begins to rise inside the car. I glance at cameraman Fred Thodal, his eyes wide, as he sits in the back seat with the film equipment.

"Get in back, Sas," says Ganbat pointing behind him as the car lists toward the passenger side. Chimedee grabs our luggage one piece at a time and hands it to Ganbat who is now in water up to the top of his legs. Fred and Battulga join him to ferry our luggage including cameras, recorders, a drone, and tripods to dry ground. They wade fully clothed through the recent snow-melt water to the shore, getting their pants' pockets wet. No one complains as they pile the luggage on the bank. Chimedee wades to shore when the car is emptied. Ganbat probably weighs thirty pounds less than I do, yet when the gear is safe, he tells me to climb on his back and carries me across the water. Only the bottoms of my jeans get wet.

Ganbat is drenched to his chest, but doesn't take time to change his clothes. He puts his responsibility to get us to Mörön first and ignores any discomfort. He walks south along the riverbank. We wait on the stony ground with the piles of luggage. In addition to the film equipment we have camping equipment, clothing, duffle bags, and backpacks.

All of us know that there is no quick fix because we haven't seen a vehicle or person on the road since we left the *guanz*, cafe, an hour before. I am the driest of all of us. This isn't the first time I feel privileged and entitled in Mongolia. I also hurt knowing this is Ganbat's first car and I doubt there is car insurance. My cell phone is useless with no service, but Chimedee's and Battulga's cell phones are wet from being submerged.

Battulga's cigarettes are totally soggy. Fred, Chimedee, and Battulga each dig into their packs and step away, facing in different directions to change to dry clothes. In Mongolia I often have to make the best of waiting time since there is nothing I can do to change or control it. We settle in. I take out my Kindle, open my back jack chair, sit, and read. The sun shines and the air is comfortable.

Battuga walks off and finds a ger, probably motivated by losing his cigarettes. He knows that all gers in the countryside welcome strangers. When he comes back, I feel good knowing there are people nearby.

An hour or so later when the sun has disappeared, we hear a rumble and Ganbat arrives sitting in a truck beside its driver. I take a deep breath, grateful for the truck.

Then I look at its tires—completely bald.

I watch Chimedee's face as she listens to Ganbat, Battulga, and the driver talk and gesture with their arms. I see her eyes widen and I ask what's happening. She translates, "The truck has no reverse gear." At once, I feel the possibility of not getting the car out, and yet, I have seen many dire situations over the years that Mongolians somehow remedied, so I stay in the present. No sense in getting overly stressed.

Then I see that there is no chain, either, just a rope that the men connect to the bumpers. The truck lines up at the edge of the river, two tires in the water, the rope barely reaches between the bumpers. The driver revs the engine, trying to pull forward. The wheels spin and the rope snaps. Ganbat's Musso SUV has not moved.

The sky gets darker. After three unsuccessful attempts to tow the car, the truck stops. A chilling wind has come up. Ganbat's teeth chatter and his body shakes with cold. He is wet all the way to his shoulders. I move into nurse mode, get him into the truck, get Battulga to find him dry clothes from his pack. Chimedee brings a thermos of hot tea. I help him take his wet things off. I am thinking about hypothermia when a heavy, cold rain starts. Now our luggage is being loaded into the back of the truck and we all climb inside and drive to the local ger. The gear is unloaded onto the ground and we cover it with our green Russian raincoats.

I go with the flow. We step into the warm, smoky, lanolin, dairy-filled smells of the ger. Night is falling.

Sixteen disparate people are inside a twenty-feet in diameter ger while sheets of rain incessantly pound the canvas and felt top. The metal of the stove in the center of the ger clangs and flames seep through the door as a mother feeds it. As I look around, I notice each space inside has its own stage with a mini-play going on. Four generations of the family each at their own station. A young mother nurses her baby. The grandmother sits beside the stove. Three teenagers giggle and flirt. The men are near the door talking.

We join the family and tuck into our own appropriate spots. Chimedee and I sit on a bed on the West side as is proper for women guests. We read, watch, wonder, snooze, try to make ourselves invisible.

Ganbat goes to check his car. The water is up to the windows, he says when he returns. Always an artist, instead of looking horrified, he says, "Well, Sas, here is another story for your book." He takes his place among the men who stand and squat around the fire.

I feel sick for Ganbat—envisioning his van in the ever-rising water of the river.

Normal life continues for the nomads. The truck driver is a vet. He goes out with the herders to check their yaks. Teenage girls come back with milk from the animals and pour it into a hand-cranked, red, metal, cream centrifugal separator. Chimedee joins in turning the crank. She comes from a herder family and knows this life.

I am working to release my expectations—a plane-ride on one hand and nature on the other. The power of the pounding rain, the river rushing, the calmness of the family members living in harmony with the land. Something will happen. We will stay here or not. Get a ride or not.

"You know how to meditate, Sas," says Chimedee, interrupting my thoughts. "Why don't you stop the rain?"

I am not about to say no since nothing else is working to get us to Mörön, so I close my eyes, find that deep place like at Quaker meeting and wait. I hold the energy of the ger, the family, my team, and then open to the outside and connect to the rain that has been pounding for three or four hours. I hold that . . . The rain sound changes, slows down. I open my eyes. I can hear the mother softly singing to her baby. The rain has stopped abruptly. Chimedee has a beatific expression. Everyone in the ger starts to talk, as if we have all been holding our breath.

After some time, Chimedee laughs. "Well, the rain stopped, now how about a car?" I laugh and close my eyes to find that peaceful place that absorbs all the ger energy—the cream streaming from the separator, the teens talking, the baby nursing, and the clang of the stove. I expand my energy to get in touch with nature. Right away we feel a vibration and hear a whine and clinking from far off. A car stops outside. Strange. A second coincidence, I think, as I open my eyes. Five men come into the ger and squat near the door. They talk and talk. I ask Chimedee what they are talking about. Each one says he can't drive us. One has a car that is not in good shape, two have no driver's licenses, another has no registration, and the fourth one says his car was flooded today when the river rose and the radiator was submerged. Plus the land is flooded between here and the city and it's not safe to drive.

Chimedee says, "Sas, can we move this along? We need a ride." I close my eyes and ask for a driver. When I open them, I read the energy of each of the five men. I focus on the one with the most clear, uncomplicated energy. I intuit that he is complaining but he could drive us. I send him energy. After some minutes, he mumbles, "Well, it would be very expensive."

"How much?" I ask.

"Two hundred dollars."

"Okay, let's go."

Little do I realize it will not be a direct ride. In Mongolia I never know who will be in the car or what will happen. That's why all I can do is be in a zone of acceptance and trust that we will eventually get to Mörön.

Along with the men, we four pack our gear in the back of the Russian jeep, then climb in along with a woman and two children. Four Mongolians in the front, and four others squished in with us in the back. The land is soggy, the streams swollen. We drop a man, woman, and the two children off and we stop for gas at a friend's. It is eleven and very dark when the car stops. I am startled by a bellowing yak walking next to me as I step out of the car. We are led into another ger. This one has two families, since one was flooded out when the river rose. The hood of another Russian jeep is lifted and the men now stand around the engine compartment. This jeep belongs to our Mörön driver. He needs to change the radiator because it was submerged in the water today. In the pitch black, with a tiny light, they change it.

By one in the morning our luggage is in the back of this jeep. Battulga, Fred, Chimedee, and I squeeze into the space where a back seat would normally be. Instead of a seat, though, there is one sheet of plywood under us and a loose piece of plywood in back of us. For the next five hours, the driver and his friend shout stories to each other and laugh in the front seat. Battulga covers his head with his deel and goes to sleep. I put my deel on because there is no heat. The driver takes the back bumpy way, through brush and flooded rivers. In case we doze off, we are immediately slammed awake by the plywood board behind us as it bangs into our backs.

And then, no more bumps. We are on paved road just outside of Mörön. The driver says, "I will let you off here. My license and registration are no good."

"No way," I say. I have a vision of the four or us sitting on our pile of luggage all day waiting for a ride. "It's five in the morning. No police are out. We need you to drop us off at the hotel."

So he does.

Chapter Forty-four

~ *Gala*

2016. Gala sits in front of a row of streamers—red and black, then softer tones of green, yellow, blue, and white all hanging from the altar in his urts in a West Taiga settlement in Northern Mongolia. Felt dolls representing *ongod*, ancestor spirits, are tucked inside the streamers. Bottles of vodka from family, a brick of tea and money along with candles and a bag of aaruul lie on the ground, partially hidden by the streamers.

Gala, the twenty-six year old son of Shaman Ganzorig and nephew of Shaman Gosta had been around shaman ceremonies all his life and has become a Dukha shaman during the past year. I knew he had been chosen when I had seen his sister sew his new costume the previous summer.

Gala has agreed to an interview and to let us film a shaman ceremony, a ceremony to bring peace, honor the spirits, and get questions answered.

"How did you find out you were a shaman?" I ask.

"Auntie told me to prepare." Auntie is Khandaa, also a shaman now.

"Did you have any sickness?" I know that shamans often have physical or mental illnesses.

"I had bad dreams."

After my questions, Chimedee asks him, "How do you feel just before the ceremony?"

"I had some dreams last night. This morning I didn't feel well. I saw mountains and land before my eyes. I am afraid of the questions my family members will ask. Some are sick and have questions about healing. I never know what spirit will come in or how the ceremony will go. I am nervous and scared."

We wait for the evening, for the stars to come out. At 11:30, when darkness finally falls, we enter Gala's urts, joining thirty Dukha reindeer herders. They bustle around, talking, taking care of business. With two palms upraised, we offer hard candies, dried fruit, cheese curds, and money to Gala for the ongod, the spirit ancestors. There is vodka on the altar, but we do not give vodka.

Gala will drum in the northern, sacred area. Since I am an elder visitor, he invites me to sit in the place of honor for the ceremony, on skins in the northwest area of the urts, closest to where he will do the ritual. My assistant and camerawoman join me. Lights are not allowed during the ceremony, so we cover the red light on the camera with tape to prepare to record only the audio. Gala sits before the altar, waiting for this mother and older brother to arrive. His younger brother, Ak-Ool, twirls the khengereg, shaman's octagonal drum, over the central stove fire. Two feet in diameter and eight inches deep, it glows from the fire, a red sun in the dark night. His father-in-law Delgermagnai lights a branch by putting it in the wood stove. The smoke and the scent of juniper *arts*, incense, fill the air, cleansing the inside of the urts along with its people and objects. This is all in preparation of the shaman ceremony.

Gala hands out cigarettes as presents to his relatives while his wife, D. Solongo, carefully unfolds his blue shaman's deel, attaches two clumps of streamers from former ceremonies, along with a metal plate of tiny metal weapons for protection. The jingle cones on his deel clang as she shakes it, smudging it with juniper smoke.

Everyone inside the urts is family except us.

The shaman cuts white cloth into strips three to four inches wide and a yard long and hands one to each relative. Someone burns more incense. Then Gala asks what questions people have for the ongod. He asks if I have any questions. I don't. I usually connect to the spirit myself to get answers. With shamans I am seeking to internalize how they shift, their way of crossing the veil between the secular and spiritual worlds.

After midnight, Gala stands, slips off his glittering, golden silk deel. D. Solongo helps him put on his blue shaman deel. He exchanges his black leather herder boots for soft leather and cloth ones. Over his shiny, short black hair and bangs, she ties a headdress with embroidered eyes, nose, ears, and mouth on the cloth. Braided string and strips of cloth hang over Gala's face and feathers bob above his head as he moves. His brother Khadbaatar assists.

Gala takes the drum and begins gently chanting, like his father Ganzorig used to do. The room is thick with incense. Each person with a white cloth streamer ties it to the back of his costume. For peace. For honoring the spirits. For the honor of asking a question. Slowly, softly, my heartbeat matches the sound of the drum. The rhythm pulses, pulses the urts and my body, two soft beats, two louder ones. Gala calls an *ongon*, single ancestor spirit, in chopped, staccato Tuvan sounds. Ha. Ka. Aha. Ora. Oye. Chavay. Hos. La. I can see a silhouette of prayer ribbons on his back, his hand on the drum beater, and feathers as he moves in front of the dim light.

The shaman's voice changes; he becomes an older man with gravelly words. It is a harsh, painful voice. Male energy. Disturbing. He twirls around, swings the drum in the air. Faster, angry. I lean back as far as I can to get away, touch the canvas of the urts wall. Khadbaatar stands behind Gala, his arms open while the ancestor flails, to prevent him from falling toward the fire. The ongod is almost crying, using coarse words, that sound like commands. Still painful. He puts his hand out, palm up. The ongon wants vodka. Or milk, or a cigarette. D. Solongo hands him a bowl. He drinks the vodka.

Gala's energy calms. He sits on the ground before me, the drum resting on my foot. Suddenly, he jumps up and swings the drum again, out of control. I have been to many ceremonies, but I am shaking with fear when this ongon is here. The shaman twirls around. Faster, full of angry energy. The ongon breathes heavily. The drum flies through the air. I glance at Chimedee, a very strong woman, and even in the dark I can tell from her shrinking posture that she is scared too. Someone in the family says, *"Myy, myy,"* bad, wrong.

He smashes the beater on the drum and a new ongon comes in. Calmer.

After two or three hours of switching from one ongon to another, he calls his cousin's name. She comes forward and he gently throws his beater while she spreads her deel skirt to catch it. She hands the beater back, saying, "*Tuurug*," please tell my fortune. The ongon answers her question about the health of her baby son. I'm relieved because I know this in the beginning of the end of the ceremony. After answering all the family members, Gala throws the beater into my fanned out deel skirt. "Tuurug," I say.

"Your grandsons are fine. Your work is fine. No problems. You will come back to us."

The drum stops. There is silence. The shaman is helped out of his costume, headdress and boots. He goes outside. When he returns, the fire is up, the light uncovered, and the family is drinking *suutei tsai*, milk tea. The person who returns is Gala; the ongod are gone. He passes food offerings, now blessed by the ongod, to his family and guests. Family members ask more questions in an informal way; Chimedee translates for me. Gala expands on the advice the ongod gave during the ceremony. Then he turns to me and says, "The reason the ongod was so angry was because you, Sas, did not bring vodka. You know my father and uncle. They are now our ancestor spirits. You know they like vodka."

I gasp, wondering if it could be true. Or if he is drunk. I want to disappear, but it is three in the morning, too dark for us to leave on reindeer. The extended family members leave. The rest of us—my team, and Gala and his wife D. Solongo—sleep on the ground in a line from west to east in Gala's urts for the night.

At daybreak he is sound asleep as we climb on the reindeer and ride back to his mother's settlement. We spend the day resting, but I have a nagging feeling of upset, wondering if the ongod's anger was actually my fault.

At eleven that evening, when his mother finishes milking her reindeer and comes for her nightly healing, she asks how I felt about the ceremony. I admit that I was scared.

Chimedee says, "Do you want to ask her?"

I do, yet I'm afraid of the answer.

"Were the ancestor spirits really angry because I didn't bring vodka?"

Silence. More silence as my hands focus healing energy on her back. Minutes pass.

"Well," she says slowly, "I guess you will bring some next time."

Yes, I think. Yes I will.

Chapter Forty-five

～ *The Why's*

*"Walk cheerfully and gently over the earth
answering to that of God in everyone
and everything."*
*~George Fox, Founder of The Religious
Society of Friends (Quakers)1656*

$\mathcal{A}$s a Quaker, I believe in "leadings" or callings to serve in a way guided by Spirit. I have been guided to prepare for my work in the world, from my rebellious childhood, hippie days living on the land, and becoming a healer and nurse, and then I arrive, finally, to marrying Mongolia. Mostly, I am guided by what comes to me in meditation, yet there are times when I am guided by others—my father and mother, my first husband, a psychic, a client, and a teacher. Abrupt changes occur when I trust.

When guided to do something, I get the idea of what to do. Then as I begin, the way opens and I see how to do it. But I mostly don't know why. An answer can come years or decades later. This kind of life is not rational. It is amorphous, requiring flexibility, persistence, and curiosity.

Here are some testimonials that help me understand why I have been guided to do what I have.

Cellular Memory. I take *Migration* on my laptop computer to the taiga settlement to show the Dukha what I have included of their life in the documentary. All the local Dukha reindeer herders are invited into the urts to see the movie. Thirty-five adults and kids pack into the twenty-feet in diameter home and I start the movie. About half an hour into the documentary, Baasankhuu, who sings a song he wrote in the movie, jumps up and places his red flip-phone beside the computer. Music from the Alash Ensemble of Tuva is playing on the *Migration* soundtrack. He says, "I feel this music of our ancestors. Since the forties we have not been allowed to cross the border to Tuva. I need it on my phone so that I can listen to and learn our traditional songs while I am out herding." After learning it, Basaankhuu will bring it back to his community.

Marginalization. We show *Migration* at the cultural building in Tsagaannuur, the village closest to the Dukha settlements. The audience includes townspeople and Dukha herders. The Dukha's faces are glowing. The townspeople have an astonished look. Dukha are marginalized in this town since they don't live on a money economy and they dress in traditional clothes. Sometimes men get drunk in town. There are no showers in the settlements. Watching the film, the locals get to see the natural beauty of Dukha reindeer herder life with its spectacular nature.

Late Bloomer. In the East Taiga, seventeen-year-old M. Solongo comes to sing while we record her on video. Her voice is pure like a bell. The next year, a donor gives us tuition funding for some taiga young people to attend a university. Solongo and her friend Batjargal have passed the entrance examinations. They write essays saying that without an education, their lives will be nothing. Solongo goes to a university to be a musician. Batjargal goes to the Mongolian Agricultural University, studies material sciences, and graduates four years later.

The second year Solongo flunks out and lends her mother the funds meant for her second semester's tuition. We cut her off. Her mother Munkhuu apologizes to me, saying she thought she could return the money in time for the second semester. Then her mother presents me with a baby reindeer to thank me for helping her daughter—a male reindeer they have named Sas. Solongo is contrite. Sas the reindeer lives in the taiga.

A couple of years later I ask Solongo to translate some songs for me. She is angry and doesn't want to help. She says, "I don't know why you come here. You are our strangest guest. What do you want? Why do you come?" I just look at her with love. The next day, she asks if she and her baby daughter can catch a ride with us to Mörön. She doesn't say one word during the two-day trip. Taiga people usually don't show emotions to foreigners. I am used to anger. Her showing it to me makes me feel part of the community.

Later I hear that she is in school studying to be a music teacher and doing well. Some years after that I hear she is teaching music in a countryside school in another province, Arkhangai Aimag.

Eighteen years after meeting Solongo, this text message comes from her:

> *Hi there. Today I wanted to express my gratitude to you, so I am writing this message. Your work and labor have contributed to my education and who I am now. I wish you happiness.*
>
> *I am sure there were times I offended you. If so, I am sorry.*
>
> M. Solongo

My heart feels light knowing that this gifted singer and musician is doing her work by encouraging children and young people. From her I learn that we never know what comes from the work we do. It may not look successful right away.

Photos. In 2009 when we photograph life in the East Taiga, cameraman Fred Thodal suggests that we let the herders use an extra camera we have. We give each family three hours to take pictures of whatever they want. Fred tells them we will develop the photos and bring them back next year. They take a lot of photos. I pack seven pounds of developed pictures in my suitcase and carry them to the taiga. The pictures taken by them show what is important. They love the pictures.

Archive for Mongolians. As Eleanor Ott, professor, ethnologist, writer, and Nomadicare board member says, "Archiving material documenting the Mongolian traditional way of life from the past three decades will enrich the lives of the new generations. But more than this, something deeper, it answers the yearning all humans share—'Who am

I?' To know and be bonded to the ways and wisdom of their ancestors addresses this profound question."

Capturing them in words. When I give West Taiga woman Otgon-bayar a copy of *Reindeer Herders in My Heart in Mongolian*, she reads the part about herself and says, "I like that these are just plain words, telling about our lives. Not beautiful words making it something else."

Transition film. Peter Mittenthal of the International Polar Institute Press, after seeing the documentary *Transition*: "Wanted to let you know your film struck at one of my largest interests, at least in relation to Arctic media . . . that is, the domestic. It seems depictions of everyday life are routinely ignored among traditional living remote peoples. Yes, we hear of climate change and mineral extraction potential, etc. in these places, but rarely how people live on the land."

Over the years, I felt an urgency to support and document the traditional Mongolian nomadic lifestyle. Since I was forty-nine when I first went to Mongolia (and fifty-eight when I went to the taiga), I knew I needed to go often and keep learning. Finding the nomadic herding lifestyle precarious, I wanted to document in every way I could. Climate change, modernization, education, the political situation, and mining all endanger this lifestyle. I feel an inner pressure, a leading, to transmit and preserve this lifestyle through words and pictures. My connection with Mongolian life is a precious and sacred experience and each year I go deeper in my understanding of it.

My goal is to bring knowledge of Mongolian traditions to others as well as preserve it for the Mongolians. From the moment I first saw countryside herders in deels living on the steppes in their gers, I was drawn to capture the unique cold climate life on film. They know how to survive.

Recently, Batbaatar, a Mongolian movie actor, teacher, and director told me that the Mongolian government does not support Mongolians to make documentaries. He held his hand on his chest thanking me for documenting their traditional life.

Chapter Forty-six

ЗӨӨЛӨН, ЗӨӨЛӨН ЗАМБУУЛИН
✒ *Soft, tender World*

If one advances confidently in the direction
of (her) dreams, and endeavors to live the life
which (s)he has imagined, (s)he will meet with
a success unexpected in common hours.
~Henry David Thoreau, Walden

Summer 2020. COVID19 has closed the border to Mongolia, so I can't go there. Film festivals are not in person. I stay home. A friend gets my groceries. In early May when I have my annual exam by telemedicine, I tell my doctor I'm gaining weight because the pool is closed and I normally swim five days a week.

The water outside is too cold, I tell her. She says, "Why don't you get a wet suit?" Being compliant, I look into it, but find that they cost $250 and you can't even try them on because of Covid. My doctor says gaining two or three pounds is not so bad, but we are in this for the duration and one pound a month over many months could cause health problems.

I haven't left my half-acre property in Middlebury. I am getting exercise by doing my own spring clean up—raking leaves and piling branches.

A Mongolian shaman Dadu writes me a message. "When the water is clear, the people will heal." This makes me think, maybe I could go a little farther back from my property where there are wetlands and I could clean up the land. When I venture out, I find planters, plastic containers, beer bottles, and a camp chair and every day bring something back to the garbage.

I hear about a two-mile walk on the Trail Around Middlebury that goes through woods and is not too mountainous. Whereas I used to go places so I would see people, now I am looking for places to go without people. I have been isolated for over two months. I find it hard meeting people on the trail. To avoid people, I go earlier and earlier in the morning. This is more in keeping with my normal exercise pattern anyway, since I like to exercise before breakfast.

When I find a tick embedded in my knee, I decide I am finished walking in the woods and cleaning up the wetlands—for now. We have a heat wave and I figure the water might be warm enough for swimming. Branbury State Park is crowded when I venture out. I am nervous about being close to so many people. Then I walk past everyone to swim alone in the deep water. The water is cold. The strokes feel like old friends, though.

Soon I have my first swim of the year at beautiful Kingsland Bay State Park on Lake Champlain. As I drive out the dirt road away from the park, I hear myself say, "I feel like a human being." Water is essential for me.

I discover I can go to Branbury State Park to swim any time—they don't lock the gate.

That solves my problem of bumping into people. I begin to swim there before breakfast. Things are becoming harmonious.

One day when my work is done and I feel more relaxed about seeing a few people, I spend an afternoon at Kingsland Bay. First, I paddle my kayak to the opposite shore and lie on a rock reading. On the way back I glide past turtles, frogs, ducks, a Canada goose, and a beaver. My kayak slides over pond lilies, known as lotus blossoms in Buddhism and in Mongolia. After I put my kayak on land, I take a long, smooth swim. I haven't had a hug in six months. I feel hugged. My cells feel awake. Water connects with all water, the whole world.

On the way home, I find myself singing Mongolian nature songs with lines like, намуун байгаль, peaceful nature, and зөөлөн зөөлөн замбуулин, soft, tender world.

❦

I am lying in a hammock in my gazebo on my half acre. I look up from reading a book about unhappy characters in London. I think: my God, I have a gazebo, with pink and white phlox blooming and lavender wave petunias just a shade darker than the paint. With purple Adirondack chairs. My house is brick and even has rose branches hand painted on the stucco of the former sunroom. I have everything I ever wanted and more.

I never imagined traveling to Mongolia, falling in love with it, being able to do humanitarian work in the world, but, to do it and have my own house and yard and family and grandchildren shows that the spirit is beyond generous. There is humor, joy, abundance, with a lavender gazebo the frosting on the cake of my life.

Mongolia has been a convergence of my various life learnings with new ways of looking at things. I sought different ways, people, places my whole life, trying to understand what being a human on the planet means.

"When all kinds of cultures interact, everyone benefits. You know that," my daughter Jasmine says. "That's why you go to Mongolia."

I surrender to guidance to make movies, write books, and take pictures, to honor and document the unique nomadic lifestyle. Everything I learned in the first fifty years of my life I use for the next twenty-six during my love affair with Mongolia. Even with the challenges of being in Mongolia, I am where I am supposed to be. In a place to listen and follow. Doing what I am supposed to be doing. Even not knowing exactly why it's happening, I love knowing that my life is being used for its own unique purpose. To be led to where I need to go, do the work I am meant to do, and be given support to do it has been an honor and privilege. I am very grateful.

❦

Harmony is moving through each step of the journey, paying attention to spiritual guidance from inside. Integrity is most important. For nearly three decades, I have journeyed to Mongolia. Said "yes" to the peaceful taiga. To simplicity, beauty, nature. To basic shelter. Basic elements—wood, fire, air, metal, and earth. To what is real and authentic.

How much can humans live without? Or is it better to think of what we live with? What does it take to create harmony in a life of extreme conditions? Are the essentials of paying attention the same? What does it mean to understand, to know, feel, and internalize cultures, realms, and people?

It comes through the senses. White, snowcapped mountains. The feel of the air. Cold, hot, rain, snow. The smell of wood smoke, damp ground, moist, cold earth, forest, juniper incense, leather. The Mongolian language, shaman song, the beating of a drum. Metal stirrups clang, shoeless horses neigh, their hooves squelching as they lift from mud. The rhythm of steps. Reindeer tendons click over the bones of their feet, they call no-ah, no-ah. A canvas urts door slaps from one pole to another in the wind, wood is cut, the river rushes, my boots slosh in the boggy forest. I lie on the wet, lumpy, ground, feeling the vibration of children on reindeer gallop past the urts. Short, white reindeer hairs cover my clothes. I ride a horse down a mountain of shale.

A kaleidoscope of experiences.

I can be in the US, half a world away, and sense it all.

Inside me, I feel the visceral connection with my past and things that matter. In Vermont I sleep on sheepskins. I hold two places, two peoples, two cultures in my heart.

I am always there. And also here. Many worlds. One.

≈

Shaman Gala tells me that I will be coming back to the taiga. During the Covid lockdown, at our non-profit Nomadicare's board meeting on Zoom, our members are silent when I tell them this. Except for Lucy who is a doctor and spent a summer in Mongolia with me. In her square Zoom box she looks at me and says, "Well, that's that then."

But when will this corona virus let me go? I am not sure. Still, when February comes, I feel the need to plan a trip to the taiga. First, I need to know the date of the new moon closest to early June. The Dukha shamans' most propitious days to perform a ritual are the fifth, seventh, and ninth after the new moon. Another consideration is to meet the Dukha before they leave the spring camp for the summer settlement, which saves me four or five hours of horse riding each way. The reindeer start to leave for the summer camp "when the needles come out on the larch trees" which is the second or third week in June. The herders follow the reindeer. I write these on my calendar and choose a date to leave, so I can follow them, too.

Epilogue

*W*hen Dad was 91, he fell again. Since Mom and Dad had been living together in an apartment in an assisted living complex, he went to the rehabilitation unit on the second floor of an attached wing while Mom stayed in their room. One day the doctor told him that because of his heart, he would not be leaving the unit. Dad got his walker, took the elevator to the first floor, walked the long corridor to the desk, told the receptionist, "I am moving back with my wife." Then he walked to the room they shared and they spent the next six months together. He was in his chair beside her watching television when his heart gave out.

I dream that Dad is in bed reading this book. The lights go off and he uses a flashlight with a greenish light. I say, "So that's my life, Dad." I feel happy about it. He turns the flashlight off with a smile.

I am just about finished with these stories. From them I understand that persistence is in our genes.

I have dreams for my twin grandsons Dune and Aidan. I wish their lives will follow their leadings and gifts.

Aidan was born an artist. When he was three, he got out of bed one the night, ripped some paper from a long roll, got paints and brushes from under the sink, and painted a colorful picture full of action. He put the tops on the paint, washed the paint brushes, placed them in the dish drainer, and went back to bed. He had already learned to heed the call of creativity.

Aidan, I wish you to keep honoring your creativity and am delighted that twenty years later, you are still doing it.

When Dune was three, he told me, "I got an idea because I was sitting and thinking." Later, as a budding actor, he realized that he needed to gain "life experience". At nineteen, he traveled to Mongolia with me as the location sound recorder for our film *Transition*. He flew around the world, met two shamans, and rode a horse eight hours each way to the East Taiga Dukha reindeer herder settlement.

Dune, I hope you continue "sitting and thinking" and follow your ideas along your life's path.

☙

To you, Dear Readers, I wish you the space to listen, meditate, and follow your dreams. They will guide you on your unique life's journey. You will learn why you are here making your own footprints on the gazar.

May you become the person you are meant to be and help create the best world possible.

> *I want to be thoroughly used up when I die,*
> *for the harder I work the more I live.*
> *I rejoice in life for its own sake.*
> *Life is no "brief candle" to me.*
> *It is a sort of splendid torch*
> *which I have got hold of for a moment,*
> *and I want to make it burn as brightly as possible*
> *before handing it on to future generations.*
>
> *~George Bernard Shaw*

Glossary

Aimag Province or capital city of province

Airag Fermented mare's milk

Arruul Dried cheese curds

Arts Incense

Balanceruu Moving toward balance

Bi chamd khairtai I love you

Bi Mongold khairtai I love Mongolia

Boodog Barbecue where meat is cooked in the animal's skin

Buu Shaman one who contacts ongod or spirit ancestors to restore balance to people, livestock, and land

Buuz Dumpling(s)

Chi khaloon osand orokh oo? Do you want a hot shower?

Chinggis Khan Mongolian hero who conquered land from the Pacific to the Mediterranean

Damaru A small two-headed drum used in Tibetan Buddhist

Dorj Brass thunderbolt used in Tibetan Buddhism

Deel Mongolian traditional gown fastened with cloth knot or silver buttons with loops on the right side. It is made of silk, wool, cotton or skin with the fur inside, depending on the season. Silk or wool deels can be any bright color for women and are often navy, black, brown, or maroon for men. Fur can be lamb's wool, sheepskin, or fur from other animals. A double layer of material in front is perfect for riding a horse because one side can wrap around each leg for warmth and protection. When a cummerbund, usually orange or yellow, is added, the top half forms a large pocket. This is useful for a herder since binoculars, baby goats, cheese, or dried meat can be easily slid in and out of the pocket, even while riding a horse. On a cold day, a parent can even tuck a baby inside.

Dukha Tuvan. People from the Tuvan republic in southern Siberia, Russia. This is the name a small ethnic group of reindeer herders living in northern Mongolia call themselves

Eej Khad Mother Rock, a sacred site in central Mongolia

Gazar Dirt, soil, ground, land, earth, world. Also place, bay, range, section, parts, office, country, soil, site, locality, station, spot, estate, grass, area, township, department, point, office, depot, camp

Ger Round, felt tent of nomadic herders. Yurt.

Guanz Cafe

Khadag Prayer scarf

Khaltar Tsarait "Dirty Face", a Venezuelan soap opera

Khashaa A fenced yard in the countryside for housing

Khengereg Shaman's drum

Khot City

Khoviin Personal

Khuduu Countryside

Khuduu aj amdral Countryside living

(K)huuchin gemtliin emneleg Old trauma hospital

Mongol uls minii nuhur Mongolia is my husband

Mongolian medicine A Buddhist system similar to Tibetan medicine, with its
roots in Ayurveda, beginning in Mongolia during the sixteenth century
and changing to include the use of Mongolian medicinal plants

Morin khuur Horsehead fiddle

Myy Bad wrong

Naadam Festival of three sports: horse racing, archery, and wrestling

Nuuts Secret

Ongod, pl, ongon, s. Ancestor spirit(s) who come to shamans during a
ritual or ceremony

Sain baina uu Hello

Sanaa-aldakh Sigh

Setgel Mind, spirit, emotions

Shagai Sheep ankle bone, used for games

Shuleg Poem

Steppe Grasslands or prairie

Sutra Holy Buddhist texts

Sum or soum County or county center

Suu tsai Milk tea

Taiga High altitude boggy forest

Tavtai morilno oo! Welcome!

Thangka God painting

Tsagaan Sar Lunar New Year

Tumsnii ulaan (Latin) Red lily

Tuurug, tuurug Response an individual gives to shamans' ongod during a
ceremony meaning, "tell my future"

Ugui, bi khuiten osand orno No, I want a cold shower

Urts Siberian teepee

Za Okay, well

Zakh Market. Used to be black market

*A*cknowledgements

As a person who has had many stories to tell, it has taken over twenty-five years to put these together. A gift to spend a month at Vermont Studio Center in 2018 got me focused on the four-part story, which has become five parts. Later in 2018 and again in 2019, I had to put the writing down to go to Mongolia and direct the documentary *Transition*. Thanks to Heid E. Erdrich for guidance in January of 2020 at the Vermont Studio Center where I was struggling to pick the thread back up. It was during the years of Covid that I could take the time at home to knit the pieces together.

Susie Cronin has supported my work as a Nomadicare board member and a donor for the trips and work in Mongolia. She became a producer for *Transition* and *Gobi Children's Song* and most recently a supporter of the publishing of this book. Susie has listened to many of these stories over the years when she, as a dear, dear friend, called me every day during the pandemic—often the only person I spoke to. I am incredibly grateful to her for believing in me and helping me fulfill my leadings and dreams.

Over the years, John Swift, Ann Barker, along with Bruce Payne and Rachel Weingeist with the Rubin Foundation have been wonderful supporters. Thanks to the Nomadicare board members Eleanor Ott, Jonathan Hodgkin, Robin Lloyd, Carolyn Schmidt, Munkhjin Bayanjargal, and Lucy McKeon, as well as hundreds of Nomadicare donors who made my experiences in Mongolia possible.

Back in the mid-nineties, I traded with Euan Bear for editing my early stories. One day in 1997, Bette Moffett stopped me on the street in Middlebury and said, "You must have a lot of stories about Mongolia. Why not join Margery Cady's group at the Ilsley Library?" Joining Marg's group, I wrote a couple of pages each week and when a decade was up, I found that I had five hundred pages. I asked some of my best mentors and writers to read them. One suggested that I use half of the Mongolian stories for a first book. I published *Reindeer Herders in My Heart* in 2012. Since then it has been translated into Mongolian and French. I am sharing the rest of the original Mongolian stories here in *Marrying Mongolia*.

This memoir has taken many teachers, writing groups, classes, and editors—starting with Don Mitchell's Middlebury College "Workshop in Nonfiction Writing" in 1985. Abi Sessions' class taught me what a memoir is. In A. Jay Dubberly's Bixby Writers'

Group with Trish Dougherty, Steve Holmes, Cliff Adams, Pat Will-werth, Beth Christian, Michelle Mertens, I learned what my writing sounded like when others read it.

Don Mitchell and John Elder's "Stories in the Land" in 2014 and its offshoot the S'warms with Alice Leeds, Jill Vickers, Sue Jeffs, Marnie Wood, Erin Ruble, and Matthew Witten opened connections to nature in my writing. And finally, deep weekly work in Di-B-Sas memoir group with B. Amore and Diane Nancekivell showed me the commonalities of women being brought up in the fifties.

Thanks to to Abi Sessions, my first reader, Shebana Coelho who edited the content, and Claudia Cooper who did the final edit and proofreading—and counseling on the last sticky issues in the book.

Thank you to all the Quakers, family members, and friends who have enriched my life, especially to Julia Carey Petro for research and Linda Waterman for answering questions.

With gratitude to Fred Thodal who takes very beautiful photos and videos.

With my star translators I am free to travel deeply into the world of Mongolia. There is a rare intimacy between who is speaking and listening and who is helping translate.

Khaliuna, Munkhjin, Zula, M. Khongoroo, Chimedee, Anuka,
Boloroo, Hagid, Michele, Davaa
This is my shuleg, my poem, to you.

You who are translator interpreter and assistant
You hold me
Without you I would not know Mongolia
Since my Mongolian is not fluent
You are my mouth and ears
You know everything first
A position of power
You don't abuse
Together twenty-four hours each day
Six weeks each year
You are my younger sisters
Daughters granddaughters
We have a rare intimacy
You anticipate needs
Allow words to flow both ways
You are my bridge
To everything Mongolian
I honor you
Za

(Za means okay . . . It is what Mongolians say to each other rather than Thank you.)

Works by Sas

Book

Reindeer Herders in My Heart: Stories of Healing Journeys in Mongolia
2012 Wren Song Press

Films

Gobi Women's Song
2001 Sas Carey, Director; Assistant Director, Oyuntungalag Ayush; Joseph Spaid, Director of Photography; Khaliuna Erdenbat, Site Translator
2002 L. Mendbayar and J. Nyamdorj, Cameras; Khagid, Site Translator.
2003 L. Mendbayar, Cinematographer; Bindrea Site Translator
2004 L. Mendbayar, Cinematographer; Zulaa, Site Translator

Ceremony
2003-2014 Sas Carey, Director; Batbayar Sumkhuu, Director of Photographer; Eric Chaikin, Fred Thodal, Ts. Altangerel, L. Mendbayar, Goomaral Uyanga Cameras; Bindrea, Zulaa, Davaa, M. Khongorzul, Boloroo, Site Translators; Battulga Solonoi, Guide

Migration
2014 Sas Carey, Director; Fred Thodal, Director of Photography and Editor; Chimedtseren Dorjgotov, Site Translator; Battulga Solonoi, Guide
2017 Urangoo Baasanjav, Camera; Chimedtseren Dorgotov, Site Translator

Transition
2018 Khongorzul Purevjav, Protagonist; Sas Carey, Director; Marcin Lesisz, Director of Photograpy; Dune Mayberger, Site Recorder; Chimedtseren Dorjgotov, Site Translator; Battulga Solonoi, Guide
2019 Jennifer Schweppe, Cinematographer; Anudari Ganbaatar, Site Translator; Horse Wranglers: Lkhavga, Sugar Lkhavga, Elbeg Erdene, Zaya Otgonbayar, Sukhbat Bazarragcha; Driver Batsaikhan Dashdondog